Co-operative Adventures
We joined the Co-op and saw the World

By

RITA RHODES

Publisher: Rita Rhodes
ISBN 9798687147453
Copyright (C) Rita Rhodes 2020

British Library Cataloguing-in-Publication Data a catalogue record for this book is available on request from the British Library.

Typeset by Chris Waite of CW Services and Amazon Kindle Direct Publishing.

Rita Rhodes has also written:

The International Co-operative Alliance during War and Peace
1910-1950

A Thematic Guide to ICA Congresses 1895-1995 (written
jointly)

An Arsenal for Labour - The Royal Arsenal Co-operative
Society and Politics 1896-1996

Empire and Co-operation - How the British Empire used Co-
operatives in its Development Strategies 1900-1970

Contents

Rita Rhodes is grateful to all who have helped prepare this joint autobiography. She particularly thanks three close friends for reading and commenting on each chapter. Thanks are also given to colleagues who worked with Bernard and Rita for their comments on sections with which they would be familiar.

Special thanks are given to Chris Waite for his sterling work with the manuscript and for helping Bernard and Rita as their computer 'guru' for many years.

Chapter One

EARLY INFLUENCES

There once was a ditty that went something like this:

"We joined the Navy to see the world
And what did we see?
We saw the sea"

Something similar could be said about the lives of my husband and myself. Even before meeting each other we had joined the Co-op and in later years this would lead to us seeing many parts of the world. Now that I write our auto-biographies for whatever reason – vanity, nostalgia, gratitude or trying to make sense of life's experiences – the Co-op is to feature large in it. Lady Eden, wife of the Prime Minister, Anthony Eden, said during the Suez Crisis of 1956 that she felt that the Suez Canal was flowing through her drawing room. For sixty years or more the Co-operative Movement has featured in our living room through books, papers, telephone calls and memorabilia. No account of our lives could be made without many references to it. Both of us were born into co-operative families, created our own co-operative family and held various positions in the Movement.

Despite this large and shared passion Bernard and I were very different. Often we reminded ourselves that opposites attract. He was shy and introverted while I was more gregarious and extrovert. Whereas he was born in the industrial city of Bradford I was born in rural Essex. He went to a Grammar School and later university while I went to a Secondary Modern School and left with no exam passes. Perhaps even more fundamentally he was ten years older and a Catholic and I went to the Congregational, now the United Reform Church.

Nevertheless we were happily married for 45 years. Despite these differences we shared many similarities. We were both

1

born into working class families and working class culture. The Second World War affected our lives in big ways and attitudes were shaped by post-war politics and the 1945-50 Labour Government.

Its election was welcomed in both families. My father, a railwayman and a member of the National Union of Railwaymen, came from a railway family, his father and later step-father were also railwaymen. Dad began as a lamp boy. Later he became a shunter and later still, a goods and passenger guard. He gained a service gold watch for 45 years' service but ended as a ticket collector. A stroke disabled him and he died at the relatively young age of 61. Happily he was never redundant but suffered wage cuts in the early 1930s. Railway nationalisation and the improved benefits it brought were warmly welcomed within the family.

Bernard's father had a more varied career and was frequently unemployed. He seemed geared more for office rather than manual work. Reckoned to be good with book-keeping, he taught himself shorthand. At one point he was the manager of a working man's club but he was given as a "retired textile clerk" on our marriage certificate. Neither of our mothers worked although Bernard's sometimes helped behind the bar of the working man's club. Both claimed that a wife who stayed at home could achieve domestic economies.

Inter-war unemployment had made Bernard's mother extremely frugal. She saved habitually in the expectation that savings would go when there was no work. Bernard's older brother, Kenneth, could not go to university because they needed his wages as quickly as possible. Like many others from the working class during the period he achieved his considerable qualifications in his own time but strongly urged that Bernard should go to university if he qualified to do so.

Both our families had left-wing sympathies. Each shopped at the Co-op and were loyal Co-op. members, Bernard's of the

Bradford and District Co-operative Society (BDS) and mine of the London Co-operative Society (LCS). When my parents married my paternal grandmother gave them two £1 shares in LCS with a membership number of 175004. Later she took a mortgage from the Co-operative Permanent Building Society, later renamed Nationwide to buy her own cottage.

BERNARD'S EARLY YEARS

I like to think that my parents might have passed Bernard in his pram. Born in 1924 he spent his early years in the Laisterdyke area of Bradford where my parents went for honeymoon in 1925, staying with cousins who lived there. Such an event is unlikely but nevertheless a happy fantasy. By the time I first knew Bernard his family lived in 95 Hastings Street on the other side of Bradford.

His parents had a mixed marriage, his mother being Catholic but his father converting only on his death bed. Both Kenneth and Bernard were raised as Catholics and went to Catholic schools. Bernard later recalled that when he arrived at St. Bede's Grammar School a master came up to ask if he were Kenneth Rhodes' brother. When he replied that he was the master said that he would do "all right" if he were half as bright as his brother. Bernard shrank with intimidation as he did again when an older pupil warned him that he would soon be doing Algebra.

His family wanted him to become a school teacher, his paternal grandfather reckoning that being a "school maister" was the best thing possible. Bernard gained entrance to Leeds University and began studying for a BA (Hons) degree but military service intervened during the Second World War. This introduced him to far rougher things than he had ever known in straight-living family life. Swearing and stealing were commonplace but Bernard's love of words and his puckish humour helped him to be amused, as when he heard a fellow private claim wife support although he and she were separated but had nevertheless been "reconciled" on the dates he now gave.

3

Bernard served in the pay corps and was not sent overseas. Many years later I realised that it was still possible to not know everything about your nearest and dearest. We were watching television and views of Buckingham Palace as the Royal family and Winston Churchill came out onto the balcony on VE night (Victory over Europe). It was a well-known scene that we had seen many times before but it was the first time that Bernard had said that he had been in the crowds outside the Palace. He had been going on leave and had a pass for a specific train. There was time to kill so he joined the celebrating crowds. Ever since, I have tried to identify him among them – without success. The incident brought home though the travel restrictions for members of the armed forces.

Happily, after being demobbed Bernard was able to return to Leeds University and to complete his degree. He seems already to have become interested or involved in the Co-op. One of his fellow students was Geoffrey Rhodes who Bernard introduced to the Co-op. Geoffrey became a well-known Co-op. figure, elected as a Labour/Co-op MP after being a Lecturer at the UK Co-operative College. A sad occurrence was the suicide of another fellow student, Mostyn Silverman. Bernard had lent him a book with his name in it from which Mostyn's parents asked Bernard to visit. Neither they nor Bernard had any idea that Mostyn was in any way suicidal. Bernard thought him brilliant and one of his most amusing colleagues, and recalled him fondly in later years.

During his university studies Bernard tapped into his working class roots. These included the Mechanics' Institute in Bradford. Founded in the early 19th century this and others set out to help educate working class men. Bernard spent many hours in the library of the Bradford Mechanics' Institute.

After graduating he studied for a further year at the Institute of Education at Leeds University and took a teaching certificate. Once qualified, he began teaching in schools although not Catholic schools as might have been expected. To some extent this reflected an independent mind but also growing doubts about his faith. These continued throughout his life and led to his not taking communion although still going to church each Sunday.

He also taught evening classes in the then Huddersfield Technical College but teaching ambitions weakened as he became more closely involved with the Co-operative Movement. In the early 1950s he was elected to the Board of Management of the Bradford and District Co-operative Society. He also joined the Co-operative Party as well as the Labour Party. He adopted a kitten born in the Bradford Society's premises which he called "Divi". They became very close. Bernard remained a fervent cat lover for the rest of his life.

Gradually his co-operative work increased. Tension grew between that and his teaching work and in 1955 the Co-op won. In the General Election of that year the Co-operative Party's Research Officer, Bert Oram, (later Lord Oram) was elected to Parliament and Bernard applied to fill the vacancy. When successful he left Bradford and teaching.

To some extent his success was due to earlier political connections. The General Secretary of the Co-operative Party was Jack Bailey, a Welshman who some years earlier had been the Political Secretary and Organiser of the Bradford Co-operative Party. Bailey knew Bernard's background. He was also friends with his Uncle Bill who regularly attended national Co-operative Party's summer schools as did Bernard who had even been the speaker at one. Bernard also had something of a head start inasmuch as he was one of the very few co-operative figures at that time to hold a degree.

He settled happily into work in the Co-operative Party's Head Office, regularly attending meetings of the Parliamentary Co-operative Group, undertaking their research requests and also drafting policy statements. There were also a number of speaking engagements and for the first time Bernard had a secretary. This was Marion Richards who became a life-long friend. Marion was active in the Labour and Co-operative Parties and was also a practising Methodist. She was a strong admirer of Dr. Donald Soper.

Bernard took bachelor digs with a Mrs. Corrigan who had a large house in Kennington Road south of the Thames: it was rented from the Duchy of Cornwall and had been built in Regency times. Mrs. Corrigan also took in other lodgers, including Tom Fraser, MP who became a Minister of Transport in one of Harold Wilson's Labour Governments. Mrs. Corrigan was a robust character. At the outset she declared she was too busy to cook breakfasts or any other meals. Consequently Bernard became well versed in the delights of Lyon's Corner Houses in various parts of London. The reason that Mrs. Corrigan was so busy was that despite her princely accommodation she was very working class, active in the Co-operative Women's Guild locally and nationally and in the Royal Arsenal Co-operative Society (RACS) which was her local co-operative. On a number of occasions she had unsuccessfully sought election to its Board: competition for such places was high.

In addition to meals taken in London restaurants Bernard also took a number at co-operative events. Besides summer schools there were weekend conferences and frequent Saturday afternoon conferences which were traditionally followed by "conference teas". Like trade unions co-operatives had strong fraternal traditions. Such teas allowed socialising and also refreshment for those travelling some distance home. It was at one such event that Bernard and I first met. Held on 29th September 1956 at the Municipal College, Southend-on-Sea, it was a Speaking Contest organised by the No.2 Eastern Federation of the London Co-operative Society's Political Committee. Bernard was one of the three adjudicators and I was in one of the competing teams.

RITA'S EARLY YEARS

I was raised in Rayleigh, Essex, which is an old town and at that time still quite small. It then had only a few thousand people but that had risen to around 9,000 in the mid-1950s.

I was born lucky, even at birth. My parents had been married seven years without children when my mother appeared to be having an ectopic pregnancy. Instead this proved to be a cyst on an ovary and both were removed. Perhaps surprisingly with only one ovary she conceived shortly afterwards. My mother was very petite and it proved a difficult birth. Sadly my brother "John" lived barely an hour. My parents had planned to call a boy "Anthony" but the hospital had him baptised immediately after birth because of his expected death. Neither Dad nor Mum could be asked so the name "John" was chosen on their behalf and we knew him ever after by that name.

Fifteen months later and perhaps finding it easier the second time round, Mum safely gave me birth. This was one on 28th December 1934 three weeks earlier than the expected date, perhaps due to much laughter over Christmas spent with my Aunt Dorothy and Uncle Bill. A great time had been enjoyed.

Mum's father was a caretaker at the Municipal College, Southend-on-Sea: Bernard and I would meet there some 21 years later. When Dad went to tell him of my arrival he threw down the dust pan and brush he was holding and declared they should "go and wet the baby's head" which they promptly did. Several years later Mum had a kidney removed and she and Dad were advised to have no more children. Sadly this meant I would have no brothers or sisters.

I recall a happy, loving and contented childhood despite the war and my parents living from "hand-to-mouth". Although never out of work my father suffered wage cuts during the 1930s. When war broke out he wanted to join the navy but could not enlist because of a childhood injury when he had fallen from a round-about and broken his left elbow. It had been badly set and although Dad was able to do the heavy manual railway work his deformed elbow prevented naval recruitment. In any event his work on the railway was considered "essential" to the war effort and he remained employed by the London Northern Eastern Railway.

His wages were paid each Friday and on Saturday morning Mum would go to the local Co-op. store to buy the week's food. As soon as I was big enough I went with her. It became regular routine and part of my childhood introduction to the Co-op. Returning from shopping Mum would count the money left in her purse and comment that it would have to last us the rest of the week. Without a 'fridge fresh food items were often bought daily. Coalman, milkman and baker also needed to be paid when they delivered to the door.

Certain meals appeared on certain days of the week. Each Sunday we had a roast joint, Yorkshire pudding and vegetables followed by stewed fruit and custard. Monday, wash day, dinner would be cold meat from the joint and potatoes as this was the most convenient for Mum to prepare. Tuesday the bone from the joint would be made into soup or any remaining meat into rissoles. Other days might require visits to the butcher for a few slices of liver, sausage meat or bones for home-made soup. All would be cheap, sometimes only a few pence. When serving meals Mum would give Dad the best portions of meat, me the next best while she took what remained. Dad had to be kept as well-nourished as possible, not only to ensure family income but also the war effort. For this he was allowed an extra ration of cheese each week.

We lived in a two up and two down semi-detached cottage built in 1864. Across its back yard was a "wash house" and next to that the outside toilet. Cut newspapers provided the toilet paper. The "wash house" had a 19th century stone sink, a gas wash copper, a black iron gas cooker that was not safe to use, and a mangle. Various items of harness hung from beams under its tiled roof. There was no ceiling. Mum washed all the pots and pans after meals in the old stone sink. Only on cold winter nights would she wash tea things from a kettle in a wash bowl on the kitchen table.

We lived in the kitchen. There was a front room but that was used only for Sunday dinner, Christmas and high days and holidays. At all other times it remained pristine as social demands of the day required. The kitchen had a black leaded kitchen range on whose top hobs food could be boiled or simmered. A grated fire lay beneath in front of which bread could be toasted on the wire toasting fork which hung at the side of the fireplace. On Friday mornings Mum got up early to black-lead the kitchen stove and clean its surrounding fender with emery paper. It was dirty work but Friday was bath night. With no indoor water we had no bathroom. I had a white enamel child's bath whereas Mum and Dad bathed in a larger zinc bath which Mum filled with hot water boiled on the stove or gas rings. Filling the bath was easy. Emptying it was far more of a problem requiring heavy lifting which my mother did – all 4ft 10 inches of her. This and lifting other heavy things caused physical problems and in 1959 she required dropped womb surgery. Baths were taken in front of the kitchen fire: in winter this was certainly cosy.

At each side of the large fireplace was a small recess. That to the left made a small sideboard as it had shelves above and drawers below while that to the right also had drawers. On its top, though, was a two-ring gas hob which Mum used to augment her cooking. Throughout my childhood years Mum longed for a self-contained gas cooker.

The kitchen floor was covered with lino but in front of the fire and its surrounding guard was a home-made rug with a sacking backing into which small pieces of material from discarded clothes had been threaded, probably by Mum or grandmother. The rug was warm and cosy but a dust trap. Mum had to shake it vigorously outside to clean it. She had no vacuum cleaner as the cottage had no electricity until 1958.

Up high a cord was hung from one corner of the kitchen ceiling to the other. Ironed washing was hung on it to air; we had no airing cupboard. Just below this above the door leading into the front room Mum hung a paper bag. In this she dried summer mint to make mint sauce during the winter months.

The wall opposite the stove comprised the right-hand side wall of the house. Within it was an enclosed and slightly angled stair case with door opening into the kitchen. Mum's larder lay beneath the stairs and had a small window. Facing the south west and catching much afternoon sun it was a poor larder. It contained a small meat cupboard with a mesh door to keep out flies. Fortunately milk was delivered daily but other items with short life also had to be bought daily. In addition the larder housed jams, pickled onions and other things Mum preserved. Blackberry jam featured prominently because nearby fields had many blackberry bushes. Horse reddish plants could also be found nearby and these went into the sauce Mum made to have with roast beef. She and Dad also collected much fallen wood for the fire.

Upstairs the cottage had two bedrooms, both with iron bedsteads. Each had well-laundered white valances hiding chamber pots beneath. Mum emptied these each morning into a pail which she then poured into the outside loo. I had the back bedroom with a window that opened with one side moving sideways in front of the other. A door opened onto a steep ladder stair case at one side of the room which led to a large attic with a low ceiling; it was used as a store room for odds and ends and maturing home-made wine.

Everything in the house was home-made or second-hand. This never seemed to worry my parents and I grew up accepting this as normal. Consequently I was moved when Mum and Dad's wedding present to Bernard and I was a complete cutlery set in a beautiful wooden case. Then their first Christmas present was a full and matching dinner service. They never had either for themselves. Knives and forks never matched neither did crockery. Mum wanted a gas stove but never pushed for it but often said she would like proper dusters and cleaning materials. Instead she cut old clothes to make dusters and made face flannels from old towels. Bed sheets with holes were cut and their sides sown to make a new middle. Once at Sunday school, I was asked to take a night dress to wear in a nativity play. Mum said I couldn't because they were 'holey' but Sunday school teachers thought I meant 'holy'!

The house had no internal water and only gas on the ground floor. To light yourself upstairs you needed to take a candle kept in a candle stick with a wide circular blue and white tin base. Amazingly we never had a fire. In 1958 Dad modernised the cottage and electricity was installed. I fondly remember my mother going round switching lights on and off and declaring electricity to be "a wonderful invention".

We lived on Crown Hill. When my parents married their address was "2 Mount Villas, Crown Lane" but by the time I was born this had changed to 23 Crown Hill. The reason was the increasing numbers of people using the railway station at the bottom of the Hill. This then became the main access to Rayleigh High Street with a T junction at its top and an unusually wide High Street. Parallel to Crown Hill was London Hill which rose to the church dating from the 1380s and around which the village had originally centred.

The background to our cottage's modernisation was long and complex. All his working life Dad was a railwayman but he had hinterlands. In the 1930s he had enjoyed sailing and had bought a 22ft yacht which he moored on the nearby river Roach. I just about recall the week's holiday we had on it shortly before the Second World War when I was four. Much of the holiday I spent with a rope tied around my waist in case I fell overboard. When war broke out, the government ordered vessels to be brought on land where they were quickly vandalised. Dad managed to get his "Catherine" to Rayleigh where it spent the war and was afterwards sold.

By then Dad was into horses, not for racing but for a small carting business. In 1943 he bought a small brown pony called "Dolly" who had previously drawn a milk float. He rented a field of roughly an acre in which to keep her. It lay on the opposite side of Crown Hill from our cottage and just below the Crown pub which lay at the junction of Crown Hill and the High Street. It was therefore central but laying half way up the hill meant it sloped. At its rear and highest point were four wooden stables with black walls red tiled roofs.

Originally Dad rented the field from a Mrs. Byford whose husband and sons ran one Rayleigh's largest building firms. Mrs. Byford died in 1953 and Dad, as tenant had the first option of buying the field. He and Mum managed to get a personal loan from a local farmer and bought the field, the only time they ever borrowed. It was a big commitment and they scrimped and saved to repay as quickly as they could. The field's value later rose when Dad successfully applied to have it zoned as building rather than agricultural land. Its central position helped.

In 1958 Mum and Dad sold the "Knoll' as the field had become called and remains so today. They had made great use of it populating it with horses, pigs, ducks, chickens, three geese and even a goat. With the horses, Dad developed a horse drawn business delivering green grocer's order to his customers and ferrying boxes of fresh fish from Rayleigh station to Britton's the local fishmonger.

Tragically Dad died in 1963. He was only 61 and I have often felt that his premature death was due to overwork. On the railway he had three shifts; 'early, late and nights' which each changed weekly: he had no regular sleep pattern. His horse drawn delivery business and running the small holding were additional though Mum helped much in feeding and tending the animals.

Fortunately before he died Dad managed to modernise the cottage with the proceeds from the sale of the "Knoll" but ownership remained a problem. It was still owned by his mother who had moved into it in 1918. She and her second husband, another railwayman, moved to Southend-On-Sea when my parents married in 1925 and moved into the cottage for which they paid rent to my grandmother. She still owned the cottage when it was modernised in 1958. Dad asked her to confirm that she would leave it to him when she died. She gave a verbal promise but Dad sadly died eleven years before she did. Consequently my mother remained a tenant, though admittedly with legal protection.

My grandmother could be admired for a number of things including leaving her body for medical research. But she could be awkward. She owned two cottages and the expectation was that she would leave one to each of her two widowed daughters-in-law. She left nothing to either. Instead she bequeathed her cottage to Holy Trinity Church, Rayleigh and Mum and Dad's cottage to her three grandchildren, Kirk, Ola and I. Sadly, Kirk a Chief Mate had recently been killed at sea and Ola had moved to New Zealand. Within a few years though she agreed to Bernard and I buying her out. Mum remained a tenant but we took no rent from her. This was a small and totally inadequate reward for the money she and Dad had spent on buying the "Knoll", selling it and using the proceeds to modernise the cottage from whose increased value Ola and I then benefitted.

Modernisation had undoubtedly raised its value. Water and electricity were installed. The attic ceiling was raised and this became my bedroom which was made into a bathroom. Dad shifted the stairs to enter the front room thus the kitchen became larger. That now had two large windows with a sink underneath one and modern kitchen under the other. The kitchen range was replaced with a new tiled one which repeated the earlier one's large side oven. Besides cooking this also heated polished bricks used to warm the beds instead of hot water bottles. Mum still lacked a gas oven although the two additional gas rings remained. The removed lino was replaced by dark green floor tiles and the fire had a new rug in front of it.

Ironically by the time the cottage was modernised I was flying the nest. I had already spent two years at College in Loughborough and in March 1959 I took a job with the Birkenhead Co-operative Society in Birkenhead. Eighteen months later Bernard and I married.

I have described the cottage at length because it played such an important part in my early life. Its frugal setting shaped my attitudes to money and much else. Other early influences included school, the Second World War, music and the 1945 General Election.

School was great. Despite being an only child I readily took to the company of other children. I loved school and was happy throughout those years. Looking back I muse on how well caring parents and teachers shielded us from the horrors of the war. In Rayleigh Primary School all teachers were women except elderly "Taffy" Sample who had been badly wounded in the First World War. Often in classes he bent double in pain but always continued teaching.

I was five in December 1939 and began school in January 1940. The larger number of pupils had begun the previous September and I was therefore a term behind them. Our year was divided into two streams. Those in the upper were expected to do well in the Scholarship exam at 10 or 11 while those of us in the lower were not. This proved true in my case. I failed and at 10 moved to Rayleigh's Secondary Modern School. Again I was happy and enjoyed school. Women teachers once more predominated but were gradually joined by men as they were demobbed from the armed forces.

The war was a constant feature in our young lives, seen in bomb damage, loss of life and in food and clothes rationing. Some seven miles from the Thames estuary and just off the German flight path to London, Rayleigh experienced bombs and deaths. Colin who sat behind me in primary school was killed along with all his family when their house was bombed. Two Sunday school friends lost their mother when she left their garden air-raid shelter during an air raid to get drinking water. The house received a direct hit and she was killed. If bombs or landmines exploded nearby we visited their craters.

A very early memory was my father picking me up from my bed and carrying me down the stairs saying "the Germans are coming". An air raid had begun and I think I remembered the incident because I did not know who or what the Germans were. We had no air-raid shelter. The general advice was to shelter under a staircase but we could not because that was where our larder was. Instead Mum and I sat *on* the stairs; Dad was frequently at work. I think Mum liked to see what was going on as when an incendiary bomb fell in our garden. Other times she watched action from a window. Perhaps her sense of adventure remained from the First World War when she had been one of the 23,000 recruited into the Women's Land Army to compensate for the agricultural labour recruited by the armed forces.

Rationing shaped our eating. Even before Dad started renting the field in 1943 he and Mum had kept ducks, chickens and rabbits in the back garden. At the very rear of this Dad built a pig sty and also started rearing pigs. One was slaughtered each Christmas and half had to go to the Ministry of Food. Dad had the other half jointed, salted and smoked for bacon. Apart from our Christmas joint the other joints were sold. Mum and Dad anxiously watched the weather because having no 'fridge they feared the mild days that sometimes occurred before Christmas. Not sold were the chit lings, the associated offal which had great flavour. For several months after Christmas we enjoyed our own bacon, mainly for Sunday breakfasts. Dad was so proud of his bacon that when we were going by train to Holyhead to cross the Irish Sea he took rashers for our breakfast. In the train restaurant Dad, a railwayman, asked another railwayman to take the bacon and cook that for our breakfast – which he kindly did. In the late 1940s we took two holidays in Ireland. Mum had always wanted to visit Killarney and Dad's rail privilege tickets helped reduce the cost.

After buying the field Mum and Dad took on more animals including two geese and a gander. We enjoyed their eggs along with those of ducks and chickens and these boosted our wartime rations. They also prompted friends and neighbours to make frequent appeals for eggs which Mum numbered, dated and recorded in a notebook to ensure freshness. All our animals required food. "Tottenham Pudding" was bought for the pigs. It was produced under a wartime scheme in which vegetable and food leavings were collected and mashed into a "pudding". Other animal foodstuffs were bought from the local mill. I often went with Dad to buy these and recall watching sacks of fodder going up and down on chains through ceiling slots in the granaries. We drove supplies back in horse and cart and stored them in one of the four stables in the field. The end one had a farrowing rail. When a sow pig was due to have piglets Dad would place her in this stable so that her offspring could roll under the low rail to avoid their mother accidentally rolling on them.

Pigs sometimes caused amusement. Once, a neighbour came rushing to ask my Dad if he had lost one as one was sitting outside the slaughter house in Rayleigh High Street. Dad quickly harnessed the horse and cart and drove up to the High Street where he indeed found Molly, one of his pigs. She was long remembered by many as the pig who went voluntarily to the slaughter house!

In the stable at the other end from the pigs farrowing stable, Dad kept "Lally" the goat. She was white and affectionate. I have since heard that goats are social animals and should not be kept by themselves. I have therefore worried whether she was unhappy. She gave no such impression as she jumped and did silly antics that made us laugh.

I was less easy with horses. Dad had four over some 15 years, each following each other. They were Dolly, Tony, Nobby and Mayflower. Dolly had been bought from a Shenfield milkman and Tony from a retired hardware shop owner named Thorn. Whereas Dolly was gentle and affectionate Tony was less so. Quite suddenly he could become irritable and try to throw or bite you. Nobby was steadier although he could also have funny moments. He could adroitly unseat you by suddenly raising a rear hock and was a practised thief. Once over the field fence he raised his head and stole a loaf from the basket of a passing lady. Happily she quickly forgave.

I was not an enthusiastic rider although Dad encouraged me to ride as much as possible. He bought various saddles including a side saddle. For me horses were a little too unpredictable. However, I rode on Nobby in a number of Rayleigh and Southend carnivals as Lady Godiva, Queen Phillipa wife of Edward III, an Elizabethan lady and other various notable figures. I could do Lady Godiva because I had very long hair.

Brass bands traditionally led Carnivals and Dad was keen that Nobby became used to their sound. So on Sunday evenings he would get me mounted and lead up to Rayleigh High Street where the Salvation Army Band would be playing. There we stood by the horse trough and joined the service. When over we followed behind as the band returned to its Citadel along Rayleigh High Street. Nobby got used to brass bands and I enjoyed the music.

At a young age music had become a passion in my life and has remained one ever since. Dad had been a church choir boy but I think he had little music skill or appreciation. My mother on the other hand was naturally musical. She recalled how delighted she was to hear a school teacher play the piano. Mum had a great sense of rhythm and a truly beautiful singing voice.

She sang much around the house and encouraged my earliest musical interests listened to on the "wireless". This was large and sat on a shelf between the stair and larder doors. It had what I believed was called an "high tension" battery which lasted several months and an "accumulator" that had to be recharged every week or ten days in a cycle shop in Rayleigh High Street. They had to be carried carefully to avoid possible injury from spilling their acid.

Besides the "wireless" my parents had a piano although neither played: they obviously had hopes that I would. Dad had also bought for 5/- a child's violin in Rayleigh market which sat in its case behind a corner chair in the front room for many years before I actually played it.

My earliest musical lessons were on the piano during the war. A great character, Madam Thornton was my teacher. She and her husband, "Uncle Henry" sailed with my parents and the four were close friends so she was a natural choice as a teacher. However, she told Mum and Dad that they were wasting their money on my lessons and I had no more. She and "Uncle Henry" were long-standing professional musicians: he played the viola and she the violin and piano. Dad had first met them when they returned to Rayleigh on late-night trains after performing in London theatre orchestras. In their earlier professional lives they played in symphony orchestras. "Madam Thornton" became a well-loved Rayleigh figure who played the piano in Rayleigh's first cinema and often led carnival processions playing the violin as a comic character. I later took up the violin at Rayleigh Secondary Modern School and also joined the School choir. My early music tastes were formed. I progressed far enough with the violin to join the second violins a local amateur string orchestra. I have happy memories of our attempting Mozart's *Eine Kleine Nacht Musik* and Elgar's *Serenade to Music*. Beethoven and Mozart became life-long friends and I was transfixed on first hearing Beethoven's 7th Symphony on the radio.

The 1945 General Election was another big childhood influence although politics were little spoken about at home. Occasional anecdotes reflected my parents' left-wing sympathies and they took; the *Daily Herald* each weekday and *Reynolds News* on Sundays. Both were pro-Labour. *Reynolds News* became an early contact with the Co-operative Movement because it was published by its Co-operative Press. Moreover left-wing sympathies in 1926 led both my parents and my father's mother to take children from destitute Welsh mining families and look after them for some months. My grandmother took "Taffy" while my parents had "Iris". They were not alone. Strikes and tough mining conditions prompted trade union and Labour members elsewhere to foster Welsh mining children. This was a happy time for my parents because their own family was still some years away.

Without being conscious of it I imbibed working class and Labour culture from a young age. It became more real in the General Election of 1945 when Captain Ray Gunter was elected the Labour MP for our Billericay constituency. My first political meeting was to go with my parents to hear him speak as a candidate in Rayleigh Women's Institute Hall. Of course it was all over my head but the atmosphere was exciting as it was also on Election Day. Then I visited a nearby Labour Committee rooms with my grandmother where I was introduced to Mrs. Pickles. I recall her vividly because she was a real part of Labour history: her late husband had been secretary to the early Labour Leader, Hardie. Mrs. Pickles lived outside Rayleigh in an area called Thundersley. To come to Labour Party meetings in Rayleigh she needed to cross Thundersley Common which she did with the aid of a lantern. Such pedigree and determination made a lasting impressing on me quite apart from the fact that she and my grandmother were friends.

The election of a Labour Government seemed such a notable turning point. Its nationalisation programme included that of the railways. For us that meant that Dad felt he had greater security of employment and enjoyed higher wages. However, politics receded as school became the larger part of my life and a happy one.

THOUGHTS ON OUR EARLY YEARS

Of course I can speak more about my early years than I can of those of Bernard but from the above I think it can be gathered that we were raised in quite different settings. Nevertheless there was much we had in common that would later bring and keep us together.

We should now therefore more on to the year that became a big turning point for us both, namely 1955.

Chapter Two

ADULT EDUCATION BEGINS –
Co-operative College

POLITICAL APPRENTICESHIPS

Bernard and I were still to meet but 1955 became a turning point for both of us: it set us along the road on which we would meet a year later.

The big turning point was the 1955 General Election. It paved the way for Bernard's appointment as Research Officer **of** the Co-operative Party in London, and for me to become a student at the Co-operative College at Stanford Hall, Loughborough.

Bernard's predecessor at the Co-op Party had been Bert Oram but he left when elected a Labour/Co-op. Member of Parliament for an East Ham constituency. Earlier, in 1950 he had stood for our Billericay constituency after its MP, Ray Gunter moved to a safer seat. Billericay still heavily rural, reverted to its earlier conservatism. Bert Oram failed to gain it in 1950. He then also left and in the 1951 General election we had a new candidate. He was Brian Clapham, a Barrister, and he made a big impression on me.

When Bert Oram entered Parliament in 1955 and Bernard followed him as Co-op. Party Research Officer I had become much involved in the London Co-operative Society. Its Co-operative Party was led by a dynamic Political Committee whose offices were in London's Grays Inn Road. Its Political Secretary/Organiser was Ted Bedford who had previously held a similar position in Birkenhead and one that I would hold a few years later.

The London Co-operative Society was the largest in Britain and indeed the international co-operative movement at that time. Its size led to its Co-operative Party being organised in four distinct federations: two in the east, one in the north and another in the west. Each had their own organiser although that for the east managed both federations of Co-op. Party branches. She was Mrs. Margaret Higgins who played a large in my early political development and whom I recall with much affection. The organiser in the north was Vic Butler whose wife, Joyce, became a Labour/Co-op. MP. Each year the London Co-operative Party held a massive Annual Conference in town halls like those at Bethnal Green or Hammersmith. These were lively events and I looked forward to them from one year to another.

I have previously described Bernard's assimilation into his new job so perhaps here I can concentrate on how the 1955 General Election proved a jumping off ground for me as well. I was excited by its rhetoric and afterwards a group of us formed a branch of the Labour League of Youth. I was elected Secretary and this linked me to the Constituency Labour Party and to the Essex Federation of the Labour League of Youth. The latter's Chair was Arthur Latham from Romford who later became a Labour MP.

I came into the Co-operative Movement through the Labour Party alongside which was a local branch of the Co-operative Party and which I also joined. Both of Rayleigh's Labour and Co-operative Party branches met in the Co-operative Hall at the back of the local co-operative "stores", a parade of grocery, butchery and greengrocery branches. At one end of the hall was a banner proclaiming "One for all and all for one".

My main activity was in our branch of the Labour League of Youth. The political attitudes of most of us were shaped by our families. For example that of Bill Drewer our chair was renowned for its strong socialist faith. His paternal grandfather had belonged to the old Independent Labour Party, as had Bill's father who was also a conscientious objector. During the war he was imprisoned but occasionally escaped. Tales were told of police approaching his house but he would escape over the back garden fence in to nearby fields. Whereas Bill was moderate his younger brother, Stephen was notably militant. He missed taking an important exam at grammar school because he chose instead to participate in a Labour Party youth conference.

The Treasurer of our Labour League of Youth was Pam Aitken. Her father was a member of the Executive Committee of the Transport Salaried Staff Association (TASSA) the white collar rail trade union. Pam's parents quickly had a large family and Pam was passed to her mother's parents, Mr and Mrs. W. J. Chambers to be brought up. They had moved from Ilford to Rayleigh when he had retired from the post office. He was an able but self-educated man enthusiastic about gardening and a founder member of the Rayleigh Horticultural Society. He was also very politically active.

Although left-wing his views and statements were always measured. His strongest criticism of the Tories was that they were more concerned to preserve property rather than people. He also frequently reminded us that right wing politicians liked the Roman practice of providing circuses to divert criticism. He nevertheless supported the Labour Government's decision to hold the Festival of Britain in 1951.

I became a delegate to the Constituency Labour Party and attended its monthly meetings. These were on Saturday afternoons and attended by some lively delegates from other Labour Party branches. I learned meeting procedures and how to speak and debate in public. I admired a powerful speaker who frequently denounced capitalism for its "booms and slumps". Later I became Secretary of the Constituency Labour Party and Secretary to the No.2 Eastern Federation of the London Co-operative Party.

In many ways I served a kind of voluntary apprenticeship. Experience was gained in administration and organisation as well

23

as through debates, youth Parliaments, speaking contests, conferences and summer schools. A highlight one year was being elected to be the constituency's delegate to the national Labour Party Conference at Scarborough. Unfortunately I was not called to speak in the debate on which we had submitted a motion but was later mollified when Jim Callaghan, later Labour Chancellor of the Exchequer and Prime Minister approached to ask what I would have said. After the conference I toured local Labour Party branches to report on the conference. Had I been called to speak to our motion I would no doubt have been very nervous but experience was teaching us how to speak in public.

Two other big events were attending the Labour Party's summer schools at Beatrice Webb House, Dorking in 1954 and 1955. Morgan Phillips was then the Labour Party General Secretary and was present at both. So too was his wife, Nora Phillips who later became a leading London Labour politician. Dining at summer schools was at large round tables and on one occasion I recall sitting near Nora Phillips when she spoke of her daughter's recent wedding and passed round photographs of it. Her daughter later became the well-known Labour MP, Gwynneth Dunwoody.

At the latter summer school I met John Collins. He and I became life-long family friends. He was then the Co-operative Party Secretary/Organiser in Sheffield, but later became a National Organiser of the Co-operative Party and a friend of Bernard. John would later help to bring Bernard and I together. At the summer school he was great company with an infectious sense of humour. At a job interview it was suggested he was too young for the position but he assured that it was something of which he would soon outgrow. He got the job.

My early Labour and Co-op. Party experiences encouraged enthusiasm and commitment. They also helped to make 1955 one of the most significant years in my life. I quite unexpectedly became an agent in its General Election and later gained entrance to a diploma course in Politics, Economics and Social Studies at the Co-operative College, Loughborough.

These resulted from a series of moves with each not necessarily pointing to what might follow. They began with constituency boundary changes. Rayleigh was withdrawn from the Billericay Constituency to become part of the new South East Essex Constituency. Organisational upheavals followed when our agent and candidate decided to stay with Billericay. A few months later the General Election was called but the new South East Essex Constituency Labour Party had not had time to appoint a secretary/organiser who would have become their election agent or to elect a prospective parliamentary candidate. I was still the voluntary Constituency Secretary and was asked to act as the Election Agent. Significant for later developments was the fact that the candidate, Edward Harby was a Labour/Co-op. candidate. I was therefore given much practical help from the Political Committee of the London Co-operative Society.

Although delighted to be asked to be the Election Agent I was only 20 and still did have the vote myself. I also had to leave my job. Since 1950 I had worked in the office of Rayleigh Windmill but was not given three weeks' leave of absence. Indeed I was told I was foolish to let politics break my work. Fortunately a Labour parliamentary candidate in an adjoining constituency assured me he could get me a job in an insurance firm after the election. For being election agent I received a fee of £75.00, £25.00 per week. I had never been so well paid.

Despite the excitement we were unsuccessful although I proved to be the youngest election agent in the country which brought some notice. For example I was invited to move to the vote of thanks at the Annual Regional Labour Party Conference held in Cambridge the following October. Gerald Orbell, the next youngest agent seconded. We had links as I had already met his father at the Labour Party Summer Schools that year.

Gerald and I became friends for a short while although my main romantic interest was then John Collins. He was visiting us for the weekend and came to the Cambridge Rally with me along with Mum, Dad and Grandma Church/ Speller and a coach load from the South East Essex Constituency. Afterwards Mum told me that Dad cried when Jerusalem was sung and he saw me sitting on the platform.

The highlight for me was a historical connection. Lady Megan Lloyd George, daughter of past Liberal Prime Minister, Lloyd George was one of the speakers and in my thanks I noted that this was in "the first year of her Labour Party membership". She had only recently left the Liberals. Another speaker was Harold Wilson later to be Labour Party leader and Prime Minister. Then he was still on his way up.

Constituency boundary changes and the 1955 General Election formed the first rung in the ladder of change. The next came on the day of the interview for the clerical job in a London insurance office. Getting there became difficult when a rail strike was called. Dad was a railwayman and I could not be seen breaking the strike by trying to join one of the few trains still running although rail was the easiest way into London from Rayleigh. Going by bus took far longer because of changes necessitated by poor roads.

In some desperation I telephoned Margaret Higgins, Organiser of the two Eastern Federations of the London Co-operative Society's Political Committee. She regularly drove to their Head Quarters in Grays Inn Road and I asked whether she might possibly be driving there that day; and if so, could she give me a lift. Happily, she agreed. That drive changed my life.

Rayleigh was 35 miles east of London so we had good time to chat and Margaret asked why I was going to London. When I explained the situation she said she thought that perhaps I should be thinking of furthering my education instead, perhaps at the Co-operative College.

26

At that time a number of adult colleges specialised in making provisions for working class students without higher educational entrance qualifications. Twenty years or so later the Open university would take on such a role but in the 1950s the main providers were Ruskin College, Oxford with trade union students while the Co-operative College at Loughborough, catered mostly for co-operative members and employees. In Birmingham there was Fircroft College for men and in Surbiton, Surrey, Hillcroft College for women. The obvious place for me would be the Co-operative College. Margaret suggested that before I went for the insurance interview she should make enquiries if and how I might study there. Once we reached her London Office two other appointments were made for me with Harold Campbell, Assistant General Secretary at the national Co-operative Party and with Reg Plant, Assistant Education Secretary of the London Co-operative Society.

Harold Campbell was known for his encouragement of young co-operative enthusiasts but his main reason for agreeing to see me at such short notice was to discuss the result of the election in the South East Essex constituency. Reg Plant, on the other hand, would know whether places remained at the College and whether it might be possible for the Education Committee of the London Co-operative Society to grant me a scholarship to study there.

The Co-operative Movement had strong educational traditions.

In the mid 19th century the Rochdale Pioneers set the precedent of retail co-operatives having "reading rooms". In these members could read assembled books or gain elementary education. A percentage of trading surplus was allocated for such provision and predated formal state education of children in the late 19th century. A century later education was highly prized in the co-operative movement and the wider working classes. As previously mentioned in support of his university education Bernard had used the library of the Bradford Mechanics' Institute. We both had co-operative and working class friends who tried to better their education and sometimes boasted of their wide reading as well as the number of books they owned. Our mutual friend, John Collins was among these. In 1919 the Co-operative Movement had established its own College first at Manchester and from 1945 at Stanford Hall in Loughborough. That purchase had been made to celebrate the centenary of the Rochdale Pioneers a year earlier and the coming of peace in 1945.

The meeting with Reg Plant, Assistant Education Officer of the Education Committee of the London Co-operative Society, proved decisive. We were now in June 1955 and it was possible that places for the coming academic year at the College were already taken. Co-operative Societies and the two Wholesale Societies would have completed their scholarship selections. Often these took the form of exams or required candidates to have already taken Co-operative correspondence courses. However, Reg arranged for me to meet the full Education Committee of the London Co-operative Society and they agreed to support my application. An interview with Mr. R. L. Marshall, Principal of the College was then arranged; it was the first time I met him. After becoming one of his students and later an employee we became long-standing friends that ended only in his death in 2008.

My first sight of Stanford Hall over-awed. It reminded me of being taken to the Royal Albert Hall for the first time during the War and on entering it becoming amazed at its enormously vast and grand interior. I had seen nothing like that only in films and very few of those. Stanford Hall was a mid 18th century manor house standing in a three hundred acre park. It was big and elegant.

Before my interview I waited in the College Library which was sited in a most beautiful large salon with two smaller rooms leading off to overlook the rear garden. Another side of the Library overlooked a mosaic Italian garden with a font at its centre. To the side of this and back in the main building was a

Badminton court which was large enough to hold College examinations.

Mr. Marshall's room was smaller but elegant and overlooked the rear gardens. It was wood panelled and lined with books. The interview took place after lunch which I was invited to join. A summer school was taking place and lunch was in one of the two dining rooms that had been a foyer leading to the theatre built by the last owner of Stanford Hall, Sir Julian Cahn, the furniture magnate. The meal was fish and chips and I recall how welcome I was made by the then Education Secretary of Ipswich Co-operative Society, Arthur Aubert. I had already found that the movement's leaders and higher ranking officials seldom stood on their dignity with young people. It was heart-warming and encouraged confidence.

I recall little of my later interview with Mr. Marshall apart from my waxing enthusiastically about *Jane Eyre* and other books of the Bronte sisters. Afterwards I thought he would consider this irrelevant so felt that I had not done particularly well. Mr. Marshall said he would inform the Education Committee of the London Co-operative Society of his decision and then me. I recall sitting in the train returning home and suddenly feeling burnt out with my political work. For the first time I doubted how far I wished to continue with it. Fortunately a new life was opening up. Within a few days I received a letter from the College advising me I had gained a place which I would take in the coming October. I also received details of my scholarship from the London Co-op. They would pay my accommodation and tuition fees and I would receive a personal allowance of £30.00 for each of the three terms of the academic year. If I made suitable progress I could apply for a similar scholarship the following year. The course I would take was for two years and should lead to a Diploma in Politics, Economics and Social Studies offered by the Extra Mural Department of Nottingham University.

Until enrolling I took a temporary job in the office of coal merchants and wondered what life would be like at Stanford Hall. Despite its beauty I feared it would not be good to be at the centre of a vast park in heavy rain or other bad weather. It was a rather isolating place.

THE CO-OPERATIVE COLLEGE

My two years at the college became a major and lasting influence. In the mid 1950s its student population was around 120, predominantly young. Many became friends for life or colleagues as their professional paths later crossed. We spent much time together in Stanford Hall and it grounds. A bus stop, ten minutes' walk away at Park Corner allowed us to catch buses running between Loughborough and Nottingham but to reach it you had to walk along a poorly lit footpath. I recall one winter's evening suddenly deciding to go to the pictures in Loughborough but walking along the path by myself I was frightened by hearing deep breathing. Eventually I realised that this came from nearby cows on the other side of the fence. Very few students had cars, neither did every tutor.

Most of us settled quickly and happily. There were many activities. . The library was usually busy. Each evening at 9pm tea and biscuits were served in the basement, organised by an elected Social Committee. Most students enjoyed although the tea from the urn was not all that good. A joke went round that it was spiked with bromide to reduce male amorous intentions.

The basement carried a number of facilities: a small chapel, a laundry and ironing room, a small TV lounge, and walls along which student notices were displayed together with a students' wall newspaper of which an early college boyfriend, John Millwood, was Editor. John had worked for *Reynolds News,* the co-operative Sunday newspaper and had journalistic ambitions. But he also had a youthful and perhaps unwise sense of humour. I recall his being reprimanded by Mr. Marshall, the Principal for reproducing two adverts in the wall newspaper. These had appeared next to each other on a large roadside hording. The first declared that VD (Venereal Disease) killed but that adjoining declared "I got it at the Co-op." In those days almost anything could be bought at Co-op. stores and indeed one wit had declared that the Co-op. had everything from "matches to MPs". John thought that the unintentional juxtaposing of the adverts was amusing. Mr. Marshall did not and told him not to include anything like that again.

John also had amusing anecdotes. As a boy he delivered meat orders for a Co-op butcher's shop in London. Several customers lived in the mews at Buckingham Palace and he took great pleasure in riding his co-op meat bicycle through the palace gates.

At a serious level my two years at the Co-operative College began my adult education. Having previously passed no examinations I was accepted for entry without qualifications. However, some other students had been to grammar schools. One had even been to the London School of Economics but expelled for immoral behaviour! These new friends brought academic competition which prompted hard work. Even so I struggled. I was soon told that I spoke better than I wrote. I had soon entered student debates and earlier political activities inclined me to be ready to express myself. I became a member of the College team to enter the *Observers* 1955 student unions debating contest where we were knocked out in the first round at Nottingham University. I found writing more difficult but tutors were patient and helped me improve.

The college environment compounded academic advances. Its grandeur and elegance I had only previously seen in films. When I first arrived I was met by Jack Dring who wore a steward's white coat and had previously worked at the Hall for the Cahn family. He treated Co-operative College students in much the same way as he had his previous employers, always with quiet deference and politeness. At the door he took my case and checked where I would stay. He then showed me along the main corridor and up a massive and elegant staircase flanked by an immense window. This overlooked a roof garden above the foyer leading to a theatre built by Cahn. By this was a landing before the stairs turned round on themselves. On it stood the life-size statue of black male called "George".

He became a prominent feature in student life as the butt of many jokes and pranks. These helped students let off steam and were generally tolerated by college authorities. For example he was dressed in cricket togs and placed outside the window of the Principal's office. Cricket ranked high at the College and benefitted from a superior pitch Sir Julian Cahn had had prepared. On another occasion "George" was placed by the fountain in the Italian garden; without clothes he looked ready for a shower.

My favourite "George" episode occurred when he was removed and a nude student took his place. The student's name was Ron Buckle although that was rigorously kept secret in the immediate aftermath of the prank. Ron came from Liverpool and was the boyfriend of my close friend, Sylvia, who would later be one of my two bridesmaids.

Ron stood nude on George's plinth and copied his stance with one arm languidly placed over his head so hiding his face. George's other hand fell equally languidly in front of him without hiding anything. Ron, however, hid his private parts with a packet of Co-op "Spell" leading washing powder. A photograph was taken on which Ron declared that he had been "Spellbound".

"I was spellbound" became a catch phrase in that year's student Christmas concert, an annual event held in the magnificent bijou theatre built by Cahn. We were fortunate to be given its use and Mr. Onions, the College engineer gave much help. There was a strong tradition of theatricals at Stanford Hall and during my time a Midlands repertory company performed plays there every third week. Amateur theatrical groups also gave shows as did photographic and film groups.

Returning to my arrival at Stanford Hall Jack Dring showed me into the first room to the top and left of the grand staircase. This was the entrance to the Adam Room, so called because it contained a genuine Adam fireplace. The room was large with two large windows on the far side overlooking the rear gardens which fell away to rolling grazing land and a lake beyond. Later exploration showed a brook leaving it which was called the King's brook. Folk lore had it that Richard 111 watered his horses there on his way to the battle of Bosworth Field and his death in 1485. Back in the Adam Room I found four beds with accompanying dressing tables, cupboards and desks. Being the first to arrive I choose the bed underneath the right hand window and politely thanked Jack who left me to unpack.

Prior to arrival I had been sent the College rules. One was that students should never go into the rooms of the opposite sex. If caught they could be expelled. So when I saw a slightly open door in the far corner of the room I did not go to see what was beyond in case it led to a student men's room. Eventually, though, curiosity got the better of me and I crept through the door into the most amazing en suite bathroom I could ever imagine. It was large in pink and white marble with a massive sunken bath, bidet, toilet, shower, weighing machine and dressing table. Again it was something I had only ever seen in Hollywood films. Initially, such luxury was overwhelming but I soon became used to it as did many other students enjoying Stanford Hall's other remarkable and luxurious bathrooms.

The other three Adam Room students soon arrived. They were Audrey Mills, Nancy Goodier and Pat Laws. It was Pat who had been expelled from the London School of Economics. They were second year Social Study students and were already firm friends. Audrey came from Huddersfield and had been active in the British Federation of Young Co-operators. Nancy came from London and had little Co-operative background that I can remember. Pat came from Derby and was clearly very bright. When some overseas students wanted a translation of an erotic book entitled *Golden Lotus,* they asked her to translate those parts written in Latin that were obviously intended to make the more salacious sections more oblique. Pat happily obliged but entertained her roommates with verbal translations along the way. My education was certainly widening.

There was further grandeur and luxury outside. A putting green lay outside the college's front door. I never played on it but many mornings saw its due being swept away by groundsmen. Further away was the high-class cricket pitch created for Sir Julian Cahn. He invited visiting cricket teams to play and put their members overnight in the bedrooms above the theatre although these were now occupied by students. The pitch was still used for college games and occasionally leading players would visit, much to the delight of Arnold Bonner, the college's resident and senior tutor. He was a cricket enthusiast and I recall him enthusiastically welcoming the prominent West Indian player, Clyde Walcott.

Near the cricket pitch was a remarkable swimming pool, elegantly encased in rock gardens. Being open it could only be used in the summer months but what luxury for ordinary students. There was also a football pitch which male students used but on which hockey was also played. I was persuaded to play in one game but embarrassed myself and the team by inadequate knowledge of the offside rules!

Some Puritanism however remained. Students were expected to give self-help in two main ways. One was ground duties each Monday afternoon when we were divided into teams and allocated certain parts of the grounds to weed or trim. On one occasion the men in our group decided to burn cuttings but the fire quickly got out of control. Another girl and mys8elf were quickly urged away so that the men could put the fire out by natural means – successfully I was told.

The other form of student self-help was washing up after main meals. We were placed on a rota and our turn came round once or twice a term. These allowed insights into the kitchen routine. In those days there were no dishwashers although I do recall a big old washer of a kind that automatically washed only heavy pans: crockery and cutlery still had to be washed by hand. Meals were served by kitchen maids although self-service was introduced in later decades. Kitchen staff was recruited locally or from abroad. I recall two very good looking Danish sisters who were very popular among students; also after the Hungarian revolution in 1956 several young Hungarian refugees were recruited.

These serving arrangements and a number of other practices point to a fair degree of formality at the College in the mid 1950s. This was perhaps not surprising being only a decade after the end of the Second World War and continuing conscription. The student population was young but many of the men had served in the armed forces. As a result they easily took college discipline and kept a personal smartness.

There were two dining rooms. The main one was in what had been the foyer between the main building and the theatre above which was the roof garden overlooked by the huge staircase window. A second dining room was in a large room near the main entrance. If anything it was even grander with a moulded ceiling and a massive stone fireplace. Two year students were first in one dining room and then the other. Each had a top table presided over by Mr. Marshall, the College principle in the foyer dining room and Mr. George Adams the College Administrative Officer in the other. They said grace before each lunch and dinner: "For what we are about to receive may the Lord make us truly thankful and ever mindful of the needs of others." They then introduced any notable visitors. Once or twice each term and from another rota students sat at the top tables thus engaging in conversation with the principal or Mr. Adams, visitors and perhaps other lecturers.

Yet another rota signed students to give readings during evening meals, a kind of secular version of readings during monastery meals. These revealed diverse literary tastes, perhaps not surprising given that each year around 30 students came from British colonial territories. They were termed "overseas students": British co-operators were uneasy about the British Empire and the term was also appropriate because some students came from countries such as Iceland. Moreover some British territories were already becoming independent. Indeed the Gold Coast became the Ghana while we were at the College and two students from there proudly wore their national dress.

The thrust of this book is that Bernard and I joined the Co-op but saw many co-operatives beyond those in Britain. We did so through actual visits and working with overseas co-operatives. My early links came through studying with overseas students at the Co-operative College in the mid-1950s. A fond memory is of the 1955 students' Christmas concert resounding to a student from Tanganyika, later Tanzania, singing a national song. Its chorus repeated the line "Tanganyika, Tanganyika, Tanganyika" which was taken up by other students around the college in the next few days.

The student and teaching part of the college formed its largest element but Stanford Hall hosted a far wider co-operative community. In addition to domestic staff headed by a housekeeper, Miss Hilda Watling, there was a college administrative office. This was led by George Adams who sat at the top table in the second dining room. He like many others working at Stanford Hall had strong co-operative credentials. His father was the President of the then Berwick Co-operative Society. The college also had Mr. Onions as its chief engineer and his supporting staff. They frequently warned that being built two centuries earlier the areas between Stanford Hall's floors and ceilings were fire risks.

There was much to upkeep. The luxury of the Adam Room was repeated throughout the Hall particularly in distinctive bathrooms. Male students slept dormitory style in large rooms, different nationalities mixing. This caused some hilarity. Most overseas students dressed like British students but a Nigerian student even more so. His usual garb was a tweed sports jacket and black Homburg hat of the kind leading politicians of the time wore. To accompany this he carried a long black umbrella which became a target for other students. They often took and hid it. One day students in his room had high jinks and beds got turned over. The umbrella had been hidden in one and became so bent could no longer be used!

Next to the hall and by the cricket pitch was a market garden. This would later be hived off but remained part of the Hall's kitchen garden during the mid-1950s. Indeed one or two teams on Monday "ground duties" would be sent to work in it.

All these additional people were regularly seen by students as were members of the staff of the Co-operative Union's Education Department also based at Stanford Hall. An attractive part of the estate was that close to the Hall and laying at right angles to it was a large stable block topped by an attractive ornamental clock. By the mid-1950s the stables had become flats and offices to which new adjoining offices had also been built.

The Co-operative Union's Education Department, of which the College Principal was also the head, was large. It comprised a number of departments. At that time the two main ones were Member Education and Staff Training. There was also a youth office as many co-operative societies' education committees still organised youth sections. The British Federation of Young Co-operators also existed and a number of its 1930s leaders were now becoming well known in the wider co-operative movement. Roommate Audrey Mills had come up through Co-operative Youth work and had won a recent national co-operative youth speaking contest.

A particularly important section of the Co-operative Union's Education Department was that dealing with correspondence courses. Typed lessons were posted to students enrolled with the Education Department or with their co-operatives' education committees. A network of markers was also had to be maintained and serviced. Candidates applying to become students at the Co-operative College usually needed to show that they had achieved certain grades in correspondence courses. I was an unusual entrant in that I had not come through this route.

Many years later Mrs. Lily Howe became a close colleague. She was then editor of the British *Co-operative News* and later became a member of the board of the National Co-operative Development Agency and a Trustee of the Plunkett Foundation. I recall her once telling me how all this had begun by her taking Co-operative Union correspondence courses.

Central to the college itself was its tutors some of whom lived in flats near the stable wing. Mr. Bonner, the Senior and Resident Tutor lived with his wife in a ground floor flat in the new wing of Stanford Hall built at the opposite end of the main building from that of the theatre. It adjoined a beautiful hedged rose garden and gold fish pond close to which were tennis courts. Residents from nearby villages, particularly East Leake and Rempstone could take season tickets to use these, the swimming pool and other facilities such as the theatre.

Many of those who worked at Stanford Hall joined students for the mid-day meal. They reminded them of the wider co-operative movement as did the college's many visitors at our time one of these was Bert Youngjohns who was researching and writing the first Co-operative College paper *Co-operation and the State;* he also gave occasional economics lectures. Several years earlier he had been a student himself at the College and then went on to Oriel College, Oxford to take a degree there.

Bert became an important figure for me for several reasons. During my second year he and his family moved to Basutoland in Africa where he became chief Co-operative Registrar. Before leaving he raised the possibility that I might later join him in a post to be created to encourage women into co-operatives. This raised many issues. I was becoming an increasing co-operative enthusiast but I was still also a political one. What kind of job I would eventually take after leaving college was not yet clear but leaving Britain and the British Co-operative Movement as well as politics for a completely unfamiliar clime was a bit too radical. Moreover, I eventually wanted to marry and landing up as a co-operative missionary in a British colony hardly fitted such aims.

I greatly admired Bert Youngjohns' Co-operative College paper *Co-operation and the State,* and to prepare it he had been a long term visitor to the college. There were also others and many visiting speakers. Among these was Prof. Jacob Bronowski, George Woodcock, General Secretary of the Trades Union Congress and Will Watkins, General Secretary of the International Co-operative Alliance.

The college was also a focal point for co-operative members who joined short courses particularly during the summer months. Elected leaders of co-operative auxiliaries also met there including the Woodcraft Folk, the Co-operative Women's Guild, the Men's Co-operative Guild, the National Guild of Co-operators and the British Federation of Young Co-operators. All reminded students of the wider co-operative movement as they were in retail societies furnishing college bedrooms and having their name on their doors. I recall an Oxford room, the Derby room and many others.

In the 1950s the British Co-operative movement was integrated and its many parts closely related to each other. The Education Department and its College were central and a major department of the Co-operative Union then the movement's senior federation.

The major point though is what the College did for me. When enrolling I was without educational qualifications. I was a political activist yet was little grounded in political and economic theory. The courses I took at the college helped remedied both deficiencies. They included British Economic and Social History, British Political Institutions, Economics, International Relations, British Trades Unions, Social Psychology and the History, Theory and Organisation of Co-operation. They were part of the syllabus of Nottingham University's Extra Mural Diploma in Politics, Economics and Social Studies with the Co-operative subjects augmenting the social studies section of the Diploma.

My favourite tutor was Arnold Bonner who took us for the Co-operative subjects as well as Economic and Social History. History was his enthusiasm and Co-operation a dedication. He was steeped in British co-operative history with family links to the Rochdale Pioneers. A great tutor, he engendered interest and enthusiasm. His classes turned me into a co-operator as distinct from the woolly minded socialist.

At that time state socialism was popular with its nationalisation of basic industries and command of the higher levels of the economy. Co-operation wooed me away from such ideas with its concepts of voluntary and open membership, democratic control and successful competition in a market economy. Over the preceding century the British Co-operative Movement had shown how these could be achieved through collective social ownership which I came to believe was superior to nationalisation and ministerial direction. In the mid 1950s British co-operative membership stood at over 12,000,000 in just over 1,000 retail societies. It was then at its zenith. Its decline was beginning although hardly yet recognised. Co-operative college students still remained its beneficiaries its scholarships. These and Co-operative adult education were funded from the success of co-operative trade and not from the state.

However education had been only one of co-operatives' founding aims. Rochdale's Law the First spoke of mutual trade being undertaken to capitalise co-operative employment and government. Initially this was to be within specially created co-operative communities but in the later 19th century these were replaced by a new kind of community formed in factories and towns. Retail societies became a notable element within these and with distinct place names in their titles.

Jack Bailey, General Secretary of the Co-operative Party when Bernard became its Research Officer noted in his book *The British Co-operative Movement* that retail societies offered greater voting opportunities than parliamentary elections. The latter could occur every five years whereas co-operative members voted more frequently in their ownership and control of their societies.

CONCLUSION

Through the Co-operative College and particularly Arnold Bonner's teaching my co-operative grounding was somewhat different from Bernard's. Despite our later compatibility I believe he found my enthusiasm for the College somewhat strange. His broader university education led him to see the college at Stanford Hall as something like a 'co-operative monastery'. Although I disagreed I could see what he meant.

Despite our different entries into the Co-operative Movement we were very much on the same lines when we met during the summer vacation between my two years at the College.

Chapter Three

COURTSHIP AND MARRIAGE

COURTSHIP

Recently I overheard a diner ask a waiter if he was still "courting" his girl. The waiter looked nonplussed and eventually asked if the diner meant was he still "dating" his girl? The exchange brought home how language has changed, as have rites of passage. Happily I can record that Bernard courted me and even wrote to my parents to ask if he could do so. Bernard was fairly formal and with his good manners these were an early attraction.

Our first meeting was on 29th September 1956 at a Co-operative Party Speaking Contest followed by a sit-down tea. The contest was held in the main hall of Southend's Municipal College where my grandfather had once been a caretaker. I was the speaker in our team from the Rayleigh branch and my father was its Chairman. Another member moved the vote of thanks. Our topic was automation and its likely future effects on working practices. I urged the formation of workers' co-operatives to help workers protect rights and control changing working conditions.

Bernard was one of the three adjudicators and represented the Party's Head Office. The other two were Jimmy Hudson who had recently retired as the Labour/Co-op/ Member of Parliament for North Ealing and Percy Bell, Chair of the London Co-operative Society's Political Committee. They sat at a large table in the middle of the hall with an audience of around 70. My first impression of Bernard was that he looked Irish and intellectual and rather sophisticated as he smoked his cigarettes through a cigarette holder. Bernard later told me that the judges' marks were in line with each other but that his were the most conservative. Together they awarded our team third place. He also said that he wrote in his diary that "Pretty Rita Church impressed." We each seemed to make an instant impression and introduced ourselves to each other at tea after the contest. This was held in a large Co-op. hall above Co-op. grocery premises in nearby Southchurch Road. When Bernard arrived Dad and I were standing near the top of the stairs and he came over to speak to us. He was perhaps in the unusual position of meeting his future wife and father-in-law at the same time!

The only thing that stayed in my memory of that first meeting was that we both mentioned our mutual friend John Collins. Later John encouraged our getting together by inviting us to see with him "Bride and the Bachelor" at the Adelphi Theatre in London. That did not immediately set us off as there was much else going on and I still had other romantic interests. But it was an occasion we both remembered fondly and later influenced the date of our wedding.

Strangely I had had a run of five boyfriends named John. My parents had sadly lost their first baby also named John and the expectation was that I would bring a John back into the family. Bernard therefore seemed to not be in the running. At college I had first stepped out with John Millwood but a very good looking John Peters soon attracted me. He was Indian and adopted by Methodist missionaries who had been working in India. When they returned home he came with them and entered the College through employment with a Yorkshire co-operative. We were probably never likely to marry. In many ways he was still immature and unsettled being caught between Indian heritage and British adoption. This little worried me as he was one of the most attractive men I had ever met. After college though, our lives gradually took different directions.

I was therefore little focused on Bernard Other excitement distracted and brought new friends. In 1957 I gained a Co-operative Union scholarship to a summer school in Denmark held at the International People's College at Elsinore.. There I met Gwynneth Llewellyn who became a life-long friend. We had a mutual friend in John Collins who I remembered speaking of a Gwynneth Llewellyn who, despite her Welsh name lived on Teesside.

It was a memorable summer school for Gwynneth because two years later she married one of its Danish tutors and then moved to Copenhagen. In those two years however we both worked in London and became close friends. The trip to Elsinore had also given me my first experiences of co-operatives beyond those I knew in Britain. They were heavily agricultural which brought new perspectives

I had left the College several months earlier. It had been a terrible wrench but for the first time in my life I had passed exams and gained a Diploma in Politics, Economics and Social Studies from Nottingham University. I had also come second in an essay competition on co-operative housing and was a member of the winning team in the college's debating contest sponsored by the Oxford Society. We were given small wooden versions of the winners' shield and I still have mine.

On leaving college a big question was what should be my work. At that time the Co-operative Movement offered few roles for women other than in the auxiliaries, particularly the Co-operative Women's Guilds in England and Scotland. Fellow women students at the College went into childcare, probation work and schools careers advice work. I was the only one seeking co-operative employment.

I hoped for an organising post in the Co-operative Party but there was no immediate opening. The London Co-op. remained helpful and offered me a temporary position in a typing pool in its large accounts department. A strong memory from this brief period was of a woman who worked as an administrator to the society's assistant accountant in a side room next to our typing pool. One day she spoke indignantly to me about investments the society proposed to make in a share-holding institution. She held this to be "un-co-operative". I found this to be perceptive given her relatively low status. I wish such knowledge was more widespread today.

This lady's boss, the LCS Assistant Accountant one day asked if I would consider becoming Manger of one of the society's funeral branches. I quickly declined. I still wanted to work in politics rather than management; and at 22 a funeral department held no appeal.

Shortly afterwards though, the position of membership secretary in the Fabian Society was advertised. I applied and was appointed. Their offices were in a house once owned by George Bernard Shaw and mine was in its basement. It had no window so I constantly worked in electric light but I did not mind. I was quickly happy. The work was interesting and colleagues friendly.

I became friends with the bookshop manager and sometimes helped him out. The bookshop had a street level entrance and one day I had an embarrassing experience. A tall, rather strange looking man came in and on looking around various displays observed that we were not featuring his book. I was silly enough to say that I was sure that we did but he immediately informed, "My name is Pakenham, Frank Pakenham". He would later be better known as Lord Longford and famous for a number of good causes. Happily the bookshop manager soon returned and immediately found the book he sought.

At that time the Fabian Society's General Secretary was Bill Rodgers who later became a Labour Member of Parliament and later still a founder of the break-away Social Democratic Party. He ended up in the House of Lords as Lord Rodgers. In the Fabian Society he was succeeded by Shirley Williams who followed a similar route through the Labour Party, SDP and the Liberal Democratic Party. Their Assistant General Secretary was Dick Leonard who later held influential backroom positions in the wider Labour Movement.

How this is related to Bernard and I getting together was that we found ourselves working near each other and could meet more frequently. I was in Dartmouth Street and he was just round the corner in Victoria Street. Moreover Bernard frequently used the Fabian bookshop. We now enjoyed occasional lunches or lunchtime walks around nearby St. James's Park. But there were difficulties. We were obviously different personalities, had different musical tastes, religious faiths and even political views. Bernard was more to the centre and believed in multi-lateral nuclear disarmament whereas I was a unilateralist. Nuclear disarmament was a divisive issue in those days. There was also a ten-year age gap between us.

Happily there were some similarities. We were both co-operative enthusiasts, both loved cats and I enjoyed Bernard's wit, humour and massive vocabulary. Each of us appreciated good food which for me in the late 1950s was a new pleasure. Bernard already knew a number of London restaurants to which he introduced me. Over one meal I recall our discussing our musical tastes. Mine ranged from Bach to Brahms and his from Beethoven to Tchaikovsky.

A taste not easily shared was that of Shakespeare and here I believe Bernard's Grammar school education and my lack of one came into play. Nevertheless he took me to see *Hamlet* at the Old Vic with John Neville as Hamlet. We were near the front and I was already attracted to John Neville who I had seen at Fabian meetings. The fact that a young Judi Dench played Ophelia went quite over my head as did much of the play.

It seemed we would remain good friends for suddenly Bernard was leaving his job and London to take a new co-operative position in Leeds. In the spring of 1958 he became Sectional Secretary for the North East Section of the Co-operative Union. His father had recently been diagnosed with lung cancer and his return north was therefore timely.

Being a political enthusiast I said that I found it difficult to understand how he would want to leave the Co-operative Party for a trading position in the Co-operative Movement. Bernard tersely replied that in having a degree, he had the ability to make the transition. Actually we were still getting to know one another and I later came to understand that he had interests and abilities more wide-ranging than I had originally appreciated. I also appreciated that he was building on his past boardroom experience with the Bradford and District Co-operative Society and was well known in that region. The Sectional Board to which he would be responsible comprised members from other Yorkshire co-operatives as well as some General Managers. Many of these already knew Bernard or had read articles he had written in Co-operative journals.

He had also written elsewhere and I recall one of his articles in *Socialist Commentary* entitled *Definition 601* in which he explored the many different definitions of socialism. *Socialist Commentary* was then edited by Dr. Rita Hinden who I had known as a member of the Fabian Society. Despite his considerable political interests Bernard never had ambitions to seek election to Parliament. Rather he mused and observed. Earlier academic ambitions had been superseded by co-operative ones. Sadly he never completed the Master's degree he began on public entertainment under one of the Roman Emperors.

Bernard's writings became a major part of his life. His prose was both eloquent and elegant. After we married we developed a "cottage industry" in which he wrote many articles in longhand and I typed them. In those days only women typed. Bernard never attempted it even when computers came on the scene. His writing spread his name and reputation and became a supplementary income that paid for a number of our holidays in the 1960s and 1970s. More importantly for me, I learned much from what he wrote and some of his literary skills rubbed off on me. Bernard's mother once observed that perhaps he took his skills too lightly because they came to him so easily. Mine were harder earned.

However, in 1958 he and I were still coming to know each other and any romantic ideas seemed premature with his move back to Yorkshire. We still met when Bernard came to London for meetings and wrote and telephoned. Both of us enjoyed writing letters. We had one disastrous evening before he left for Paris the next day to attend a meeting on behalf of the Co-operative Union. Over dinner we disagreed on almost everything, with increasing irritation. Fundamentally Bernard was a pessimist and I an optimist. For him a glass was half empty, for me it was half full. We still had to learn that opposites really do attract.

I had a memorable distraction with a co-operative trip to Austria. Thirty members of the London Co-operative Society made an exchange visit with the Austrian Trades Union Congress and I fell in love with Vienna. I was bowled over by its music, architecture, and wine villages in the nearby Vienna Woods. We stayed in a Trade Union centre where the food was great. Our first lunch was of grilled chicken of an excellence I had not previously known served with a salad also dressed in previously unknown ways. A gorgeous light cherry sponge followed.

After the Second World War Austria, like Germany had been split between and governed by the occupying Allies. These left in 1955 only three years before our visit. Much war damage remained and I was shocked by the number of war-wounded we passed. We also learned much about Vienna's struggles before the war between Fascists and Marxists and of the Anschluss when Germany and Austria merged in 1938. We drove by the Karl Marx Platz, a large block of municipal flats, where bullet holes from Fascist attacks in 1934 could still be seen.

Despite such recent terrible history Vienna encouraged a light-heartedness I had not found a year earlier in Copenhagen. Viennese humour came through despite translation and there was an ambient theatricality. Men wore their jackets lose over their shoulders as if they were capes. At a dinner in the Kahlenberg

Restaurant atop a hill overlooking Vienna, the lights were dimmed and then through a door came an accordionist singing "Vienna, City of my Dreams". We were urged to turn round our chairs to look out of the huge windows looking down on the city and the Danube which now sparkled with lights. It was magical.

We were also taken to the Volksoper theatre to see an Austrian operetta, Der Vogelhandler, or *"Bird Trader"*. This introduced me to a kind of Viennese folk music somewhat different from that of the better known Strauss father and sons. Viennese manners also appealed, particularly the kissing of hands. Once several of us enjoyed coffee at a pavement café and when a nearby man and his son got up to leave they bowed as they passed our table.

After a week in Vienna we had a day in beautiful Salzburg and then a week at another Trade Union centre on the outskirts of Innsbruck. All in all it was a memorable visit which led me years later to persuade Bernard to visit Vienna. Along with Paris and Lisbon it remained one of our favourite cities. We became long-standing members of the Anglo-Austrian Society and I still remain a member. Through its music arm we were lucky enough to obtain tickets for three Silvesterabend concerts played by the Vienna Philharmonic Orchestra under Willi Boskowsky in the 1970s. These concerts were the same as those performed on New Year's morning and broadcast world-wide. They led us to join the Johann Strauss Society of Great Britain and to assemble a great many records of music by the Strauss family and their contemporaries.

I wrote happily about my Vienna visit to Bernard who was now settling well among Yorkshire co-operatives although his father's health worsened. Strangely this brought us closer together as Bernard's letters and 'phone calls became more frequent. After his father died on 7 November 1958 Bernard came down to London. We spent much time together and our courtship began. Always formal he even wrote to my parents seeking agreement for us to do so. Although not enthusiastic they agreed. They possibly thought it would not last.

Although I worked happily in the Fabian Society it was a job without prospects. I was likely to remain Membership Secretary indefinitely. I wanted a more politically active job. An organisational position in the Co-op. Party appealed most and I had already unsuccessfully applied for the position of Political Secretary/Organiser of the Enfield Highway Co-operative Society on the outskirts of London.

I had also developed a sense of co-operative geography which grafted onto physical geography. As I was conscious of the counties around Essex I was also conscious of the co-operatives around the massive London Co-operative Society. To its south were the large South Suburban and Royal Arsenal Co-operative Societies, to its north was the Enfield Highway Society and in Essex the smaller Chelmsford Star Co-operative. Further out were the Colchester and Ipswich Co-operatives.

Enfield Highway was renowned for the high number of national co-operative leaders elected to its Board of Management. In the mid-1950s these included Jack Bailey, General Secretary of the Co-operative Party, Harold Campbell, the Party's Assistant General Secretary and Ted Graham who had come into the co-operative movement through the British Federation of Young Co-operators before the war. He was currently the Southern Sectional Secretary of the Co-operative Union but in the 1960s would succeed Harold Campbell as General Secretary of the Co-operative Party. Another Enfield board member was John Gallacher, a Scot and past student of the Co-operative College who would later become a Sectional Secretary of the Co-operative Union and later still its Parliamentary Secretary. Bernard would succeed in that position when John became a Life Peer in 1983. Muriel Russell also sat on the Enfield board having also been a past Co-op College student and was prominent in the Co-operative Women's Guild. She became more widely known in the 1960s when she became the Women's Officer and Secretary of the Women's Committee of the International Co-operative Alliance then based in London where it had been formed in 1895.

To apply to become the Political Secretary/Organiser of Enfield Highway Co-operative Society with such an eminent co-operative board of management was therefore somewhat presumptuous and it was perhaps not surprising that I was unsuccessful. However, I had become noticed and this helped me to success a short time later when I applied for a similar position with the Birkenhead Co-operative Society.

We did not know the result of this application when Bernard and I started courting but we decided that I should not withdraw. If I was not appointed our courtship could take its natural course but if I were we would have to think things out again, which in fact was what we had to do. I was appointed in March 1959 and quite quickly took up the position. The Society's area and its Political Committee covered four Parliamentary Constituencies one of which had Selwyn Lloyd the Foreign Secretary and Conservative Member of Parliament. Although our marriage was delayed my move north facilitated our courting. Most Sundays we met in Manchester and it was easy for me to cross the Mersey to Liverpool and then onto Manchester or Bradford for occasional weekends.

All in all we had quite a rich social life in this period. We got on well and enjoyed each other's company. Most Sundays in Manchester we went to an early evening Mass at St. Mary's, "the Hidden Gem" just off Albert Square and for a meal afterwards. In Bradford Bernard introduced me to his friends. To one, Peter he had earlier lent quite a large proportion of his savings when Peter was getting married. Happily this was repaid in time to help Bernard put a deposit on a mortgage for our first house.

We also had good times with John Collins and his "bride". Much to the astonishment of his many friends John had finally been caught. I was bowled over by Pauline, the daughter of a

Leeds Labour Councillor. We first met at Queen Street Station, Leeds where I was awed by her prettiness and elegance. She had, and still has a great dress sense. In other ways Pauline proved to be a high flyer with, it must be said with John's support behind her. After marriage they were both active and later prominent in the Leeds Industrial Co-operative Society. Pauline was elected to its Board of Management and several years later became the youngest President of any British co-operative society. A sharp mind and a good speaker she also gained election to a number of national co-operative committees including the Co-operative Union's National Education Executive which had ultimate responsibility for the Co-operative College and the Union's Education Department.

John and Pauline were obviously making a good marriage. The four of us became quite close after Bernard and I married a year or so later. Before that John had been appointed the Co-operative Party's National Organiser for the North East and was based in Bernard's Leeds Sectional Office along with Harry Harrison, the Section's Education Officer. John and Bernard were already close friends and John asked Bernard to be his Best Man when he and Pauline married in September 1959.

Six months later when Bernard and I became engaged we travelled down to London for him to give me the ring in Trafalgar Square. We caught a train from Leeds where Bernard's Sectional Board was meeting but as that had not ended by the time we were due to catch the train, John kindly took over for the rest of the meeting; he was attending it as a sectional officer.

I had not seen the ring before Bernard put it on my finger. I had asked him to choose it because I knew he could not afford an expensive one but that I would feel cheapened if he paid what I thought was too little. I would rather not know and still do not know to this day, but I have valued it greatly. After Trafalgar Square we celebrated with dinner in a Greek restaurant where the Head Waiter gave Bernard a knowing smile and I simpered. We enjoyed Chicken Maryland which now seems less popular or even little known.

MARRIAGE

Bernard had proposed three times, on 3rd and 16th January and finally on 19th March. I think we both liked his doing so because I never once said "no". We planned a relatively short engagement and it was Bernard who chose the date of our wedding. This was set for Thursday, 18th August, 1960 at St.Annes, Rock Ferry, in Birkenhead. We would then spend our first night at the Midland Hotel in Manchester so as to remember all our courting days in Manchester. The next day we would travel to London and stay at the Great Eastern Hotel overlooking Liverpool Street station as that had been the terminal for trains to Rayleigh. On Saturday we could celebrate the third anniversary of our first date and seeing *Bride and the Bachelor.* Then on Sunday we would travel by the Golden Arrow from Victoria Station, London to Paris and stay there for a week. Bernard loved Paris but this would be my first visit.

It all worked out as Bernard proposed. On the Saturday evening we went to see a revue entitled *Pieces of Eight* starring Fenella Fielding and Kenneth Williams. A fond memory is of Bernard laughing uncontrollably during one of Kenneth Williams' sketches.

Our week in Paris was wonderful. We passed many military bands celebrating the anniversary of the liberation of Paris 16 years earlier. On the actual anniversary we joined crowds at the Place de Ville to see a parade headed by General de Gaulle, the French President. We never actually saw him because the clouds burst and with many others we were drenched. We chased back to the hotel.

One morning we had an amusing incident at breakfast. Two Americans at a nearby table asked in French if we could pass them our sugar. Hoping we might also speak I said when passing it that we were English so no need to speak French. Shortly afterwards we heard one mumble to the other that "I come over here to speak the lingo and what do I find, God Damn Limeys". We were amused rather than offended.

Bernard already loved French cuisine, I was quickly becoming enthusiastic. The evening we arrived we ate in a nearby restaurant where we enjoyed cheese and onion soup followed by a peppered steak and finished with wood strawberries and cream. The strawberries were smaller than any I had previously tasted and were accompanied by a rich golden cream from an earthenware jug.

Our Hotel Normandy was towards the Louvre end of the Avenue de la Opera which we walked along many times towards the Paris Opera House by which was the famous Café de la Paix. We also ate there in its Edwardian splendour but we also enjoyed drinking coffee at its pavement tables and watching Paris traffic. I was particularly taken with buses with curling exterior stairways and street urinals that could then be found at convenient intervals along Paris streets. Sadly both have disappeared but can happily be recalled when re-reading the Maigret stories.

MARRIAGE AND THE CO-OP

I must admit that not once did the Co-op intrude on our honeymoon. It did appear in various ways during our engagement and wedding. Our engagement ring was bought at Leeds Co-op and the actual engagement introduced me to many of Bernard's co-operative friends and colleagues. Our wedding "breakfast" was held in the restaurant of the Birkenhead Co-operative Society and our early furniture was bought at Harrogate Co-op. The mortgage for our first house came from the Co-operative Permanent Building Society, shortly to be renamed Nationwide.

A number of big co-operative events in 1960 were also memorable. One was the annual conference of the Co-operative Party held at Llandudno at Easter. In those years this and the Co-operative Education Convention were held at Easter and the national Co-operative Congress at Whitsun. Hundreds of delegates and observers attended each and in those days the national press reported. Bernard and I were photographed at the Co-operative Party conference by the *Daily Herald* headed, with the caption that *They Voted for Love.*

The conference was chaired by Jim Peddie, a Director of the Co-operative Wholesale Society who later became Lord Peddie. A dynamic figure he aroused conflicting views. Some liked him, others did not. Bernard and I were invited to move the vote of thanks at the end of the conference. Bernard did so from the platform and was near to Peddie when a hand vote was taken. Peddie quickly declared it passed but Bernard had doubts. He was upset when he heard Peddie quietly admit that he had thought the vote lost! The anecdote brought home the difference perspectives of conference floor and platform as well as political ruthlessness.

In his vote of thanks Bernard thanked those who had congratulated us on our engagement. He recalled the anecdote of Sidney Webb that when he and Beatrice married they agreed that he would decide on important questions but that she would decide which were important! Bernard thought something like that might also happen with us.

Another major gathering was that year's Annual Co-operative Congress. There Bernard introduced me to more of his work colleagues. Like the Trades Union Congress in relation to trades unions the Co-operative Union was the umbrella organisation of co-operatives. Besides its policy making and representative functions it was also a trade and employers' association and had many departments. I have already made several references to its Education Department. As an Employers' Association it had a Labour Department and its trade association functions were supplemented by the offices of its Sectional Boards which co-ordinated societies' trades within particular trades associations: these were again assisted by the Union's Head Office in Holyoake House, Manchester.

Perhaps the Co-operative Union's most important representative function was organised through its Joint Parliamentary Office which also included the two Wholesale Co-operative Societies, hence the title "Joint". Many years later Bernard's final position before retirement was as its Parliamentary Secretary and head of its Parliamentary Office in London. The Joint Parliamentary Office had two main functions. One was to make representations on behalf of the movement to government through its departments and civil servants. The other was to keep the movement informed of legislation and changes in regulations etc. that affected co-operative societies.

The Union was also the parent of the Co-operative Party which it formed by decision of its 1917 Congress. Party staff was thus Union employees although the Party was party political. Through it the Union had concluded periodic electoral agreements with the Labour Party and through these a number of co-operative sponsored parliamentary candidates stood in General Elections as Labour/Co-operative candidates. If elected they formed a co-operative parliamentary group which also included predecessors elevated to the House of Lords. Both the Party machine and the Parliamentary Office worked closely with this group.

All these interests and departments reported to the movement's annual congress. They did so first in the Union's large annual report and then by presentations of their officers to sessions of Congress where delegates representing primary retail societies comprised the largest group. There were also representatives from smaller co-operative groups such as the Co-operative Productive Federation. Agricultural co-operatives also existed but formed their own federals. In addition to the above mentioned departments above the Co-operative Union also had what might be described as service departments such as Publications and an extensive co-operative library. All were reported and represented at the movement's annual Congress. It was therefore a massive event. In those days it began Whit weekend and continued in the following week. Many cultural and social events took place in the evenings after the close of formal Congress sessions. It was at one of these that I first met many of Bernard's work colleagues.

In one way the event presaged later married life and a difference between us. Bernard never wanted to waste time being early for anything whereas I could not bear being late. Catching trains became a disaster area. We almost missed the Golden Arrow from Calais to Paris on our honeymoon. A forerunner was the social evening at the 1960 Congress. We were the last to arrive and as we entered we were welcomed with much clapping of hands and later we received many personal congratulations on our engagement.

The evening reflected the structure of the Co-operative Movement as it was in 1960. The chief officers of the Co-operative Union were there, Bob Southern, General Secretary, Clarence Hilditch the Assistant General Secretary and Winston Mulliner, the Head of Accounts. Present also were Secretaries and Chairmen of the Union's Sectional Boards. One I recall with affection was Norman Stevens who was Bernard's counterpart in the South West Section. Bernard was close to him and his wife, Margaret. Heads of Union Departments were also present and I came in touch with staff from the Publications Department for the first time. It was good to be able to salute Desmond Flanagan, the renowned Head of the Library who I had previously seen and heard speak at the Co-operative College.

Bernard was often amused by traits that he considered "typically feminine". One of mine has been recalling past clothes or those I have worn on special occasions. That evening I wore a navy chiffon dress with big low white collar and an unusual flounced knee-high hem. Being able to recall this underlines my strong memory of the occasion.

I had taken the next day as holiday to be able to attend Congress as an observer. I sat in a gallery and looked down on proceedings, a little like watching those in the House of Commons from the "strangers" gallery. Around me were many women, wives of delegates and officials, all stylishly dressed; most wore hats and there seemed a strong element of competition. A year later I would be one of the wives. Men predominated at Congress although there were some women delegates. Often they were active members of the Co-operative Women's Guild. Later as an accompanying wife I argued that Congress should include some wives' activities. Pauline Collins, who had by then become a member of the Board of the Leeds Industrial Society and by rota a Congress delegate in her own right, supported the idea but it did not go very far.

Congress debates allowed me to hear some good speeches from the rostrum. I even recognised some of the contributors from photographs in the weekly *Co-operative News,* I particularly recall Tom Taylor, a Director of the Scottish Co-operative Wholesale Society rising to speak who had a mellifluous voice and announced himself as "Tom Taylor....ESSSSSSS CEEEEEE W ESSSSSS. Another was Arthur Jupp of the Co-operative Productive Federation who I found as good looking in the flesh as I had found him from *Co-op. News* photographs. I felt a bond with him because, like me, he was a past student of the Co-operative College. It was also good to hear Mr. Marshall, college principal answer delegates' questions after his Chairman Fred Abbots had delivered the Education Department's report. Fred Abbots had recently endeared himself to me by calling in my office at Birkenhead to see how a recent student of the College was progressing in co-operative employment.

My day at Congress also included breaks for coffee and lunch. Then I saw in the flesh figures I had only seen reported in the

Co-op. News. Memorable among them was the uncle of Dick Douglas, a fellow student at the Co-operative College. His uncle was another Mr. Douglas and I wondered if he had inspired Dick to follow him into the Co-op. Many people spoke to him. He seemed well-known which perhaps could be explained by his having been a past Congress President as well as an earlier President of the Birkenhead Co-operative Society where I now worked.

The 1960 Co-op. Party Annual Conference and the Co-operative Congress were big events for me in our relatively short engagement. But of course the Co-op. would figure much in the setting up of our first home.

OUR FIRST HOME

This would be in a 1938 estate built just off the main road between Bradford Bernard's home town and Leeds where he now worked. Naturally Bernard obtained a mortgage from the Co-operative Permanent Building Society. I believe the price we paid for the house was £2,300.00 which was also Bernard's annual salary.

I have previously mentioned that sometime earlier Bernard had lent a close friend much of his savings to help him marry and set up his own home. Fortuitously, the loan had just been repaid and so helped with the deposit for our mortgage and in buying basic furniture. That came from the Harrogate Co-operative Society whose General Manager Dick Shepherd allowed Bernard to buy at staff rate. Dick sat on Bernard's Sectional Board and they obviously had a high regard for each other.

Over the years I enjoyed Bernard giving pen pictures of colleagues with whom he worked. The first of these came from his Sectional Board. Its Chairman was Bill Cranfield, the President of a south Yorkshire society who was a powerful lay person and had been elected to the Central Executive of the Co-operative Union.

Bernard could mimic people well, invariably kindly. He often quoted Bill Cranfield's remarks. One was that "they won't have "unilateral" in connection with divisions over whether Britain should adopt unilateral or multilateral nuclear disarmament. Another remark Bernard believed was aimed at Dick Shepherd which was that Cranfield he had known lay people "with ten times the ability of some managers" Despite such jibes Bernard noted that few on the Sectional Board ever challenged Cranfield. This also seemed to be the case in his local politics. Once displeased with his local Labour MP he threatened to call him into 'yon little room' to tell him of his objections.

Sadly Cranfield fell from prominence in an unfortunate way. Several years later at another congress he was a platform speaker in the early afternoon. No doubt he had had something to drink with lunch which had lowered discretion and he made an overtly sexual joke. In later years it may have been more readily accepted but at that time, the Co-op. still had strong Methodist and temperance elements. Consequently his joke caused offence and within a short while he had disappeared from the sectional and national co-operative scene.

With hindsight we can see Cranfield as the kind of powerful lay leader who then still had influence in the Co-op. Bernard got on well with him, admiring his undoubted ability and sharing his multilateral nuclear disarmament views.

Bernard also got on well with other board members but particularly Dick Shepherd who had a far quieter personality. Dick, his wife and daughter came to our wedding along with Arthur Richardson who had previously held Bernard's position as Sectional Secretary to the Co-operative Union's North East Sectional Board. Arthur had since become Secretary to the Co-operative Retail Services which had formed as a CWS subsidiary and ambulance service to retail co-operatives in difficulties. When he retired some years later he was succeeded by Alan Rhodes Bernard's assistant in the Leeds Sectional Office when we married in 1960. He had taken the position after Lloyd

Wilkinson had left to study at the Co-operative College. Lloyd would later become Chief Executive of the Co-operative Union and thus Bernard's boss. All this illustrates how career paths crossed and re-crossed in the Co-operative Movement at that time.

We had planned a small wedding with only family and close personal friends but Co-op. friendships enlarged it considerably. Although it was true that the Co-op did not feature in our honeymoon, it did as we returned. Walking along the platform to catch the train to Bradford we sensed someone watching us. It was Mrs. Corrigan, Bernard's London landlady when he was Research Officer to the Co-operative Party. Fortunately there were seats near hers and so we joined her on the train. She was travelling to Bradford to stay with a long-standing friend, a Mrs. Hool, who was married to a school caretaker and was a member of the Bradford Co-op as well as a prominent Co-operative Guildswoman, which was the basis of her friendship with Mrs. Corrigan. Bernard knew her from when he had also been a member of the Bradford Co-op board.

When we arrived in Bradford Mrs. Hool was at the station to greet Mrs. Corrigan. When she saw us as well and learned that we were returning from honeymoon she urged us to join her, her husband and Mrs. Corrigan for tea the following Sunday afternoon, which we did.

That tea stays in the memory because it prompted my early co-operative research. Over tea Bernard quite quietly mentioned some of the pre-Rochdale co-operatives that had formed and still survived in West Yorkshire. Two in particular stuck in my mind, Meltham Mills (1827) and Ripponden (1832). I wanted to know more.

Later when writing to Arnold Bonner, senior tutor at the Co-operative College I mentioned them and he urged me to research them.

I did quite a bit of work on Ripponden and wrote an article for it for *AGENDA,* a journal then produced by the Co-operative Press for the interest of Co-operative Directors. It had whetted my appetite for co-operative history although later research lay well into the future.

The tea with Mrs. Hool and Mrs. Corrigan launched us into married life, with all the excitement of getting our home together, developing new routines and strengthening new friendships. In each the Co-op would continue to figure prominently as it had in our courtship and marriage.

Chapter Four

LEEDS, MANCHESTER, LONDON AND GLASGOW

OUR LIVES IN DECADES

When considering how to structure this joint biography I realised that it might be helpful to do it in decades. The main reason was that each decade tended to be different. For example the 1960s were quite turbulent. There were various strains including living in six different locations. Each move was due to Bernard's work. From our first house between Bradford and Leeds we moved to Manchester and from there to Forest Hill in south London. Then we had two addresses in Leeds and in 1969 we moved to Glasgow.

By contrast the 1970s were more settled and until 1983 we remained in the same address in Glasgow although my work was beginning to take me to different places.

EARLY MARRIAGE

Recalling our early married life underlines how far personal and marital relations have since changed. For example in 1960 many women left work to become housewives. Indeed some professions required women employees to resign on marrying. Men were considered the main bread winners which also helped explain why women's wages and salaries were lower even for the same work. Another reason why so many women remained at home was that they were soon raising families.

I now find it difficult to recall my expectations when Bernard and I married. Ours would be a Catholic marriage and we expected to soon have a family. It therefore seemed a good idea to get used to having only one income.

After engagement I thought I should see whether I was able to make a shift to the Catholic Church. Bernard had been brought up in a mixed marriage and suffered problems from that. I was anxious that our children would avoid these. Happily I found I could make the change and was received into the Church seven weeks before our wedding.

As far as a family was concerned we agreed we would have three and then review the situation. The sad irony was that we would have no children but I remained happy in my conversion. One reason was the fact that Pope John xxiii and the Second Vatican Council in the 1960s inspired. Later I was morally and spiritually helped by a number of generous parish priests. Today Catholic Social Teaching remains close to my centre left political and economic views.

The Co-op was central to our early married life. It paid Bernard's salary and we were active in the Bradford and District Co-operative Society which brought me into touch with many of Bernard's earlier colleagues. Within a very short while the Co-op would cause us to make our first move.

CO-OPERATIVE UNION

Several months after we married suggestions were made with seeming official blessing that Bernard should apply for the newly created post of Development Officer in the Co-operative Union's Head Office in Manchester.

This post came about from the recommendations of an Independent Commission. Co-operative Congress had decided this should be appointed and initially its remit concerned only co-operative production. It was later widened to explore other problems the Movement was facing in the post-war world. The Chair of the Commission was Hugh Gaitskell, leader of the

Labour Party and of Her Majesty's Opposition in Parliament and its Secretary was Tony Crosland, a Labour MP who would hold ministerial posts in future Labour Governments including that of Foreign Secretary.

It was therefore a high-ranking commission whose report and recommendation were seriously considered at Co-operative Congresses in the late 1950s. Against the background of changes occurring in the distributive trades industry the Commission analysed trades in which co-operatives were strong, those in which they were less strong and those where they were weak. It also pointed to co-operatives' small markets resulting from their multiplicity and therefore the small size of many retail societies. These usually reflected how they had come into being. Changes in post-war distribution, particularly the increasing competition of large-scale retail competitors meant that they were becoming increasingly inappropriate.

The Commission proposed and Co-operative Congresses accepted massive rationalisation including the amalgamation of societies to reduce their number and increase the size of their markets. Overseeing this would be the Co-operative Union which would also create a Development Department to advise societies on how to improve their performance in different trades.

This was the Department that Bernard might lead. Some felt that it should have been set up in the Co-operative Wholesale Society (CWS) rather than the Co-operative Union. Moreover, Bernard's appointment was opposed. He was interviewed by a sub-committee who then proposed his appointment to the Co-operative Union's Central Executive but before it met, John Stonehouse, a member of the Central Executive indicated he would speak against his appointment. Over the years our paths had crossed, mine with John and his wife in the London Co-operative Society and Bernard's with them in the Co-operative Party. Personal relations were amicable but John thought that Bernard had too week a managerial and trading background for the position. And given that Bernard's background was more academic than managerial, he certainly had grounds.

However the Co-operative Union set up the Department and confirmed Bernard's appointment. He had obviously been helped by his co-operative track record and degree. At that time, few co-operative members and officials had degrees. Nevertheless, John Jacques, a member of the Union's Central Executive and General Manager of the Portsea Island Co-operative Society invited Bernard to spend a weekend with him and his wife to go over things on which he thought Bernard might need guidance. Bernard recalled that when they arrived, Jacques's pet dog rushed to greet them and that Jacques and his pet then rolled round together on the hall floor.

He and Bernard remained close. Jacques later became a memorable Co-operative Congress President his Presidential address delivered without notes. Harold Wilson, then Labour Party's Fraternal delegate was so impressed that when Prime Minister he proposed Jacques to become a Life Peer in the House of Lords. He thus joined the Co-operative Parliamentary Group that Bernard had helped service when Research Officer to the Co-operative Party in the mid-1950s.

THE MOVEMENT'S POST-WAR PROBLEMS

At the time of Bernard's appointment as Development Officer in the Co-operative Union the Movement had a growing unease about a number of issues but no clear grasp that their overall influence heralded decline. Over the previous century the movement had grown and grown. It had achieved economic and social success and created new wealth among the poorer sections of British communities. Earlier success had created a mind-set that made it difficult to recognise the need to change or how to do it.

There were many external changes such as the need to build thousands of new houses to replace those destroyed or damaged in the war and to clear numerous slums. Massive rebuilding resulted often in completely new towns. Co-operative societies often had to build new and larger stores in new catchment areas and to close stores in areas from which members had moved.

Additionally a number of previously family or privately owned retail businesses became public enterprises. Their improved access to capital prompted them to build larger stores and to begin negotiating directly with suppliers. Wholesaling therefore reduced in retail distribution. Given that the co-operative movement had two massive wholesale societies at its core this development had consequences.

Changing competition and the need to build new stores in new places caused heavy demands on co-operatives' capital but at a time when co-operative societies' cash flows were becoming less certain.

Traditionally co-operative members' main savings were held in their society share accounts. In the post-war world though, National Savings and building societies began to attract working class savings. To some extent co-operatives were bound by their history in which capital had been recognised as a necessary factor of production but was held to be subservient to labour. That was represented in a co-operative member so his or her share capital received only a pre-determined and limited interest. In post-war Britain, National Savings and building societies provided similar security along with greater flexibility. Moreover, the significance of the latter grew as improving living standards allowed workers to save to take out mortgages to buy rather than rent their homes.

Attitudes to capital also began to change within the co-operative movement itself. Some felt that although other forms of capital were more expensive they could be more reliable than members' share capital which could be was easily withdrawn and was repayable on death.

This new thinking weakened the previously strong link between co-operative membership and capital. Member loyalty, the bedrock of the movement also suffered and eroded further in the 1960s when Resale Price Maintenance was abolished. The greater price competition thus encouraged and hit trades like furniture and footwear in co-operative department stores.

Retail societies tried to maintain member loyalty in a number of ways. Some did so by sustaining dividend rates at artificial rates above what was actually earned, perhaps believing that this would be a short-term measure. Others dropped dividend but tried to attract trade by issuing trading stamps. In doing so they turned on its head the earlier co-operative principle of a division of trading surplus pro rata to trading loyalty. Instead, the cost of stamps became an element of price before sale.

Whether dividend should continue to be paid became a question at the highest level of the movement. Ben Parry, father of my best friend Sylvia was the General Manager of the Blackburn Co-operative Society and a member of the Co-operative Union's Central Executive which he later came to chair. During this period I recall his declaring that the dividend was a "sacred cow" to which co-operatives should no longer necessarily tie themselves.

BERNARD AT THE CO-OPERATIVE UNION

This was the background to Bernard's work in the Co-operative Union in the early 1960s. His small Development Department began work in December 1960. We moved to a slightly grander house in Stand on the northern outskirts of Manchester. Bernard could catch a local train from Whitefield to work and we were also on bus routes into Manchester. Other co-operative officials lived nearby and included Ron Byrom, a CWS Employee and later Director, Clarence Hilditch, Assistant General Secretary of the Co-operative Union's General Secretary and Alf Sugar who worked in the Co-operative Union's Publication Department.

Despite this friendly co-operative environment Bernard never settled well into the job. There seemed to be various dissatisfactions. Overall I think he feared that the Union was insufficiently dynamic and that it's General Secretary, Robert Southern, was too far laid back. An episode I had experienced earlier suggested that Bernard could be right. It happened while I was still working for the Co-operative Party at Birkenhead when I had a meeting with Jim Trotter, the Party's North West National Organiser in Holyoake House. During it Southern came in and stayed to talk to me at some length. Of course I was gratified but was surprised he could spare the time. I have already mentioned that at that time co-operative leaders gave time to younger co-operators and that was no doubt what I thought Southern was doing.

I also thought favourably of him years later when researching my Ph.D thesis. Trawling through past ICA Congress reports I read speeches Southern had made in the late 1940s. They were obviously well prepared and verbatim Congress reports reflected powerful deliveries in which he enunciated the ideas of democracy on which western co-operative movements were based and how these differed from those on which co-operative movements in the Soviet bloc had been formed.

Sadly Bernard remained less warm to Southern. He disliked the cautious wording of official documents and overall feared for the future of the Union. In this he was remarkably perceptive but way ahead of his time.

He was happy with his own department, particularly with Sid Ainsworth who became his Senior Assistant. They remained good friends until Sid's untimely early death. Bernard also had a strong regard for John Hough the Union's Head of Research. Like Bernard he had a degree and their research backgrounds no doubt added to their affinity. Bernard laughed when recalling how Hough told him that he also disliked the Co-operative Union's cautionary approach, of how he drafted papers "like a lion at midnight" but later toned them down.

Bernard was more critical of other members of Union staff, disliking the way they stuck rigidly to office hours and not being prepared to work late. On one occasion when he did so he found that the building was so tightly locked he could not get out. He eventually did so by crawling through a basement window and making a somewhat acrobatic leap to the pavement above. Despite such working to rule and the Union's cautious nature Bernard picked up rumours of a grandiose idea to build a new upper floor. It was built and came to be nick-named HMS Mulliner after the Union's Accountant, who had proposed it. Sadly, in later years it became something of a white elephant.

Bernard's main role in his new department was to implement the recent Independent Commission's recommendation that co-operatives needed to adapt to changing markets. There was outside interest in his work. Brian Groombridge of the Research Institute for Consumer Affairs (RICA) asked Bernard to write an essay on contemporary co-operative trade. Since we married Bernard had written for many different Co-operative and trade publications and it became our "cottage industry"; he wrote by hand and I then typed his drafts.

In the RICA essay Bernard wrote that the Movement was failing to adjust to changing consumer demands and was becoming increasingly vulnerable to stronger competition. It remained strong in areas where average transaction values were high and where durables such as furniture had a strong pull. It also retained trade in goods that were in constant demand such as milk and cigarettes, as well as those in which co-ops could provide good delivery services like bread, milk and coal. However, the movement was less successful in trades where fashion, flair and style were important, as in clothing and footwear. It was even poorer in semi-luxury trades such as jewellery and photography. The post-war economic emancipation of the working classes was increasing demand for these and for goods and services like catering, hairdressing and motor transport. Co-operatives needed to recognise these new demands and then seek to meet them.

Marriage had already taught me that Bernard was a very hard worker. At home in the evenings he often prepared trading guides for areas in which co-operatives needed to improve. He was also heavily engaged in freelance writing as well as visits to co-operative societies to advise them on developments they were considering. In this connection I became something of a co-operative grass widow although Bernard encouraged me to begin my own research and writing.

I returned to an earlier interest in the history of West Riding co-operatives formed before Rochdale in 1844. An article I wrote on the Ripponden society appeared in the *Agenda*. Bernard and I also wrote together an article on the biographical details of Co-operative directors which I had researched from various co-operative journals. This showed that in the early 1960s Co-operative directors were predominantly from the working class with very few having been to university. Their attraction to service in the movement was still class oriented and many had links with the Trades Unions and Labour Party. Many also served as Councillors on local authorities or as Justices of the Peace, the latter being particularly the case among women Co-operative directors. Our article was published again in *Agenda*, the journal produced by the Co-operative Press at that time for co-operative societies, particularly their boards of management.

Despite Bernard's uncertainties about the Co-operative Union we remained happy at home. I still did not go out to work and no family had appeared but we had taken a black and white kitten from the PDSA. To remember this Bernard suggested we call him Pizza. At that time neither of us had eaten a Pizza and probably didn't have a great idea of what it might be. Pizza, the family pet became a character and much loved. Fortunately he proved to be a good mover. On one occasion we lost track of him while furniture was still being moved in. After a frantic search we found him snoozing in a warm airing cupboard. He had sussed out a comfortable place and seemed to wonder why we were so alarmed.

As will have been seen, though, work entered home life. Throughout our marriage the Co-op was a large and constant element. Unhappiness in work therefore led to domestic repercussions. My first experience came when Bernard decided to look for another job. This turned out to be with the College for the Distributive Trades in Charing Cross Road, London.

Perhaps this could have weakened our links with the co-operative movement but happily Bernard remained well thought-of. In 1969, six years after he had left the Co-operative Union Peter Bushell became a senior assistant in the Development Department. He observed that Bernard was remembered "as a prodigiously hard worker and that his "persona remained firmly imprinted on the character and operational procedures of the department."

COLLEGE FOR THE DISTRIBUTIVE TRADES, LONDON

The position at the College for the Distributive Trades was Head of its Department of Management and Merchandising. Bernard was very much undecided whether to apply and left making his application so late he had to put it through the College door the evening before applications closed.

He was appointed and we moved to Forest Hill in June 1963. I was delighted. My father had died three months earlier and the move took us nearer to my mother. Against that, however, the move had long term property ramifications. London house prices were so out of line with those we had known in Manchester we decided to rent. Bernard was then offered a flat by Mrs. Weedon who, besides being a lecturer in his department was also a director of St. James, a London-based laundry. They could offer us an unfurnished flat above one of their shops at a reasonable rent.

We enjoyed life there. Both of us loved London and most Sunday evenings we went to church in central London and had dinner afterwards. Many restaurants became well-known to us as did a number of theatres. Some Saturdays we would also shop in the West End. Simpsons in Piccadilly became a favourite and one Saturday another customer there was Gerald Gardener, then Labour Attorney General. Such shopping also meant that we met some of Bernard's students who came from stores like Simpsons and even Harrods.

He was therefore dealing with retailers who were quite different from the Co-op. This was at the time when industrial training boards had been set up by government. Firms were required to pay a training levy to support such boards and that for the Distributive trades helped bring London students to the Distributive Trades College.

Bernard's work there was heavily administrative. Managing a department required good relations with lecturers and to a lesser extent, students. A function Bernard found most difficult was time-tabling classes allocating rooms and tutors. This was before computerisation and was done by hand. I recall several times his working through the night with papers and draft timetables spread out on our dining table. Sometimes I helped him double check drafts to see that neither lecturers, nor classrooms had been double booked. Bernard also arranged students' study visits which sometimes included co-operative societies. One group visited the then successful Nottingham Society where Bernard had good links with Cyril Forsyth, its General Manager.

We did not realise that in fact Bernard was heading for ill-health. From time to time he felt less than well although in generally unspecified ways. Despite feeling under the weather he kept a speaking engagement one evening at the Royal Arsenal Co-operative Society. I went with him and we were collected and brought home with a chauffeur-driven society car. These made me feel uncomfortable although many retail societies kept them for use by their board members. I found it incongruous to see a strongly working class person sitting in the back of a chauffeur-driven car.

Shortly after this meeting Bernard sickened with jaundice but its cause was not diagnosed. We assumed that he had caught it. When it recurred a few years later he was even more poorly and landed up in hospital for a week. For some time afterwards he needed to watch his diet and limit his alcohol intake. An operation to remove his gall bladder was proposed but he refused to have it. I then found that even though I felt he should have had it, I could not urge him to do so in case there were adverse consequences. Then and later I felt I had to leave such a decision to him.

This second bout of jaundice did not happen until late 1967 by which time we were living in Leeds. While Bernard remained with the College for the Distributive Trades in London two other important elements in his career were his extensive writing and being invited to join Harold Whitehead and Partners. They were Management Consultants with a strong retail section. They wanted Bernard to advise and introduce them to co-operatives. He quickly became uneasy about the latter and he remained with them little more than a year. Their invitation showed how his reputation was growing; his writings undoubtedly helped. Our cottage industry continued and along the way I learned much about retailing.

LEEDS INDUSTRIAL CO-OPERATIVE SOCIETY

I like to think that because of his earlier co-operative work in Bradford and Leeds Bernard might have been head-hunted for this job. Instead I have to admit that his appointment as Assistant General Manager in the Leeds Industrial Co-operative Society initially owed much to our close friendship with John and Pauline Collins.

The Leeds Co-operative had had interesting history. Perhaps it is surprising that political parties have not realised how co-operatives' policy of "open membership" has made it potentially easy for them to be infiltrated and subverted. In the 1970s when Bernard and I worked in Scotland we witnessed an SNP membership thrust into Scottish societies. It was not sustained and had no lasting effect.

An earlier example had occurred in Leeds where Conservatives gained leading positions in the Leeds Industrial Co-operative Society. This was led by a Conservative Constituency Election Agent by the name of Wallace who served as the Society's President for a number of years. John Collins, National Organiser for the North East Region of the Co-operative Party and based in Leeds rallied opposition. His wife, Pauline gained election to the board of the Leeds society. Pauline had already become prominent in a number of national co-operative bodies. Eventually she was elected President of the Leeds Society thus defeating Wallace.

Unfortunately the society faced increasing problems. The new General Manager, Vincent McGeehin, had previously been the Manager of its Pharmacy Department and had no overall managerial experience. The board of Management felt that he needed the support of an Assistant General Manager and appointed Bernard. We moved back to Yorkshire.

There should have been so many things right about this move. It brought us near to Bernard's mother once again although taking me away from mine who still lived in Rayleigh, Essex. Yorkshire was Bernard's home county and he loved it, as did I. But the job soon revealed personal and employment difficulties. It was Bernard's only managerial appointment and although his managerial knowledge based on advisory work and teaching equipped him for it his temperament did not. He could see the need for restructuring and rationalisation but shrank from having to tell employees that they were redundant. On top of this he and McGeehin, the General Manager did not always see eye to eye.

Initially Bernard was collected at 7.30 each morning to be driven to work in a chauffeur-driven car. He soon stopped this. We lived on a good bus route into Leeds and were used to moving around by public transport.

Once again we seemed lucky with accommodation as we were let a maisonette above a Leeds Society grocery shop in Swinnow, a Leeds suburb. It seemed a good deal probably because we expected it to be long term but we were there only a short while, In fact it delayed our return to the property market which would have adverse consequences.

Some redecoration was needed and I was delighted when two Leeds Society employees who had decorated our first house turned up to do it. They remembered me and I them. It was interesting to catch up with what had happened to them since. With Bernard being the Assistant General Manager we also got good service from other departments, including the furnishing which made new drapes for the flat.

Despite all this the job soon proved a mighty strain for Bernard. He slept badly and suffered dyspepsia which rather limited our entertaining. We were happy though to renew close contact with old Bradford and Leeds friends. One sign of the stress Bernard was under was that he asked me to join him for lunch in his office each day. I would take in sandwiches and we would spend a quiet hour chatting. This seemed to ease him but added to tensions I was feeling. Swinnow was not attractive, nor was Leeds at that time. I still typed Bernard's articles but essentially I remained a housewife. I did not go out to work and we still had no family.

FREELANCING

Things came to something of a head when Bernard resigned after disagreements with Vincent McGeehin. He felt able to do this because he still gained income from free-lance writing and believed that this could be increased. The change would also give him a much needed rest. I was happy to go along with this because I was worried about his health.

We had to find new accommodation and although we would have liked to have returned to London we knew we could not afford to do so. So we decided to stay in Leeds and rent. We found a delightful flat in Oakwood, a suburb on the other side of Leeds comprising the first floor of grand detached family house. Its owners lived in the ground floor flat; her wealthy parents had been the earlier owners but she had married into the wool trade. We learned much about suit making from her husband who had now retired. Most summer afternoons they took tea in the garden from a silver tea set. A single lady lived above in an attic flat. We nicknamed her "Thumper": she practised Judo and often gave parties.

It proved an agreeable arrangement. Bernard was already writing for many trade journals, co-operative and otherwise. Two of the latter included *The Grocer* and *Grocers' Gazette.* Among the Co-operative journals were the *Co-operative News* and the *Scottish Co-operator* which paid contributors in those days. The Co-operative Press also produced other journals. One was *Agenda* geared mainly for Co-operative Society directors while another was *Marketing and Management* which as its title suggested had a stronger technical and trade side. The Co-operative Union also produced a monthly gazette for its national and sectional staff and the Co-operative Productive Federation published a monthly *Review.*

Bernard often wrote in his own name but also used a number of pseudonyms such as Peter Cotton, Donald Williamson and Autolycus, a Greek mythical figure famous for commenting on "this and that". Donald Williamson had family derivations, Bernard being William's son and his middle name being Donald. In the *Scottish Co-operator* Bernard wrote under his own name but also that of a fictional character he created whom he named Archie Tastrel, believing that the term "tastrel" described a mischievous wit. He particularly enjoyed writing those articles. They became a bit of light relief and brought out various aspects of Bernard's humour and verbal wit. We enjoyed working together, he drafting and I typing. I also kept records of when articles were published and when payment was received.

Strangely although we lived and worked together at home we still got on well. Bernard's income was enough to keep us going in the short term. The big worry was, however, his health. It worsened rather than improved. It deteriorated to the point where he could not work. We had to decide what to do in these new circumstances. A return to education seemed sensible and we began looking each week in the *Times Educational Supplement* for posts for which he might be considered.

We did not realise it at the time but this in fact became the first rung of a new ladder for me. We saw teaching posts advertised for which I was also qualified but Bernard was not keen that I should return to work and we still hoped for a family. Nothing had happened in that direction. Each of us had been born to our mothers when they were 35 and rather stupidly thought I might do the same.

Looking back at how we thought in those days makes me realise how far things have since changed. You did not discuss such difficulties even with relatives and would hardly know what to say to a Dr. I recall a close friend who already had a son but no other children asking her doctor what might be possible. When he told her that her husband would also be required to take tests she took it no further. She had not told him she was seeing the Dr. and in any event she feared he would not agree to any tests.

The problem weighed more heavily on me than on Bernard. I seldom mentioned it because I did not wish to add to his problems particularly when his health worsened. Even then his Dr. could not diagnose the problem. In an emergency call he said it was best if we ran "horses for courses" and asked us to agree to his calling in a consultant. He visited Bernard at home, charged £40 and called an ambulance to get him into hospital right away.

That was frightening but it was the point at which a possibility emerged. On leaving the hospital I turned to kiss Bernard goodbye and noticed that his eyes were beginning to turn yellow.

Once before that had been the first sign of jaundice and so it turned out to be so again this time. A weak gall bladder was diagnosed. He remained in hospital for a week and was then discharged with arrangements made for the operation to be done later. However, once home, and feeling less bad Bernard decided not to have it.

In any event his health improved and amazingly the problem never returned. He still looked ill and this made me fear that soundings that were being made from the Scottish Co-operative Wholesale Society as to whether he would consider taking a position with them would come to nothing. Happily they still wanted him. He obviously retained a good reputation in the movement, even north of the border. No doubt it was helped by his earlier visits and extensive writings.

The position offered was that of Head of a new Department to be known as the Central Research and Planning but its name was quickly changed to Central Planning and Research. Apart from his final position as Parliamentary Secretary to the Joint Parliamentary Committee, I believe that this job was Bernard's happiest.

Many tributes were paid when he retired. One was that he was a discerning recruiter and had assembled good staffs. From comments Bernard made at home I think he felt this one in Glasgow was the best. Sid Ainsworth who had worked with him in the Co-operative Union in Manchester joined as his deputy. Bernard also recruited younger assistants including Peter Bushell, who later spent the rest of his working life in co-operative service in national co-operative organisations such as the Co-operative Wholesale Society, Co-operative Research Services and the Co-operative Union.

Bernard was well received by Scottish co-operators. He had included a number of Scottish societies in the series *Successful Societies*. He had also written articles for the *Scottish Co-operator* and was on good terms with its Editor, Arthur Oakes and his assistant Willie Lawson, a Director of the Kilwinning Society. One day, shortly after arriving in Glasgow we had lunch with them. Although I had heard of both it was the first time I had met either of them. I fondly recall them walking towards us: Arthur short and with a twinkle in his eye, Willie a foot or so taller, thin and far more lugubrious. Nevertheless he proved most genial. He and his wife later invited us to their home for tea when I found that the Scottish "tea" was what we Sassenachs might call "high tea".

An issue that soon presented itself was whether Bernard should accept the offer of a staff car. The problem was that he had never learned to drive. When an earlier offer had been made I had very stupidly begged him not to accept and not learn to drive. I very much feared that if he returned home late I would wonder if he had had an accident and that would scare me. In any event Bernard himself was not keen to drive so never took up the offer.

With cars all around us today that decision must seem strange. It was less so in those days. Cars were becoming more popular but we and our friends came from the working classes among whom cars were still relatively scarce. We were more used to public transport which was plentiful in places we lived like Leeds, Manchester, London and Glasgow.

Bernard continued using public transport throughout Scotland. It worked very well because invariably he was met at bus and train stations by a driver sent by the society he was visiting. If on a train he could work or read. Occasionally a work colleague accompanied him and if he had a car they drove. Peter Bushell recalls a number of such trips and the lively conversations he enjoyed with Bernard along the way.

The new job worked out very well and Bernard was happy in it. He also enjoyed living in Glasgow with its libraries, theatres and restaurants. Indeed he was happy to be in Scotland and I think part of this came from his love of words and language. The

Scots had many dialects and idioms. Bernard had been familiar with Robert Burns but now he came to know him even better. This and his use of colloquialisms helped endear him to existing friends and to make new ones.

I was happy for Bernard but my position was somewhat different. The move complicated the tentative start I had made in teaching.

RITA GOES INTO TEACHING

This had begun earlier, almost by accident in Leeds when Bernard was ill. Neither of us anticipated what might follow. Our friend Pauline Collins had taught a class in a retail course at a Harrogate College of Further Education. Other commitments, including Presidency of the Leeds Co-operative Society, led her to withdraw and she proposed that Bernard take her place. Unfortunately he was poorly and could not accept. Both he and Pauline then suggested to the College that they consider asking me. Although I had no retail or teaching qualification I did have the Nottingham University Diploma in Politics, Economics and Social Studies and had gained considerable retail knowledge from typing Bernard's many articles.

The Head of the College department invited me to meet him. Happily, he had various co-operative connections and was familiar with the Movement which possibly explains why he had invited Pauline Collins to take the class in the first place. He agreed I should take it. I hastily studied the syllabus and started preparing lessons. The class, held one afternoon each week, comprised young retail employees from the Harrogate area. I was easily able to make the journey from nearby Leeds.

I took to the new experiences like a duck to water. Teaching was satisfying. The syllabus proved manageable but above all I identified with the young people I taught. At the end of the course the Head of Department suggested I think about a career in Further Education and that I should apply for a place at the nearby Teacher training college at Huddersfield. It was part of the Institute of Education of Leeds University and trained Further Education teachers.

I applied and again Co-operative connections played their part. The Head of one Department had earlier been the General Secretary of the National Guild of Co-operators and decided he would like me to enrol in his department. We later enjoyed many conversations on the movement during my one-year course.

I began as a day student the following September. It meant a big change because each morning I rose at 5am had a quick breakfast, caught a bus into Leeds and then a train to Huddersfield. Fortunately I was soon able to team up with other Leeds students who offered lifts.

That autumn prospects of the Glasgow job opened up for Bernard and when he decided to take it we readily accepted that he needed to move right away. Fortunately I was able to become a resident student at Huddersfield and we vacated the Oakwood flat.

Although I enjoyed my time at Huddersfield the college did not make the lasting impression on me that the Co-operative College had made. There were no long-term friendships. It proved merely a stepping stone. However, there were to be difficulties starting my teaching career in Scotland.

Education in Scotland, like its ecclesiastical and legal traditions, was different from English education. Many Scots held it to be superior to English education. Some Scottish universities made a four-year Masters their first degree and traditionally teachers were required to hold degrees. I had only a two-year Diploma.

My first appointment was a fluke. It was with the General Studies Department of Coatbridge Technical College where an unusual situation had arisen. Mrs. Margaret Crane MA had been appointed Senior Lecturer in the Department after teaching in the

College's Commercial Department for many years. A number of the male lecturers in General Studies who had also applied took such strong exception that they applied for and were appointed to positions in other Scottish Further Education Colleges. Three vacancies resulted and the Lanarkashire Education Authority struggled to fill them during the summer holidays. In desperation they appointed me two weeks before the beginning of the autumn term.

It would turn out to be a good move. Above Margaret Crane was Patrick Murtha, the Head of the Department. They made a great team and supported and encouraged me. Sadly Pat died several years later but happily Margaret succeeded him as Head. I had such respect for her that I never addressed her other than "Mrs. Crane". Only after I left and our friendship grew did I call her "Margaret". We remain good friends today.

The first week at the college was spent getting to know the set up. When I received my first time-table I felt reasonably confident about taking English and Economic and Social History. I was less confident taking "Pre-Apprentice" classes. These were part of a year's course for students who had left school but were too young to begin their apprenticeships. I took these for General Studies which gave me scope to pick and choose from their syllabus. However, discipline was the problem; also my understanding what they were saying and their understanding what I was saying. My days as a school prefect returned. I became as happy ordering them around as I did commanding fellow pupils to come up the stairs in single file and on the right-hand side.

The really big challenge came with two subjects that a class of policemen were taking in the Scottish National Certificate in Business Studies. These were Industrial Relations and Scottish Government. A quick reading and mastery of sources was now urgent. Industrial Relations proved easier because there was so much going on nationally at that time. Comparisons had to be made with a foreign trade union movement and I was able to obtain information on the Austrian industrial relations system from contacts I still had in the Austrian Trade Union Movement.

Scottish Government with Scottish students was more intimidating but it provided a useful incentive. Teachers have a phrase about being "only a paragraph ahead" of students and that was certainly the case here.

Another fluke was that one of the police gained the highest marks that year in the Certificate Industrial Relations course and he was given a special award in Dundee. With the agreement of my Head of Department he invited me to accompany him and his wife to receive it. As gratifying as this was I felt I was somewhat cheating. I had been ill and had not taught the full year. He therefore owed much to the teacher who filled in for me. Moreover, the student was particularly bright and assiduous.

The reason I had not taught the full year was that I had suddenly been taken ill and had to have an unexpected hysterectomy. This was catastrophic. First, I was poorly; secondly, it was a big shock, and thirdly it meant we would have no family of our own. For quite some time afterwards I was depressed. The following spring, Pizza, our much loved cat died and that summer we toured Italy by coach. In Milan I cried and cried and told Bernard I felt 60. Now in old age I would happily be 60 again but at that time such age seemed a long way off. Part of the problem was that I felt different from friends and even Bernard who presumably still had the ability to create which I did not.

It was of course also a terrible shock for Bernard. I don't think he had been over-worried about not having a family until that point. But it hit when he visited me in hospital. It was a "women's" hospital and to enter he passed someone handing out details of nappy services he was never going to need.

Despite the trauma my time in hospital brought me conflicting experiences. We were in a large ward with beds down each side.

The layout prompted good contact between patients and brought many laughs, sympathy and support. Several patients were natural comediennes. One entertained us with calls home on a mobile telephone unit that was wheeled between beds. She did so in the style of a Hollywood film star, waving back Veronica Lake style hair with a languid hand. Another came from a family of funeral undertakers who rang home asking "anybody there?" I laughed so much I risked bursting stitches and a nurse had to teach me to protect myself. This was by lying on my back, raising my knees and gripping my ankles to hold myself together when laughing. There were also serious discussions as when one young woman argued that when her husband knocked her around he was doing so because he loved her.

I laughed but also cried to previously unknown depths. A patient opposite me had given birth but complications led to her having an immediate hysterectomy and to her being brought into our surgical ward. She was so ill she did not want to see her baby. Eventually a down to earth ward sister settled the issue by bringing her son to her one evening in front of all of us, although the curtains were pulled around her bed. I was greatly upset because this could never happen to me. I cried under the sheet and one of the older patients came up and gave me a good talking to while others gathered round. Sadly I later learned that the new mother and her baby never properly bonded. Before I left hospital I was told that I could never have had a full pregnancy. I had too many fibroids. They had caused no trouble until the near blockage that landed me in hospital.

Bernard and I now faced our biggest decision yet. Did we adopt or not? Many factors were taken into account. Adoption at that time was not easy. A friend had adopted a mixed race daughter and sent information about such children as well as those incapacitated in various ways. It seemed that their greater needs made them were more readily available.

Even if we had been able to adopt then and there other factors came into play. One was that Bernard was 45 and I 35. If a child went to university as we might hope, Bernard would be nearing retirement and meeting the financial needs of a child at that time could be difficult. Moreover, our mothers were both in their seventies and neither could be of little help. In any event they lived far away and no other immediate family lived nearby. My having just entered teaching was also a major factor. I loved the work and it helped rebuild our depleted finances.

After much agonising we decided not to adopt. It was a major turning point in our lives and one we spoke little about after we had recovered from the shock. Bernard was at last in a position in which he felt he was doing a good job and I had entered teaching.

We therefore began the 1970s in somewhat unexpected circumstances but in ways that would help us to become more settled. With two regular incomes we were once again thinking about re-joining the property market.

Chapter Five

COATBRIDGE AND GLASGOW

INTRODUCTION

Our first home in Glasgow was in Westbourne Gardens in the city's west end. We had a ground floor flat in an elegant terraced town house in a beautiful area. It had a fenced central garden for which we had keys. Nearby neighbours were professional or business people or those comfortably retired, as was the lady in the garden flat below us. Opposite us Sir Alex Gibson, conductor of the Scottish National Orchestra, lived with his attractive wife and young family. They had a complete house. When they gave parties we sometimes heard opera singers arrive singing a few bars of music rather than ringing the doorbell! Sir Alex's study was in the front of the house on the ground floor and often through its window we saw him working.

Our town house was divided into four flats: garden, ground floor, first floor and second floor. In the flat above us lived a young man who was so attractive that I took a second look at him the first time I saw him. He drove a Jaguar car which had to be parked outside as we had no garages. Innocently I thought the numerous young men he had around him were Jaguar enthusiasts, as they may well have been. "Lady Strathclyde", a neighbour across the road, had other ideas. She was not really Lady Strathclyde but the mother of a Dr. who lived with his wife and two young sons in the two upper floors of the house, while she had the ground floor and the basement. Throughout our two years in Westbourne Gardens "Lady Strathclyde" urged us to join the Conservative Party, invited us to Conservative gardens parties and other events and gave us frequent updates on the real Lord Strathclyde. She must have been perplexed by our consistent refusals because we were always polite and gave her warm smiles. Actually we liked her for she was always a character who took her small dog with her everywhere. I forget the dog's name but remember that she was so well-loved that "Lady Strathclyde" said that they could eat from the same dish!

Westbourne Gardens was in walking distance of Hyndland Station from which we could take the "blue train" into central Glasgow or I could travel onto Coatdyke for the Coatbridge Technical College about 40 minutes away. The train took me through east Glasgow and areas quite different from those in which we lived.

BACK TO THE PROPERTY MARKET

Between Westbourne Gardens and Hyndland station were acres of pink stoned Glasgow tenements. Built in the Edwardian period they had four floors, usually with a central staircase with two flats on each floor. Although their sandstone had darkened over decades they were internally attractive. Rooms were large and often had corniced ceilings. Some flats even had small rooms for live-in maids. Quiet streets and several central garden areas interspersed so that the area, being so convenient was an obvious place to consider buying a property.

First we had to save and to recover from our straightened period in Leeds. In October 1971 we bought a second floor flat in Polwarth Street near its junction with Clarence Drive. We were on several major bus routes so Bernard could travel easily to his work in Centenary House. This was on the south side of the Clyde in Morrison Street just past Glasgow's Central Station. After its formation in 1868 the SCWS had built there a vast complex of imposing buildings and warehouses. A little further out was Shieldhall where the SCWS had built factories to produce its own goods. Together these sites gave the SCWS a considerable presence in Glasgow reinforced by the fact that it was also one the of the city's major employers.

We lived happily in Polwarth Street for 14 years. The flat had a spacious entrance hall with a large bedroom to the right and beyond that an even larger lounge. Across the other side of the hall was a second bedroom which became Bernard's study. In between that and a large kitchen with a walk-in larder was a narrow bathroom and toilet. Photographs of the period show that we papered the walls in bright and strong patterned wall-papers, and even painted our lounge ceiling purple with its cornices trimmed in white!

House prices rocketed in the 1970s and our flat soon appreciated in value. This was pleasing but we recognised that if we moved we would have to pay correspondingly high prices somewhere else. As it was we were uncomfortable when we learned that a young couple who bought the flat beneath ours three years later had to pay double what we had paid.

Another area for celebration was that Bernard was happy in his new work and that helped us settle in our new home. Sadly, Pizza, our cat, died while we were in Westborne Gardens but throughout our married life we always had one or two pet cats. Dainty was the next cat, followed by Sherpa. Bernard chose both names: Dainty because she always looked elegant as if she were walking in high heels; and Sherpa because she saw our large windows and decided that their curtains were her natural playground. We loved both but sadly each was killed in road accidents. Fred came in 1976 and I gave him his more prosaic name. He lived until 13 so more about him later.

BERNARD AT THE SCWS

Bernard was quickly at home in Glasgow. For the first time in our marriage neither of us was near our early roots but Scottish co-operators, both officials and lay members welcomed us. Important among the former was Fergus Wilson, Head of the SCWS's Property Department with which Bernard worked closely. Fergus and Bernard became life-long friends; similarly with David McCallum a Senior Assistant in SCWS Accounts. Among SCWS staff I had the pleasure of renewing contact with several ex-students I had known at the Co-operative College.

These included Henry Fairlie the SCWS Funerals Manager, Ron MacInninie a Manager of one of the Scottish societies, and Benny Morgan who would later head the SCWS computer section. It was a particular delight to meet Benny again. He and two friends had got into many student scrapes at the college. One, Billy Proven had been appointed Grocery Manager of the Leeds Society during Bernard's time there. Henry Marshalsea the other friend went to work in a joint CWS/SCWS tea estate in India after leaving the Co-operative College but was now a further education lecturer in Kirkcaldy: we met again at an educational conference in Edinburgh. I was then struck with how maturity had dulled these three friends of my youth.

We also made close friends among co-operative lay people. Notable among these was Willie and Norah Bargh. He was a headmaster but was also heavily involved in the Co-op; a long-standing Chair of the Glasgow and District Co-operative Association which brought together co-operative societies in the Glasgow area; he was also prominent in the Scottish Region of the Co-operative Party having unsuccessfully fought a Parliamentary election as a Labour/Co-op candidate. His wife Norah had visited me in hospital and was also an enthusiastic co-operator. Jim Craigen, the Labour/Co-op MP for Maryhill, noted how complementary they were. He once wrote that "Mrs.Bargh and secretary ship were... synonymous in the same way as Willie Bargh seemed to be chairman of almost every organisation, and a rather good one." Jim considered Norah less of a speaker but nevertheless "an organiser with a personal touch that persuaded people to do things..."

Memories of Willie and Norah lead me to reflect that Sidney and Beatrice Webb, Willie and Norah Bargh, Bernard and Rita Rhodes illustrate married couples sharing interests, even passions but bringing different aptitudes to them.

At the SCWS Bernard was joined by Sid Ainsworth who had been his Senior Assistant in the Co-operative Union's Development Department in Manchester in the early 1960s.

Together again in the SCWS they identified and recruited younger staff members. Bernard's work in the Co-operative Union had been shaped by the recommendations of the Independent Commission. Now in the SCWS it was influenced by recent Scottish co-operative history.

Whereas the English and Welsh Co-operative Wholesale Society had entered retailing by establishing Co-operative Retail Services to rescue societies in difficulties, the Scottish Co-operative Wholesale Society had entered retailing earlier and deliberately by recognising that the Scottish Highlands and Islands had fewer and more widely spread populations with smaller markets and consequently fewer traders. Wanting to meet needs and bring co-operation to people living in those areas the SCWS opened a number of stores in the 1920s. By the 1960s a new need was emerging. Some long established retail societies faced difficulties and the SCWS decided to add an ambulance service similar to that offered by the CWS in its Co-operative Retail Services. Scottish Retail Co-operative Services (SRCS) was launched in 1966. Both this and its southern counterpart reflected a strong co-operative tradition. This was to save failing societies to preserve their members' goods and services and also to head off bad publicity harmful to viable co-operatives.

By the time Bernard and I arrived in Scotland in 1969 a number of independent societies had already joined SCRS including two large Glasgow societies, Glasgow South and St. George. Their loss was mourned nostalgically but the need to rescue them pointed to growing problems. Few yet spoke publically of co-operative decline. Hope remained that implementation of the Independent Commission's recommendations of massive rationalisation would ease problems.

Widening the functions of Scottish Co-operative Retail Services impacted on the rest of the Scottish Co-operative Wholesale Society and this led to Bernard's Planning and Research Department being asked to examine the Wholesale's constitution and future functions. Bernard led the project and I recall his working long hours, even some weekends. Often he arrived home in the late evening,

The changes that Bernard and his team proposed were accepted in 1972 and the SCWS was renamed the Scottish Co-operative Society (SCS). This was possibly misleading as a number of independent Scottish co-operative societies traded alongside it. Significant though was its acknowledgement that wholesaling was a declining distributive function and that retailing had become a significant element in SCS's operation. It still remained a federal and secondary society whose members included primary retail societies like St. Cuthberts in Edinburgh, Falkirk and District United and Paisley Co-operative Society and some 70 others.

Despite attempts to adjust to changing market conditions catastrophe was just around the corner.

CATASTROPHE

The Movement's appointment of the Independent Commission, acceptance of its recommendations, and the re-structuring of the Scottish Co-operative Wholesale Society acknowledged that changes were occurring in retailing prompting harsher competition. The catastrophe that hit the Scottish Co-operative Society in early 1973 was totally unexpected and left no time for a gradual response.

It stemmed from the failure of the Scottish Co-operative Bank to master national banking changes. Consequently a mismatch arose in its investment portfolio: it over-committed to substantial forward deals in Sterling Certificates of Deposit at a time when the government was attempting to control money supply by raising interest rates.

In February 1973 the SCS Board was warned that because of this severe problems of liquidity were imminent. Moreover rising interest rates and other factors would make it difficult for the bank to borrow sufficient amounts to meet commitments.

Bernard was an internal eye witness to the crisis but it began for him with IRA bomb threat leading to SCS staff being evacuated from Centenary House. He was joined in the holding zone by a close friend, David McCallum from the accounts department. David looked pale and Bernard feared he was sickening for the flu or something mundane.

Days later David revealed the reason. He told Bernard that the bomb threat had interrupted fevered attempts to try to determine the extent of the liquidity crisis. It was so large that new calculators had been purchased because their existing ones had "too few noughts". David also told Bernard that the crisis had been revealed by chance and that SCS could have been insolvent within six days.

The danger had become apparent when J.S. Marshall, SCS General Manager had visited the bank manager. While there he overheard a large withdrawal of Sterling Certificates of Deposit being requested and casually asked what might be the position if there was a quick succession of similar requests. Fortunately he was not satisfied with the answer and asked SCS accounts to look more deeply into the question.

A dire situation was revealed and the Bank of England was immediately involved. Through quiet and quick negotiations a merger was agreed between the Scottish Co-operative Society and the Co-operative Wholesale Society in Manchester. The speed of this agreement helped avoid much adverse public comment.

Internally, though the upset was immense. Bernard spoke of heated rows in the SCS board with its Chairman throwing the board room keys across the board table to any director who would replace him. Directors had reason to be upset because Marshall, the General Manager and the board had not known of the impending disaster. Accountability had been weak. However, doubt was growing whether SCS Directors were sufficiently versed with banking to have understood the risks even if they had been told. Further criticisms were made for their having appointed a Bank Manager who was not up to the job. He had been an internal appointment who was well known, liked and respected but later shown not to be up to the job.

Generally the fear grew that some co-operative organisations were becoming conglomerates that were failing to develop adequate systems of accountability. This proved to be even more the case, compounded by a weakness of institutional memory when the Co-operative Bank failed forty years later.

For SCS employees including Bernard the bank's collapse was a personal tragedy. Jobs went yet only a few months earlier Bernard had joked about the bank being the most successful part of SCS but 'no one understood why'. Many a true word is spoken in jest – or ignorance. Bernard was offered a new position in the CWS in Manchester which he accepted and we prepared to move to Manchester. I gave in my notice at Coatbridge and we started looking for houses in Manchester. However, Bernard sensed problems and decided to opt for redundancy instead.

This meant we could stay in Glasgow. Fortunately a lectureship in retailing was advertised at Glasgow's Central College. Bernard applied and was appointed. Happily I could withdraw my notice to leave Coatbridge Technical College.

While we were able to make satisfactory personal re-arrangements the co-operative movement in Scotland was devastated. Its presence in terms of employment and property were considerably reduced. SCWS/SCS archives and library were taken to Manchester and the massive co-operative buildings in Morrison Street were pulled down.

BOTH OF US AT THE CO-OPERATIVE UNION'S SCOTTISH SECTIONAL OFFICE

Perhaps Bernard and I made co-operative history in the mid-1970s when we both joined the Co-operative Union's Scottish Sectional Office, he as its Sectional Secretary and I as its Sectional Education Officer.

Bernard had spent only a year teaching at Glasgow's Central College but throughout followed moves his staff made in his SCS department to find alternative employment. Bernard was angry at its loss. The one consolation was that his lectureship at the Central College provided income. When, however, the position of Sectional Secretary in the Co-operative Union's Scottish office in Glasgow was advertised he immediately applied and was happily appointed.

His new office was in 95 Morrison Street, an historic Victorian co-operative building. Massive and grand, it had once been thought to become Glasgow's City chambers. Instead it remained the headquarters of the Scottish Co-operative Society until Centenary House replaced it in the SCWS centenary of 1968.

I arrived a year later in something of a surprise. Coatbridge Technical College had changed and I was now less happy there. A new college at been opened at Hamilton to which staff and courses were shifted.

New staff joined our General Studies Department and its earlier good relations had declined. Sadly Pat Murtha, its Head had died and Margaret Crane became his excellent successor. This meant there was a vacancy and the Labour mafia became influential in filling it.

I had gradually become aware of its influence in Coatbridge, its surrounding area and its college. Despite being traditionally left of centre I did not like them or their effect on the college. A new principal and his deputy were both part of the Labour mafia with repercussions on General Studies. When Margaret Crane became its head her previous position of senior lecturer had to be field and the one appointed was endorsed by the Labour mafia. But he was not up to the job and problems soon arose. These were compounded by three new members of staff becoming increasingly militant and actually leading a strike in the college.

There were still reasons for me to remain at Coatbridge. I loved teaching. "Do as I say, not as I do" summed me up well. Teaching encouraged my bossy elements. Moreover I had begun studying for a degree with the Open University and a change of job would complicate this. I therefore did not apply for the position of Sectional Education officer when it was first advertised. No appointment was made and it was re-advertised. This time and with Bernard's agreement I did apply. He withdrew from the appointment process.

Co-operative Union Sectional Education Officers also operated in other sections of the Union and were often past students of the Co-operative College. Dick Douglas, one of my fellow students had previously held the position in Scotland.

It seemed that I was considered well qualified for the job but questions were raised about my being married to the Sectional Secretary and how well I might work with him. Nevertheless I was short listed and interviewed. Robert Marshall, the Co-operative Union's Chief Education Officer chaired the interviewing panel which also included the chair of the Sectional Education Council and one of its members.

I was appointed and took up the post in December 1975. For the first time I had a secretary. On my first morning I was rather taken aback when she appeared with my post. I soon became used to dictating replies which she took down in shorthand, typed and then brought to me to sign. "May J" had been secretary to the previous Education Officer's secretary and filled me in with much useful information.

I worked with the Sectional Education Council which met once each month. My work divided between member education and staff training. The former was carried out through the elected Education committees of independent co-operatives. For the latter I worked with the Personnel Officers, shortly to be renamed Human Resource Managers and training officers in local co-operative societies. Besides reporting to the Sectional Education Council I was also responsible to Robert Marshall the Chief Education officer based at the Co-operative College and his departmental heads in Member Education and Staff Training.

I also had relations with a number of external education bodies including the Scottish Distributive Training Board and with the Scottish Business Education Council to whose board I was later appointed by the Scottish Secretary of State. Meetings of the Scottish Institute of Education were also attended and we had ongoing relations with the Scottish Workers' Education Association.

It was a much more diverse job than that I had at Coatbridge Technical College. I represented Scottish Co-op education on or liaised with a number of other adult education bodies in Scotland including the Adult Education Department of the BBC. I was later appointed to its national Adult Education Committee which held meetings at the BBC in London. The travel I enjoyed most, though, was back to the Co-operative College for meetings with my boss, Robert Marshall; also with Les Fox, Senior Staff Training Officer, and Len Burch, Head of the Member Education Department. I enjoyed working with Len and his two assistants but less so with Les with whom I was later to cross swords. Les was a Director of the Co-operative Wholesale Society and therefore carried quite a bit of weight. Marshall used him as a kind of side-kick to deflect awkward situations. Les had a reputation of rushing aggressively at problems, of charging through walls rather than finding their doors. With ultimate responsibility Marshall was usually more conciliatory.

My job also included being secretary and organiser of the Scottish Section of the Society for Co-operative Studies. Bernard and I had already joined when the Society had formed some fifteen years earlier. It aimed to create a forum to bring together academics interested in co-operative theory and organisation and lay and managerial co-operative practitioners. It published a quarterly journal edited by Marshall and Prof. Tom Carbery of Strathclyde University and held an Annual Conference which elected its officers, editors and committee.

Professor Carbery was our Scottish convenor and he, Bernard and I were became great friends. He had taken his first degree and Doctorate as a mature student while working and raising a family. His intellectual brilliance was accompanied by great humour, working class loyalty and dedication to co-operatives and the wider Labour Movement. As a co-opted member of the National Co-operative Education Executive he had close links with Robert Marshall, its Chief Executive but also served on our Sectional education council whose meetings he regularly attended. He helped me organise a Strathclyde business course for co-operative managers, based on the model created by Dr. Ted Stephens in Leeds University. With Robert Marshall Ted had also been a founding member of the Society for Co-operative studies. Tom introduced me to other Scottish academics interested in co-operatives which led to our mounting a course for members and co-operative directors with the Extra Mural Department of Glasgow University. In those days such courses had the label of "lay leadership". As Sectional Education Officer I organised a one-day symposium on this at which one of the speakers was John Atkinson, Education Secretary of the London Co-operative Society. A national organisation called Co-operative Education Secretaries' Association (CESA) brought me in touch with him and many other secretaries and organisers of co-operative societies' education committees. Its annual meeting was held during the national Education Convention held each Easter and hosted by a co-operative society in either a city or some coastal resort like Scarborough.

With Bernard I also attended, as an observer a number of annual Co-operative congresses. At one Bernard introduced me to "the Wily Bird", his nick-name for John Gallagher. Scottish by birth and with a brother still active in the Scottish co-operative movement, John was the Co-operative Union's Parliamentary Secretary and Bernard's present and earlier jobs brought him into close contact with him. Bernard had an amusing and always kind knack of nick-naming friends. He called John "Wily bird" which reflected respect. I was pleased to meet him.

As the Co-operative Union's Parliamentary Secretary John nominated co-operators for public positions. I was surprised but chuffed when he later telephoned to ask if he could submit my name for service on a Scottish Industrial Relations Tribunal. He had obviously known of my teaching industrial relations at Coatbridge, election to the Committee of the Society of Industrial Tutors and articles I had written in the *Co-operative News* on recent industrial relations legislation. I happily agreed and when appointed came into quasi-legal work. I sat as one of three members on a board that considered cases not settled by mediation and arbitration.

My main work though remained as Scottish Sectional Co-operative Education Officer. I now did far less teaching as the job was more administrative, organisational and representative. I worked a lot through the Education Committees of individual co-operative societies to help them draw up syllabuses for their courses and programmes. Important among these were youth and cultural activities and a national co-operative consumer education programme.

Being rooted in communities, retail co-operative societies had long cultural traditions. These were reflected in many ways including activities with members' children, drama groups, brass bands, orchestras and choirs. In Scotland in the 1970s I was responsible for branches of Playways for young children and Pathfinders for the slightly older. The Sectional Education Office employed a Youth Officer, Hugh MacLean who was an uncle of Billy Connolly, the comedian. Each year we had a Youth Day and a Music Festival in which young and older choirs competed. I owed much to my secretary, May J's previous experience and knowledge of these events.

An interesting event was the Queen's Silver Jubilee in 1977. Our groups joined with other youth groups in an event attended by Her Majesty in an Edinburgh stadium. I was struck by two things. The first was the influence of the crowd running into thousands. When the Queen arrived the cheering was tremendous and with some surprise I found myself cheering as loudly as anyone! The second was that I was quite near the royal limousine and saw how the driver stood watching events and paying little attention to children playing near the car which could have been so easily damaged or sabotaged. No doubt security is tighter today. At the youth rally the atmosphere was relaxed and enjoyable.

Hugh MacLean remained in the youth exhibition in which we had a stand. He saw the Queen look at it and probably wondered what we were. She seemed to have a sharp eye. Some years later she attended the service in Westminster Abbey to commemorate the centenary of the Co-operative Women's Guild and noticed that Guild banners divided between those that said "Women's Co-operative Guild" and others which said "Co-operative Women's Guild." She asked the Guild President about this difference. It was explained that original branches used the latter was while younger ones realised an advantage could be gained from coming higher up the alphabet. Her Majesty had spotted the difference. More will be written about this event later.

Consumer work was another big area of activity. The national Education Executive had recognised the growing significance of consumerism within retailing and through Marshall its Chief Education Officer and Len Burch with his Member Education Department had constructed an educational programme. Each year three consumer subjects were chosen. Study materials for each were prepared and distributed to co-operative education committees throughout the country and these arranged teaching, research and discussion on them. Their findings were co-ordinated and reported to annual National Co-operative Consumer Conference.

On the first day findings were brought together and framed in consumer recommendations. I recall the frantic work of Co-op. Union education staff in typing these up overnight to be distributed and presented to the full conference the next day. The conference attracted observers from national consumer bodies showing that the co-operative movement was making its presence felt.

Consumer education was a recent manifestation of co-operative education. Another one was involvement in encouraging the formation of new workers' co-operatives in Scotland. George Brown, the Co-operative Party's National Organiser in Scotland and I helped set up the Scottish Co-operatives Development Committee (SCDC). The first of its kind in Scotland, it had seminal influence helping to influence subsequent co-operative developments. It encouraged the formation of workers' co-operatives and representatives of Scottish voluntary organisations joined because believing these co-operatives assisted job creation. Representatives from the Industrial Common Ownership Movement (ICOM) also joined along with a few from actual workers' co-operatives. The Co-operative Union endorsed George and I serving on the Committee and gave practical assistance including room space.

Enthusiasm for common ownership had recently grown and owed much to the work of the Industrial Common Ownership Movement which reflected three main influences: Christian socialism, workers' control and contemporary alternative ideas. The Labour Government also showed sympathy. In 1975 it passed the Industrial Common Ownership Act which gave ICOM £100,000 and the Scottish Co-operative Development Committee £50,000 to encourage new workers' co-operatives. In Scotland we quickly appointed a development worker, Cairns Campbell. He was young, able and enthusiastic and proved successful despite tensions on the committee.

ICOM representatives and some of the new co-operatives looked upon the ageing consumer co-operative movement as hardly a true co-operative despite the personnel and facilities it contributed. The voluntary Scottish representatives mediated but interest in co-operative history, reminded me of the late 19th century debate on the competing merits of consumer and producer co-operation; consumer co-operation won because it was so successful and gained support from some prominent economists including Prof. Charles Gide; also Beatrice Web. Yet some notable co-operative leaders such as Edward Vansittart Neale, Edward Owen Greening and the fourth Earl Grey, the first President of the International Co-operative Alliance, recalled Robert Owen's belief that producer co-operation was intrinsic to a moral economy.

The success of consumer co-operation convinced many contemporary co-operators, including Bernard, that retail societies were the true co-operatives. They were universal because they operated open membership but many other kinds of co-operative were sectional because they needed to restrict membership for trade or economic reasons. Of course I subscribed to open membership as far as it related to race, colour or creed but I also felt that more sectional enterprises could still be co-operatives. I therefore became actively involved in trying to promote workers' co-operatives. I became secretary of the Scottish Co-operative Development Committee.

George Brown the Scottish Co-op Party Organiser and I attended a number of meetings to advocate workers' co-operatives among different organisations. These included trades unions and one was with the Motherwell Trades Council arranged by Jeremy Bray, the local Labour MP. The Chair of the Trades Council greeted us with the comment that he had hoped his members "would not come to this", in other words co-operatives to save jobs. We readily understood this and it was already policy not to propose them in redundancy situations where workers' redundancy payments might be lost in capitalising a business that could still fail. Workers' or producer co-operatives were undoubtedly more speculative than retail societies.

The Scottish Co-operatives Development Committee argued the case for workers' co-operatives among policy and decision makers and in the wider public. For example we organised a large public meeting in Glasgow which drew Members of Parliament, local authority councillors and representatives from various co-operative and public bodies. It attracted media coverage with my first BBC radio interview.

My work with SCDC became an important stepping stone. Ideas for a national Co-operative Development Agency were already around. ICOM and Industrial Common Ownership Finance (ICOF) were actively campaigning for it but it would require legislation and the Co-operative Party also became involved.

Despite all this I had doubts. History showed that some governments could become too controlling and limit co-operatives' voluntary nature as well as their democracy. Governments could also have national programmes that subsumed co-operatives even where the programme was for the common or national good. Above all I feared that the relationship between co-operatives and state was still not fully settled.

I went back to the Rochdale Principle of religious and political neutrality, as well as warnings from early co-operative leaders like Dr. William King that government influence should be avoided. Moreover co-operatives had multiplied in the late 19th century through their own self help, observing only governments' legislative and taxation frameworks. Admittedly there had later been protracted debates about their entering politics and they did so defensively in 1917. They then developed a dual approach. One was political through the Co-operative Party and the Co-operative Union's electoral agreements with the Labour Party; the other was through representation through its Parliamentary Office. That pre-dated the Co-operative Party and represented the Co-operative Union's employment and trade association interests with decision and policy makers. The Parliamentary Office also briefed co-operatives on legislation and government policies that would affect them. It was an operation with which I would become familiar. Bernard's final position before retiring was Parliamentary Secretary which meant he headed this office.

That was in the future. In the meantime it was possible that the Labour Government would set up a national Co-operative Development Agency. It was already being mentioned that it would include an education post for which I would be considered if I applied.

Faint ideas of moving south had already risen between Bernard and myself. A growing problem was my mother who was showing early signs of senility. The various forms of that were not given public label in those days but whatever it was caused us worries.

Out of the blue another job prospect in London appeared and my applying for it strengthened chances that we would move south. It was as Education Officer with the International Co-operative Alliance in London and Bernard supported my decision to apply.

My mother was one factor. Another was the retirement of Robert Marshall, Principal of the Co-operative College and also Chief Executive of the Co-operative Union's Education Department. As Sectional Education Officer I was within the latter and responsible to Marshall. Sadly I soon found that I got on less well with his successor. Tensions were rising which meant that I would at least consider changing jobs.

I was not appointed to the position with the International Co-operative Alliance but heard through the co-operative grapevine that I had been the runner up. Several years later this would become significant. In the meantime that application set a precedent which eased an application being made with Co-operative Development Agency when that was advertised a year or so later.

This was in 1979 and I was appointed. I took up the post a few weeks before that year's General Election. Margaret Thatcher headed a conservative government but it soon became known she disapproved of quasi government organisations and the national CDA was one. Immediately there were question marks over its future.

In taking up the post I moved back to live with my mother in Rayleigh. . Possible job opportunities arose for Bernard in London. One was with the International Co-operative Alliance in charge of its accounts but on asking to see details he decided not to accept. So we waited for some other opportunity. We could not then realise that we had begun a 10-year commuting marriage which amazingly we survived.

Chapter Six

GLASGOW AND LONDON

INTRODUCTION

The 1980s was a defining decade in that it set patterns for the rest of our lives. Bernard was promoted in 1983 to become Secretary to the Joint Parliamentary Committee of the Co-operative Union and Co-operative Wholesale Society, making him a departmental head in the Co-operative Union. His new office was in London and we settled in our house at Rayleigh in Essex commuter land. Bernard retired at the end of 1987. During the '80s I had three ostensibly good jobs but each proved difficult and ended in redundancy.

BERNARD AS SCOTTISH SECTIONAL SECRETARY

Bernard remained Secretary to the Scottish Section of the Co-operative Union until 1983. It was his longest job and he was reasonably happy in it. He settled well among Scottish co-operators both lay and professional and seemed well regarded. The position was similar to that of other Sectional Secretaries in the Co-operative Union although Scotland's greater number of small markets prompted a higher number of small co-operatives with place names such as Alloa, Bo'ness, Kelso, Markinch and Prestonpans. These maintained strong member loyalty which led to a higher trade penetration and profitability than co-operatives enjoyed in other parts of Britain. In 1974 when Bernard became Sectional Secretary, there were around 70 retail societies in Scotland.

Larger ones existed. Glasgow had several but Edinburgh had only one as did Paisley, Grangemouth, Perth and Falkirk. However, Scotland's distinctive situation led its Sectional Board and the SCWS to ask for special treatment when the 1968 Co-operative Congress voted to reduce the number of British societies to around 50. Scottish co-operatives would find this difficult because of their greater number based on small local markets. The compromise was to create five co-operative regional councils to encourage and facilitate mergers which might eventually become five regional co-operatives.

The process would be serviced by the Sectional Office so making this an important part of Bernard's work. He was not totally happy with it. On the one hand he knew that retail competition had not yet grown as strongly in Scotland as it had south of the border; and that when it did Scottish societies would need to adapt. On the other, hand he disliked proposing to board and society members that they merge so losing place and possibly weakening member identity and loyalty. Privately he wondered whether the movement still had its earlier ability to innovate as when societies federated to perform specialist functions.

Amalgamation objectives led to Bernard travelling all over Scotland. He still did not drive which worried neither of us. He was not in the least mechanically minded and Scottish visits were relatively easy. Morrison Street was still an important co-operative hub visited by many society officials who often offered him lifts. Yet he did not mind using public transport because he could work on trains. Local societies invariably arranged for him to be met at stations and he often returned with anecdotes, quips and jokes about the personalities he met. He could be more scathing though about auditors. For example he disapproved of one who asked the society he was visiting to fill his petrol tank but offered no payment. It appeared to be a routine practice.

Bernard's hands-on relations with many Scottish societies prompted a series of humorous articles under the pen-name Archie Tastrell. "Tastrell" was a Yorkshire term for an imp or a mischievous person. "Archie" had a Scottish ring. The amusing situations and characters Bernard kindly described were inspired by his visits to Scottish societies and his great regard for Robert

Burns. He was still writing many other articles and we had an evening routine. After dinner Bernard would rest for an hour, then begin writing and I typed each page. He could write straight off with very few changes and had picked up a journalistic trick of ruling pages to enable a quick calculation of how many words had been written. Few knew that Bernard was "Archie Tastrell".

Back in the sectional office and in addition to his advisory functions Bernard had a considerable administrative role. He serviced the Sectional Board, its monthly meetings and its relations with the Co-operative Union in Manchester as well as a number of co-operative trade associations and the Sectional Wages Board.

The office had a long history. In the mid 20th century the British Consumer Co-operative Movement still had few women officials but the Co-operative Union's Scottish Section had already had two women secretaries, Miss McQueen and Miss Wylkie. Either they were very impressive or Scottish co-operators were particularly enlightened in appointing them. Happily I met Miss Wylkie who although now retired was much respected and frequently present at co-operative gatherings.

Co-operative Union Sectional Secretaries met together once or twice a year and in the evening would go to a theatre or have a meal together. Miss Wylkie was still Scottish Sectional Secretary when Bernard held the similar post in Leeds in the late 1950s. He found her staid and correct and somewhat perplexed when one evening, after enjoying a rousing chorus in *The Merry Widow* he said he would rather be up on the stage than a Co-operative Union Sectional Secretary! In the 1960s and 1970s the Co-operative Movement was still sufficiently an economic and social force for its leaders to feature often in the Queen's Birthday and New Year's Honours lists. Miss Wylkie had been awarded an MBE.

Bernard was happy with his staff. They supported him well. His deputy was Maria Blackstock who was Finnish by birth but had married a Scot. She had previously worked with Bernard in his SCS Planning and Research Department and she had so impressed him that he later sought her to persuade her to re-join him. It says much for her ability for Bernard was of medium height and avoided being close to tall people; yet Maria was over six feet tall!

His secretary was Ellen Crossan. In those days sectional correspondence, circulars and reports were dictated and later typed or duplicated on a Gestestner machine. Alongside Ellen worked Jess Marshall who handled the Section's finances and kept the books. Both she and Ellen were in their late 40s or early 50s and had worked for Bernard's predecessor, Dick Bluer who was now the Co-operative Union's Deputy General Secretary in Holyoake House, Manchester.

Bernard's staff also included two junior members who played supporting office roles in photo-copying, copy typing, filing, answering the telephone and tea making. The General Office had an early photocopier that was so complex I find it difficult to describe. Cumbersome and slow it had only limited use.

A feature of the co-operative movement in those days was its friendliness, probably derived from earlier beliefs in equality and fraternity. Officials and lay members visiting the Sectional Office were always welcomed and offered tea or coffee. Refreshments were also provided to those attending meetings of the Sectional Board and other committees, part as a "welcome" but also because they may have travelled some distance. Where expenses were involved Jess Marshall handed them out based on the Co-operative Union's well established rates and procedures.

Bernard was reasonably happy in his position of Sectional Secretary as I was with being the Sectional Education Officer. Changes were on the way however and these would lead to our having a commuting marriage and a need to find new ways of keeping ourselves together.

RITA JOINS THE CDA

The first break came when I was appointed Education Liaison Officer to the newly created national Co-operative Development Agency (CDA) in April 1979. This was in London and I moved back to Rayleigh to live with my mother. The Agency would not mount its own co-operative educational programmes but rather liaise with co-operative educational bodies that could. Identification of training needs and curricula development ranked high in my job description.

Early gossip suggested I was a strong candidate. The CDA board included well known co-operative figures and I had close links with some. George Brown was one based in the Scottish Sectional Office as the Scottish National Organiser for the Co-operative Party; we had also worked together in founding the Scottish Co-operative Development Committee. George's service on this probably led to his being appointed to the CDA board and he was also able to become its Scottish representative. Other board members I knew well were Harold Campbell from his days at the head of the Co-operative Party and Lily Howe, the Editor of the *Co-operative News*. The Board's Chair was Lord Oram and as Bert Oram he had been the Labour/Co-operative candidate for Billericay 30 years earlier when I had been active there in the Labour League of Youth. We heard that Bert hoped I would apply and that he was also taking soundings about a possible co-operative job for Bernard in London. One turned out to be Finance Officer with the International Co-operative Alliance (ICA) but as I said earlier when Bernard was interviewed and saw the books, he decided against it.

After I was appointed to the CDA he remained in Scotland and we began a commuting marriage. We little suspected how long it would last or what twists and turns there would be. Fortunately we had always communicated well. Letters and telephone calls now increased and we began to enjoy weekend or holiday reunions in different places. It was also good to be able to live with my mother in Rayleigh. A closer eye on her was becoming necessary and I could easily commute between Rayleigh and London.

A month after I joined the CDA a Conservative Government was elected and Margaret Thatcher became Prime Minister. She disliked QUANGOS and the CDA was one. It had also been created by the previous Labour Government. We felt threatened which bred caution and inhibited strong moves. It therefore proved a frustrating and disappointing appointment. I was less personally happy in it than I had been in earlier jobs in Coatbridge and Glasgow.

Moreover tensions arose from it having been set up under legislation which engendered a strong civil service influence. This affected its structure, policy and decision making. Board members largely failed to counter this. Relations with local Co-operative Development Agencies were also prejudiced by the agency's top down approach as against their more democratic procedures and concern with local interests. Essentially the national CDA had to be top downwards because it made annual reports to government through the Department of Trade and Industry and had to satisfy a funding audience.

This could be seen in the Department of Trade and Industry wanting it to encourage the development of workers' co-operatives as job creation initiatives. Consequently the CDA concentrated on these to the exclusion of other types of co-operative although these had been mentioned in discussions leading to its legislation. I also came to realise that I was the only member of staff with a Co-op background and that I had very nearly not been appointed.

When short listed I was called for interview with Lord Oram and the recently appointed CDA's Director, Dennis Lawrence. He had just retired from the Department of Trade and Industry and seemed an eminently sensible appointment as he had headed the department's role in steering CDA legislation through parliament. The interview went well until pay was mentioned.

Then I learned that the rate being offered was lower than my existing salary which had recently risen under a new agreement between the Co-operative Union Ltd., and the National Association of Co-operative Officials. Lawrence said he was sorry but the rate being offered could not be raised. It needed to be within the agency's overall salary structure as well as the civil service grade to which I would be appointed. Sadly I said I could not accept.

There was something of an aftermath. Several CDA board members expressed concern. George Brown had an additional agenda in that he hoped that if Bernard moved to London to be with me, he might succeed him as CU Scottish Sectional Secretary. Pressure was brought on Lawrence and a few weeks later he wrote saying that the pay grade at which I would be invited to join had been raised and offered me the position of Education Liaison Officer. I accepted.

I later found the staff structure was strongly influenced by the civil service and had little in common with a co-operative institution. For example we never had staff meetings. Information of what was happening elsewhere came through the circulation of a weekly "float" containing copies of correspondence and reports.

Beneath Lawrence were two Deputy Directors, one for co-operative promotion and the other for external relations: neither had any previous co-operative experience. One had strong Labour Party links and Parliamentary ambitions; the other had worked in local government to encourage small businesses which might have included a few co-operatives. Dennis Lawrence had a full time secretary, retired from the civil service while his two deputies shared one.

The Deputy Director responsible for co-operative promotion had three assistants, two men and a woman who were recent graduates with strong Labour Party links. They may have had co-operative enthusiasms but they brought academic skills to their drafting of co-operative model rules rather than co-operative experience.

The Deputy Director responsible for external relations oversaw a communications officer and me as Education Liaison Officer. The communications officer had been a journalist and was thus used to keeping his own records. He had a decorative woman assistant who again had no previous co-operative experience. I had no secretary or assistant but was self-reliant because I could type, file and telephone.

Over time the communications officer and I shared an increasing dislike of the agency's direction and structure. He was genuinely enthusiastic about workers' co-operatives, visited and reported on some and became close to several of their leaders. His frustrations with the agency led to a row with Lawrence after which he left and was not replaced. To some extent his functions were taken over by two further civil service type appointments. One was seconded by the Department of Trade and Industry and became Lawrence's assistant, conveying his wishes to staff, taking board minutes and drafting reports. The other was later recruited when the first needed an assistant but was not seconded from the civil service; he also had a strong background in the Labour Party.

Finally there were three administrative assistants, each previously with the Department of Trade and Industry. One controlled finances, another kept the books and distributed salaries, the third, a retiree was a filing clerk and messenger.

Personal relations were not easy. I might be wrong but I suspected that members of staff with no co-operative background wanted to distance themselves from someone who did. Fortunately we had a lightening conductor in Nora Stettner who was secretary and personal assistant to Bert Oram. They had been close friends for many years and had worked together on a number of issues. Bert had collaborated with Nora when she had been the ICA's Research Officer, and it had been his links with the Alliance that had helped explore possibilities of Bernard gaining an employment there. Bert and Nora shared an office in the CDA although Bert spent much of his time in the House of Lords. Nora was there most days and was always approachable, kind and diplomatic. Most importantly she was enthusiastic for and knew much about co-operatives.

My personal relations with Bert remained good. He obtained for me a ticket to the state opening of Parliament after the 1979 General Election. I stood in the Waterloo Chamber and watched HM the Queen and members of the Royal family move to the House of Lords. Before the procession the royal crown was set on a cushion a few rows in front of me. It was the nearest I had ever been to state jewellery and I was transfixed by its beauty and symbolism. Wearing it a short while later, the Queen, accompanied by Prince Philip passed in front of us. They were followed by Princess Anne and Earl Mountbatten. I remember being impressed with her regal walk. Three months later he was assassinated.

Bert was always approachable and once when we had lunch I aired my CDA frustrations. He listened but said little. Later he was considered by some to have been a weak chair. I suspect though that he had been constrained by Lawrence because of the threat of the CDA being closed or having its funding reduced.

I found that time and order had different connotations in the CDA from what they might have had in co-operative environments. Fraternity was then still strong in the Co-op but in the CDA you related closest to those in your grade or section. Time lost urgency as when I was asked to survey the training needs of worker co-operatives and propose training and education courses to meet them. I argued that a survey was not needed as I already knew most of the answers from earlier experiences. It was suggested however that a survey could help my relations with training bodies but I suspected it was also seen as a way of increasing co-operative knowledge among other CDA staff.

Civil service hierarchy entered into reporting the survey. A meeting of around 20 co-operative educationists was called and I knew all. It was my report but the Deputy Director to whom I was responsible would present it. I would take notes and perhaps answer questions. Afterwards several friends asked why I had spoken so little.

Despite my co-operative antecedents I was later surprised to realise how far ideas of civil service hierarchy had entered my soul. I first met Andre Saenger, the recently appointed director of the International Co-operative Alliance (ICA) at a conference in London. At a coffee break several of us were introduced and he asked questions about British co-operation including the CDA. He was interested in its development work and asked if I would call to see him at the ICA to tell him more. My immediate thought was that CDA director Dennis Lawrence should do that. The civil service tradition was to speak to someone of the same rank. I debated whether to tell him but decided to not do so. I kept the appointment myself, with some interesting consequences.

Despite disappointments and frustrations my time in the CDA had some pleasures. I was able to keep many of my earlier co-operative education connections including the Co-operative Union's annual Co-operative Education Convention held each Easter. I delivered greetings from the CDA and spoke on the growing number of worker co-operatives. While there I attended the fringe meeting of the Co-operative Education Secretaries Association comprising education secretaries of retail societies. Sadly their number was declining through co-operative mergers but many present were active in local co-operative development agencies. They were thus a significant network with which it was useful to have links.

Some, together with the education and training officers of other co-operative organisations joined with the CDA to form the Co-operative Education Working Group (CEWG). Under its legislation the CDA had forum functions through the co-operative movement. Sadly, apart from the Co-operative Education Working Group little was done. The main thrust came a few years later with the work of Keith Brading following his retirement as Chief Registrar of Friendly Societies.

Links between co-operative educationists were already pretty good and we were able to develop a forum without too much difficulty. Other members included the recently formed Co-operative Research Unit of the Open University, ICOM, Commonweal the co-operative training centre set up in Kent by members of the Wates building family, the Plunkett Foundation, and a number of local co-operative development agencies.

I tried to persuade the International Co-operative Alliance to be involved in the hope of developing links with their Co-operative Education and Materials Advisory Service. Sadly they declined because they felt they should concentrate on their international remit. I was also disappointed that the UK Co-operative College did not join. Its Principal, Bob Houlton was sceptical of workers' co-operatives' likely progress which led to an awkward situation for me. I voiced my disappointment at the College's non-involvement at what I thought was a private meeting but when Houlton learned of this he complained to Dennis Lawrence CDA director. For once we shared a slight joke in that his only discipline was to read Houlton's letter to me without further comment.

Members of the Industrial Common Ownership Movement played a valuable role in CEWG, particularly Freer Spreckley who was young, dedicated and very much an activist. He ran a training centre for workers' co-operatives on the outskirts of Leeds.

Another lively member was Edgar Parnell, the Education Officer of the Plunkett Foundation. An earlier student of the Co-operative College, Edgar had had a varied co-operative career, mainly in co-operative retailing in Britain but also in colonial co-operative development. Bernard knew him well when both had worked in the Scottish Co-operative Wholesale Society and had a high regard for him.

At that point the Plunkett Foundation was in transition. It had been founded by Sir Horace Plunkett, the pioneer of Irish agricultural co-operation in 1919 as a general co-operative research and educational body, although it continued its preoccupation with British agricultural societies. Additionally, during the interwar years it became an advisory body helping the development of co-operatives within British Empire by drafting co-operative legislation, running training programmes and providing a resource centre in Oxford for colonial co-operative registrars. The 1970s renewed interest in workers' co-operatives led the Plunkett Foundation to focus on these. In any event the British Empire was rapidly becoming history.

Although the International Co-operative Alliance had not joined CEWG the CDA had several links with it. I and another member of staff visited its library to see whether it might be of use to us. In this connection we had also been asked to review other co-operative libraries in London, Oxford, Loughborough and Manchester.

The ICA library was headed by Anne Lamming who warmly welcomed us. She was steeped in the co-operative movement as ICA Librarian and also because her father had been head of the Co-operative Branch of the International Labour Organisation in Geneva. During the meeting one of her remarks suggested the subject of my later Ph.D thesis. Anne thought a number of the books in the library could help explain how and why the Alliance survived the two world wars and the cold war when similar international working class organisations that also espoused peace and the brotherhood of man split under the pressures of total war and divisions of doctrine.

This was way in the future but in late 1979 we also had other links with ICA. One was through Trevor Bottomley, head of its Department of Development and Education. He and I were past students of the Co-operative College as was Bert Youngjohns who tragically died following a severe heart attack while working in Nepal. At his funeral I represented the CDA and Trevor the ICA. He and his wife kindly drove me there.

We also kept in touch with the ICA in connection with the project it was conducting on industrial and workers' co-operatives. This was of course of mutual interest and comments were exchanged on findings. I represented the CDA at its concluding conference which was memorable because it was held at the Royal Society of Arts, John Adam Street, London where the ICA had been established in 1895.

My time at the CDA also brought me into contact with other organisations that would figure prominently in later years. Important among them were the Co-operatives Research Unit of the Open University and the Plunkett Foundation.

Among personal links I particularly valued a growing friendship with Will Watkins, director of the ICA between 1951 and 1963. Despite being in his late 80s his book *Co-operative Principles Today and Tomorrow* had recently been published. His family was rooted in the movement originally from the Plymouth Co-operative Society and his father had chaired the Co-operative Party when formed in 1917. Will met his future wife when she worked in the Co-operative Union's library and he was a tutor at the Co-operative College; in its early days based in Manchester. During the interwar years Will worked for the International Co-operative Alliance and joined the co-operative Sunday newspaper *Reynolds News* during the war after which he was appointed co-operative advisor to the British military governor in Germany. At that time it was divided between French, British, Soviet and American sectors. Will closed his career as director of the ICA after which he wrote a history of the Alliance's first 75 years.

Will was to play an important part in events about to unfold. Despite old age, a widower and living outside Oxford he remained active in the Society of Co-operative Studies. He participated in one of its working groups examining changes then occurring in retail society membership. Seven or eight of us met in the offices of the Greater London Secondary Housing Association (GLSHA) whose Chief Executive was Harold Campbell. When he resigned his position with the Co-operative Party Harold moved into co-operative housing although he remained a member of the board of the Enfield Highway Co-operative Society and was appointed to the board of the CDA. Working with him in GLSHA and also participating in SCS working group meetings was Archie Macintosh. Another past student of the Co-operative College Archie had been recruited by the Colonial Office to work with co-operatives in West Africa. He was now in co-operative housing.

I also joined the working group and was interested in the outcome of its deliberations because I was shortly to become chair of the Society for Co-operative Studies. Quite frequently after our meetings and before catching his train back to Oxford Will visited long-time friends Andre Saenger and his wife. They had recently moved to London after his appointment as director of the International Co-operative Alliance. Will and the Saengers had met years earlier when Will was ICA director. Those links led him to be asked if he supported Saenger's appointment which he said he did. The earlier friendship was renewed after our SCS working group meetings and I became a topic of conversation.

Frequent mention was made of CDA problems which was natural with Harold on its board and me on its staff. A third round of redundancies threatened and I was likely to be included. Will said he would speak to Andre Saenger to see if there might be a vacancy in the ICA for which I could be considered. However nothing materialised. In any event I was likely to meet Saenger to let him know about the work of the CDA as requested at the recent London conference. It was difficult to get a date from him because he was travelling to parts of the ICA in other countries.

We met eventually and he remembered Will's enquiry but had been unable to respond because considerable change was occurring in the ICA. No new appointments were being made. Indeed proposals had been made to move the alliance from London although a new location had not yet been decided.

So no opening there and tensions were rising in the CDA. Economies led to reduced accommodation with a greater sharing of rooms, telephones and filing cabinets. It thus became easier for staff to muscle in on each other's work to increase one's work load and possibly avoid redundancy. It became something of a relief when I was finally made redundant in January 1982.

Several suggestions were made that I should claim unfair dismissal. Despite past industrial relations experience I felt my nerves would not stand up to that and did not proceed. The suggestions arose from a strange situation. Previously a third of the CDA board were replaced at any one time but at the time of my redundancy the whole board had been replaced with a totally new one. There was surprise, disbelief and annoyance compounded by the minutes of the last meeting of the previous board being changed. One issue was my redundancy and that when proposed had been voted against and defeated. A stupid situation arose. While board members could say what they believed took place they had no formal record apart from personal notes they took during the meeting. Neither could new board members challenge the minutes of a meeting at which they had not been present.

I have to say that I was glad to be away from the CDA and no longer followed what happened next. However, I believe that shortly after a new director was appointed. I needed a rest. My nerves were in a bad way from the CDA and growing problems with my mother's health. In those days doctors spoke less openly than they do today of Alzheimer's or senility but she clearly had one of these. She was now an increasing danger to herself and to others. Going to bed one night she turned off the lights but turned on the gas stove without lighting it. Most fortunately I was there and could turn it off.

I became depressed and broke down completely when my mother one day trashed the kitchen wasting much food and necessitating a massive clean-up. A friend got me to my doctor who prescribed anti-depressants and contacted Social Services about my mother. I had come to a complete standstill. I could do nothing, not even open a packet of cornflakes for breakfast. Bernard came rushing down from Glasgow and helped us over the crisis. Several weeks later it was decided that my mother needed to go into a local nursing home. Looking back and keeping in mind the difficulties we have today in adult social care, I am amazed that that happened so easily. It was straight-forward and I cannot even recall what payment had to be made. I think my mother's state pension was taken for her care.

Bernard and I decided that I should not immediately seek another job. One was already in prospect although not until the following autumn. With a redundancy payment of around £2,000 and a need to have a rest I chilled out.

INTERREGNUM

The next possible job was that of General Secretary to the Co-operative Women's Guild; the present recumbent would shortly retire. I was already being tipped as a strong candidate. In the meantime I had two major commitments: membership of the Co-operative Employment Commission and Chairman of the Society for Co-operative Studies. Expenses were paid but each was voluntary, involving meetings and behind the scenes activities.

The Employment Commission had already begun work. It comprised a number of leading co-operators including Labour/Co-operative Members of Parliament. No woman had yet been appointed and I possibly became a token woman although my CDA work was clearly relevant to its work. An added pleasure was that Dick Douglas MP with whom I had been a student at the Co-operative College almost thirty years earlier chaired the commission.

Much of 1982 was strange inasmuch as I was busy but not in full-time employment. Worries about my mother eased because she was becoming more settled and had fulltime care. My own health improved although I was still on anti-depressants. I was cheered to receive an invitation to present a paper to a conference on workers co-operatives to be held in August at the Coady Institute, St. Xavier University, Antigonish, Nova Scotia and I looked forward to crossing the Atlantic for the first time.

A big surprise was a greatly moving spiritual experience. Day surgery for a gynaecological problem landed me in hospital and in a ward with three other women. Recovering in the late afternoon I realised that two had just had abortions. Bernard and I prided ourselves on being rational beings and while we were not easy about legalised abortion we could accept some justification. The difference here was that I was very close to it and it sparked a strong reaction. I was horrified that in the morning there had been six souls in that ward but now there were only four. I have since heard that profound spiritual experiences cannot always be put into words. This was one. It led me to return more seriously and regularly to the church's sacraments and to join the Society for the Protection of the Un-born child.

Another surprise was being offered a six day assignment by the International Co-operative Alliance. It was to take and write the minutes of an executive meeting shortly to be held in London. Robert Davis, the Deputy Director, asked me to meet him when he gave me papers and explained the nature of the meeting. He also told me that I might hear a constant buzz from members requiring an interpreter who would sit next to them with a small mike while they received translation through connecting ear pieces. The resulting buzz could be disconcerting if you had not previously experienced it.

I was happy to accept the assignment but said I was surprised to have been asked. Davis explained that traditionally verbatim reports were taken in shorthand by retired Parliamentary Hansard reporters but the Alliance could no longer afford these. A member of staff would not be asked because one of the questions to be discussed was whether the Alliance should move its head office from London and arouse fears of redundancies; hence the need for strict confidentiality. He also explained that the question arose because the lease of the head office had only another 16 years to run and was rapidly declining in value. New premises in London were likely to be higher than the alliance could afford because property prices had risen greatly since it moved to Upper Grosvenor Street in Mayfair in the 1950s.

I later saw how the issue became caught up with the change of director. It had been expected that John Roper, a Labour/Co-op Member of Parliament would succeed Dr. Saxena. He had applied because he was leaving the Labour Party and giving up his parliamentary seat. Shortly before doing so however, a group of Labour Party members also broke away and formed the Social Democratic Party. Roper joined them and changed his mind about leaving parliament. He decided to retain his parliamentary seat which meant that he then had to withdraw from the ICA. Some later believed that had he remained he would have wanted the ICA to stay in London and would have worked hard to find ways of doing so.

His leaving the scene precipitated strengthened French influence. The substitute director was Andre Saenger. He was from the Swiss Co-operative Movement but was French-speaking and was close to Roger Kerinec, the Alliance's French President.

Little of this was clear to me at the time that I was to take the minutes of an ICA Executive meeting. My main fear then was that I might not be up to the job. I was still on anti-depressants and uncertain how they affected performance. Fortunately I had taken notes since student days and lost count of how many sets of minutes I had also taken. Happily all seemed to go well. The British representative on the ICA Executive was CWS Director, Hedley Whitehead. He told me that when asked whether he thought I would be a suitable person to take the minutes he replied "none better". I smiled and thanked him but kept in mind his nick-name of "Deadly Hedley" as he had the reputation of not always meaning what he said.

The meeting proved fascinating. I saw first-hand co-operative leaders from USA, Canada, Germany, Norway, France, Austria and USSR. I expected it to be a one-off assignment but several weeks after submitting the draft minutes Robert Davis called to ask about what committee work I had done. The ICA was considering appointing someone to service a number of its committees and he asked if I might be interested in this. He emphasised though that ICA staff restructuring was not yet complete and that it could be some months before it was. This was therefore a tentative offer.

I agreed to an interview although Bernard and I were hesitant. While experience might qualify me for such a job, professionally I was an educationist. We decided to explore and if nothing materialised the position of General Secretary of the Co-operative Women's Guild was still to be advertised although that would also take me away from education. We also acknowledged that the Guild did not have the drawing power of the ICA but would offer a co-operative job opportunity. Sadly, having campaigned over many women's issues for many years, the Guild was now declining. Women's positions were changing in society. More were becoming wage and salary earners and no longer just housewives. Consequently fewer were joining the Guild and its membership was ageing. Nevertheless it remained an important auxiliary within the British Consumer Co-operative Movement and that attracted me.

However, I agreed to the interview because the International Co-operative Alliance was more attractive. It brought together at international level many co-operative movements; it had a long and distinguished history, and it espoused peace and the international brotherhood of man.

I was interviewed by Saenger, Davis, and Ted Ryan, the Alliance's Finance Officer. They offered a temporary position ahead of the completion of staff restructuring. Not every ICA committees had administrative back up and some such as the ICA's Women's Committee were loudly calling for help. The Women's Committee had been without a secretary since Muriel Russell retired two years earlier and would shortly meet in Iceland. Arrangements for this were being made by Raija Itkonen, one of its Finnish members. Ulla Jonsdotter, Sweden, the committee's chair had recently been co-opted onto the ICA Executive. She was its only woman and probably a token one but it helped strengthen her appeals for a secretary.

The job would be temporary and part-time with immediate emphasis on the Women's Committee meeting in Iceland. Its job description might later change in the light of staff re-structuring but in any event I might not wish to stay should the Alliance moved from Britain. A pro rata annual payment of £10,000 for three days a week was offered and accepted. This arrangement gave me time to continue with the Co-operative Employment Commission due to report that autumn and to complete my year as chair of the Society of co-operative Studies.

I began work with the ICA in May 1982. A month later the ICA Executive met in Paris and agreed to ask the Central Committee to vote in favour of moving the Alliance's headquarters from London to one of four cities: Manchester, Paris, Geneva and Vienna. The vote should have been taken at the next meeting of the Central Committee to be held in Rome in October. Instead, the Executive decided to take a postal vote which ICA rules allowed. This was an adroit move reducing both personal contacts between national delegations and the power of speeches to sway votes.

Soon afterwards the Austrian co-operative movement withdrew Vienna and the French movement, although it had proposed Paris indicated it could accept Geneva. The vote was thus between Geneva and Manchester.

Geneva won. Staff structures were finalised and I was offered the joint position of Education and Women's Officer, servicing both the Women's Committee and the Advisory Group for International Training of Co-operators (AGITCOOP). The latter was a working group formed in 1973 to advise ICA authorities on co-operative education and training in developing countries. It worked closely with the ICA's Co-operative Education Materials Advisory Service (CEMAS) and the International Labour Organisation's Material and Techniques for Co-operative Management (MATCOM).

The salary would be in Swiss Francs. Several officials had already been to Geneva to plan early arrangements and returned with horror stories of high prices. Ted Ryan thought I would be in difficulties and advised either I withdraw or ask for higher pay. I tried the latter and it worked, possibly because the option remained of a job with the Co-operative Women's Guild. Despite many fears Bernard and I decided that I should ask for a two-year contract with the possibility of renewal if things worked out. This was agreed and I moved with the ICA to Geneva in early October 1982.

Chapter Seven

GENEVA

INTRODUCTION

My joining the ICA was a big upheaval in terms of profession and marriage. With the latter I think we adjusted quite well. Geneva is a most attractive place and new to both of us. We therefore enjoyed it. Bernard came over whenever he could although air fares were not then as cheap as they would later become. Both of us had become strong letter writers and each Sunday we had lengthy telephone calls.

It is more difficult to judge the move's professional outcome. I survived almost three years which was longer than my original two year contract. In the sense that that did not lead to permanent employment it could not be deemed successful. Yet it heralded new directions that would bring interest and satisfaction.

My time in the ICA coincided with internal upheavals. One was the massive disruption caused by the move of its headquarters from London to Geneva. The other stemmed from changes in its membership. Mass membership consumer co-operative affiliates were declining necessitating changes in the Alliance's subscription formula. These proved difficult to agree and added to its growing instability.

THE ICA'S MOVE TO GENEVA

It was hard having left a position in the CDA where there had been bad staff relations to begin a new job where they were even worse. ICA staff was torn by rows after the vote had been taken to move to Geneva. There were fears of redundancy which exacerbated deteriorating relations with the new director. While

127

he could be urbane, polite and suave he had a sharp temper and could be devastatingly sarcastic. Two events made him more unpopular. A bad disagreement he had with the editor of ICA publications led the editor to resign. Fortunately the retired editor, Hans Ollman returned temporarily.

The other dramatic event was Saenger's dismissal of his secretary for supposed lack of confidentiality. She had worked for the Alliance many years and had risen through its secretarial ranks to become the "Senior Secretary". She was popular whereas Saenger was quickly becoming unpopular and controversial. In the uproar staff divided. Those threatened with redundancy were more openly hostile than those moving to Geneva. A dangerous situation arose when a valuable antique French clock disappeared from the boardroom. Some accused Saenger of taking it because he had a declared interest in antiques. Ted Ryan, the finance officer tried to diffuse the situation by suggesting that one of the viewers possibly interested in taking the property's lease could have stolen it. Nevertheless a note of accusing Saenger was placed on a wall in the tea room. Saenger never joined others for tea and coffee breaks so did not see it which was as well for those putting it up refused to take it down.

Ryan, the Finance Officer, the position Bernard had turned down, suggested that to limit friction these two groups keep a distance so breaking the long held tradition of shared tea and coffee breaks. Now the lady who managed post and stationery became a tea lady bringing refreshments to those not joining breaks. Dr. Saxena the previous director had always joined the collective tea and coffee breaks but Saenger did not.

News of head office difficulties quickly spread throughout the ICA. Long established staff had developed good relations with members of the executive, central committee and national delegations. They were also in touch with staff in regional offices and international departments of national co-operative organisations. London difficulties quickly aroused sympathy.

Unexpectedly I found problems closer to home. Some friends and colleagues in the British Co-operative Movement disagreed with my agreeing to move to Geneva. I was also unpopular for arguing that London rather than Manchester should have been the British candidate when the alliance voted to relocate.

I had several reasons. Trevor Bottomley had declined to join the earlier Co-operative Education Working Group because he believed the alliance's international remit meant it should avoid too close an identification with any national affiliate and historically this had been the case. The ICA was based in London but the headquarters of the main institutions of the British Co-operative Movement were in Manchester and the North West. However, by the 1980s changes in British co-operation prompted changes in the Co-operative Union and it now had surplus space in its headquarters in Holyoake House. Letting some of this to the ICA would ease the problem and in any event many international co-operative visitors passed through Manchester on pilgrimage to Rochdale.

My moving to Geneva under an increasingly unpopular ICA administration and my views on the Manchester candidature sparked ill-will. For the first time in my co-operative career I was snubbed. In October 1982 I attended my first meeting of the ICA Central Committee. Held in Rome it was preceded by a grand opening reception and naturally I went to speak to British members. I was surprised when two with whom I had previously had good relations turned their backs and walked away. In time good relations would resume but it was all rather a shock at the time.

Over and above my disagreement with Manchester as a new location I believe British co-operators had failed to understand how strong a competitor Geneva was. At that time the Swiss had a strong consumer co-operative movement with a department store in Geneva that was a little above Selfridges and a whisker below Harrods. It traded within a rich market comprising many well-paid employees of governmental and non-governmental international organisations.

Geneva had been the original home of the League of Nations and now accommodated a major complex of its successor the United Nations. The ICA had had strong links with the League and now the United Nations. Links with UN agencies were also important particularly with International Labour Organisation set up under the League in 1919. Its first director, Albert Thomas, was a prominent French co-operator as well as a longstanding member of the ICA's Central committee. In 1920 he set up a Co-operative Service within the ILO with functions to complement those of the ICA. Relations between the two had always been good but were likely to become stronger if the alliance moved to Geneva.

As far as the United Nations was concerned the ICA had a foot in the door from its formation. This stemmed from its involvement during the 1939-1945 war in the embryonic UN's schemes for rehabilitation and regeneration; also its plans for post-war employment and re-development. In 1946 it was one of the first three non-governmental international organisations to achieve category A Consultative status, allowing it to appoint representatives to UN bodies in New York, Geneva, Paris, Vienna and Turin.

Geneva's strong international pull was an ostensible factor in the ICA voting to move there rather than Manchester. A less obvious one was a decline in the earlier strong British influence in the ICA. As yet it was hardly apparent but by the 1980s the number of its members and volume of sales turnover were declining: also within the ICA power was shifting to affiliates in its regions, particularly Asia and Africa.

ICA regional offices had been established in New Delhi in India, Moshi in Tanzania and Abidjan in West Africa. The Swedish co-operative movement had been prominent in the founding of the Asia and South Pacific Regional Office as well as that in East Africa, while the French and Norwegian co-operative movements had assisted that in West Africa.

It was true that the British co-operative movement had also been involved in third world co-operative development but in other ways. Some had been through individual projects sometimes arranged through the British Council but the most significant were those mounted by the British Colonial Office which saw co-operatives as a means of building civic society in colonies moving towards independence. Although still hardly mentioned, the decline of British influence within the ICA was most likely reflected in the fact that its Presidency since the 1950s had alternated between the Swedish and French.

GENEVA SET UP

Settling down in Geneva, I found staff levels similar to those in London at around 20. Designations were changed however. Saenger remained director but had a new deputy, Francoise Baulier from the French Co-operative Movement. Her position was somewhat ambiguous in that she was also personal assistant to Roger Kerinec, ICA President and spent two weeks with him and then the next two with Saenger. Without a full time deputy, Saenger had a personal assistant, Serge Guillame who was young, recently married and in his first job after graduating. He was also hard working with great attention to detail but relieved by a good sense of humour. Serge became well-liked.

Two new members of staff were Malte Jonsson from Sweden and Vladimir Kousmine from the USSR now Russia. Malte had been the Deputy Director of the Swedish Co-operative Centre (SCC) and had had extensive experience in co-operative development in India and South East Asia. He now became head of development. In London, Development had been linked to Education but was now given greater importance because of the increasing significance of the ICA regional offices.

Vladimir had worked for Centrosoyus the central organisation of Soviet co-operatives which were closely linked to the Communist party. Despite that Vladimir proved to be relaxed and amiable. He became a good friend for whom I still have fond memories. Sadly he died in late middle age. His father had also died young from stomach cancer believed to have resulted from near starvation in Stalingrad in World War ll. Vladimir's wife, Valentina was allowed to come to Geneva with him although their son remained at school in Moscow, possibly as a hostage to their good behaviour. They lived in Soviet leased accommodation and it became apparent that they needed approval for any social activity they might take with other members of ICA staff. Vladimir headed the Alliance's link with the United Nations and liaised with its representatives to UN bodies in New York, Paris, Geneva, Vienna and Turin.

Another senior member of staff was Francois Kister, a Swiss who became Head of Communications. He had previously worked for MIGROS a Swiss retail organisation that could be likened to John Lewis in that it had co-operative characteristics but was not fully a co-op.

My position was Education and Women's Officer and I worked with counterparts in ICA regional offices. With Education I also liaised with co-operative colleges in the developed and developing world and represented the Alliance at international education conferences, particularly those organised by UNESCO whose scholarships to co-operative members I administered. I also worked closely with the Co-operative Education Materials Advisory Service (CEMAS) that was funded by the Swedish Co-operative Movement and had moved with the ICA from London to Geneva. Another important link was with Materials and Techniques for Co-operative Management Training (MATCOM) that was again funded by Swedish co-operatives but as part of the Co-operative Branch of the International Labour Organisation (ILO) and based in the UN offices in Vienna rather than Geneva.

Ted Ryan remained finance Officer but based in London. That seemed strange but the reason given was that a major ICA account remained in a British bank which prompted speculation that the Alliance might return to Britain. Strong criticisms of its move to Geneva were still being made. Ryan was frequently in Geneva.

The two big London casualties of the move were Robert Davis and Trevor Bottomley. Both were in their early 60s. Being near retirement might have influenced their not being invited to transfer. Robert seemed sanguine but Trevor became bitter and remained so for many years.

The rest of the more junior staff in Geneva was Swiss and were helpful and supportive. Some long-term friendships were made. Sadly Saenger's reputation for poor staff relations was soon reinforced when he had a massive disagreement with his new Swiss secretary and head of administration. Both left, whether by their own option or dismissal I do not know. News of this new rupture travelled quickly and added to his unpopularity. At a practical level the need to find replacements meant he had to postpone a visit planned to the East African Regional Office.

Apart from such upsets the physical part of the move seemed to have gone smoothly although doubts were soon raised as to whether the archives and library had been fully moved. Too much space seemed to have been allocated for them. However it was decided to delay checking until we moved into permanent accommodation some months hence.

Despite the upsets I was happy to be with the ICA. It differed strongly from the Co-operative Development Agency in London. Whereas that had been a newly created national organisation, the ICA was almost 90 years old and large. It had well established routines and conventions. Membership comprised 165 national or apex co-operative organisations in 70 countries plus three regional offices. I liked the broad international and co-operative environment. Having no foreign languages I was relieved that the working language was English. Moreover co-operative terms were commonplace whereas they had not been in the Co-operative Development Agency.

The first big challenge was a meeting of the ICA Central Committee to be held in Rome only a few weeks after the move. It was held in the Palazzo Barberini and at that time the committee was around 300 strong which necessitated a massive meeting space. A Roman palazzo was quite something. Around the meeting room were magnificent wall paintings with Roman antiques beneath.

The Executive of the Women's Committee also met in Rome. This was the second time I was meeting them. The first had been at the meeting of the full committee in Iceland the previous July. That had taught me how suddenly dangerous diplomatic incidents could arise and how quickly they needed to be defused. One occurred at a lunch given by Mr. Einarsson, Chief Executive of the Icelandic co-operative movement and his wife. They had a beautiful home and their daughter, a concert pianist played for us on a grand piano. Suddenly she launched into a bravura performance of Chopin's Revolutionary Study its nationalistic tone of anger and opposition writ large. Afterwards, a Polish committee member with tears streaming down her face rushed to thank her and gave her a tight embrace. The choice of music may have been innocent but the gesture of thanks was clearly anti-Soviet. Fearing consequences I was relieved when two Scandinavian members suggested a series of choruses and I sang as loudly as anyone, "I like to go a wandering with a knapsack on my back...."

By the time the Women's Executive Committee met in Rome I realised that they were adroit at avoiding diplomatic incidents. Tolerance and personal friendships existed as evidenced by western members sometimes taking medicines for eastern members when these were not available in their own countries. I also came to admire the business-like attitude of the latter. They came to meetings well prepared and wanted accurate and detailed minutes which was fine by me as that was the way I had been trained. I believe Soviet and eastern bloc members needed minutes to show the positions they had taken and also to show they had acted as briefed. I was also impressed with the excellence of the interpreters accompanying them who were always charming and linguistically gifted. Much later I became aware they could have other functions such as keeping a delegate or official in line or reporting any deviations. I quickly became aware of the delicacy of east-west relations particularly in relation to the alliance's strong commitment to world peace. From 1913 it had regularly passed peace resolutions. Drafting these at the height of the cold war in the 1980s became a triumph of drafting as well as diplomacy as I later found when I became involved in that drafting.

My work was heavily administrative as in the award of scholarships to women co-operators in developing countries. Funded by Scandinavian and French co-operative movements they enabled recipients to participate in meetings of the Women's Committee. Additionally work arose from the award of various UNESCO scholarships. These involved links with regional women's officers who I first met at the meetings in Iceland and Rome. My work was also representational when attending conferences on behalf of the ICA or at speaking engagements when I realised I had to give interpreters time to translate.

Rome also enabled me to meet other regional staff. Among them were some engaging personalities. One was Eli Anangise, director of the East Africa based in Moshi, Tanzania. A great character he was adept at fitting into many different environments. Sadly though, years later he was the first person I knew to die from AIDS.

My work seldom involved Saenger which lessened chances of disagreement. However problems arose about a meeting in Rome to which I thought I should have been asked or at least my views sought. It was a breakfast meeting between Saenger, Francoise

Baulier and Alf Carlsson, Alf was the Swedish chair of AGITCOOP and I would work with him as Education Officer. I liked him as soon as we met. He was gentle and a good natured person with a strong co-operative background, being director of the Swedish Co-operative Centre. During the meeting it was agreed to drop next year's summer school.

I told Saenger that I thought my views should have been sought. He seemed rather surprised and replied that it had been an informal meeting to allow him and Alf Carlsson to become acquainted. During it and without notice Francoise had suggested that because of extra commitments arising from the move next year's school should be dropped. Saenger and Alf had agreed. Since then the question had dropped from his mind. He assured me however that this decision did not jeopardise future summer schools which were an important tradition in the alliance having been held since 1925 apart from war years. He added though that they would have to be considered in the light of future programmes. Reluctantly I agreed.

Fortunately other relations proved more successful including those with the Co-operative Branch of the International Labour Organisation (ILO). The ILO was based in a magnificent modern building across the road from the permanent office to which we moved in November 1983. Contacts were quickly made and ICA employees were given the option of renting car parking space in ILO grounds.

I had previous personal links with Liam Pickett in the Co-operative Branch. Basil Loveridge had carried out a number of co-operative assignments for the ILO and knew Liam well. He had asked him to help me apply to join the ILO's list of consultants and experts recruited to undertake short-term assignments and Liam had kindly done so.

A completely new contact was Dyonisis Mavrogiannis who was in charge of the Co-op Branch's documentation centre. He also had a special responsibility for women in co-operatives which gave us a mutual interest. He attended many meetings of the ICA's Women's Committee as an observer. Mavro, as he was widely called was Greek and although he had strong political skills he also had Greek excitability. One learned to be quiet and wait for him to quieten down. He had been a child during the war and despite working with many languages in the UN system he hated to hear German spoken because it reminded him of wartime occupation.

Mavro's work had helped him make many international co-operative friends. He had close links with the French among whom he particularly valued that with Prof. Henri Desroche, a founder member of the International Co-operative University which organised training in French for co-operative leaders in developing countries. Perhaps surprisingly his relations with Francoise Baulier were far less cordial.

Besides establishing personal links in the ICA's new setting its staff had to learn to work with each other. There was considerable camaraderie. Most working days six or eight of us lunched together in nearby cafes and restaurants. On Friday afternoons we finished work at 4pm to have a drink together before going home. We were conscious though of strains arising from the move and of deeper problems hardly being voiced. I was struck by the fact that Executive members or members of the Central Committee did not visit the Geneva offices. Indeed the ICA President, Roger Kerinec did not do so until six months after relocation. A sense of crisis festered.

INSTABILITY – THREE DIRECTORS

I worked for the ICA almost three years and in that time there were three directors: one from Switzerland, the second from France and the third from America. There were of course a number of factors in each appointment but I believe a major one to have been the forthcoming presidential election which aroused competition between the French and Swedes. For some time the apparent front runner had been Yvon Daneau, head of the international department of Desjardin movement in Canada and a member of the ICA Executive: he had recently become one of the Alliance's two Vice Presidents. Daneau was closely identified with Kerenic and Francoise Baulier as part of the French speaking influence. It was also believed he had the support of ICA director, Andre Saenger.

Saenger's influence in the election of a new president was probably lessening as he seemed to be on his way out. Unwittingly and with much embarrassment I became caught up in this. Ulla Jonsdotter, Sweden and I met before meetings of the Women's Committee to discuss the agenda and what might come up. Prior to a meeting in Worthing in 1983 Ulla and I met in London and she told me she would table a motion calling on the ICA Executive to advertise the position of the Director. If passed I would then be required to send it on behalf of the committee to the ICA Executive. If they endorsed it would become a vote of no confidence in Saenger who could then resign or be dismissed.

It was unlikely that Ulla would make such a move by herself, suggesting she had support, but where and how much. We might know this sometime in the future but I had immediate problems. Ulla's resolution was adopted unanimously. I had to send it to the ICA Executive but courtesy suggested I warn Saenger. What a thing to do! But it was necessary as he read the minutes of all committee meetings and would in any event know what had happened. I approached the meeting in some trepidation but surprisingly he took what I said calmly. I later wondered if he had already known and had reason to believe the Women's Committee resolution would not even be received by the ICA Executive, let alone voted on. Nevertheless rumours persisted and Saenger's downfall came some months later.

In the meantime other important things happened to the meeting of the Women's Committee in Worthing in 1983. It was held in conjunction with the centenary celebrations of the English Co-operative Women's Guild which begin with a service in Westminster Abbey attended by HM the Queen. The ICA women's committee was invited and its members asked to wear their national costumes. These certainly gave colour particularly so in the abbey's choir stalls where the committee's officers and executive were seated.

Her Majesty's entrance was something of a surprise. Instead of advancing up the central aisle she entered by the altar, presumably having come up a side aisle. She took her seat in one facing the altar at the rear of the choir stalls. Next to her was a prominent Guilds woman, Dorothy Fisher, a life peer. She later told how Her Majesty asked why some Guild banners read Women's Co-operative Guild while others said Co-operative Women's Guild. Dorothy was able to explain that the latter had replaced the former when the Guild realised it gave them alphabetical advantage. HM smiled, readily seeing the point.

I resisted glancing sideway towards her but I did see that she wore a light wool green coat over a green Paisley dress with a belt that she adjusted several times. The idea that she carried no money was trounced when the collection was taken and she contributed.

Afterwards the executive of the ICA Women's Committee was invited to join Her Majesty for tea in the Jerusalem chamber along with the Archbishop of Canterbury, Robert Runcie. There were several amusing moments. Some of us were presented and in front of me a very stout and overdressed leader of the UK's Co-operative Union's Central Executive made a surprisingly deep and reverential curtsey. She looked like an over-dressed dumpling and I expected her to topple over. Another smile was curbed when Ulla Jonsson and I were presented to the Queen by the Guild's President. Perhaps confused by Ulla's Swedish dress or tiring with all the ceremony she introduced us as coming from Finland. I think we remembered to curtsy but both forgot that Her Majesty speaks first. Ulla explained she was from Sweden while I added and, "I, Ma'am, am one of yours." No annoyance was shown and indeed we received a lovely smile.

I think there was brief conversation but I do not remember what was said. Instead I was fascinated to find that Her Majesty was a little shorter than I when I found myself looking down into remarkably clear ice blue eyes. I also noted that she was drinking tea without milk, a practice I immediately followed and have maintained ever since.

As we left Westminster Abbey Her Majesty was being driven away without ceremony and I recall the pleasant smile she gave us. We needed to hurry to Victoria Station where a special train was waiting to take Guild representatives and members of the ICA Women's Committee to Worthing.

The second strong memory I have of the Worthing meeting was a speech by a prominent Japanese co-operator. The horrors after atomic bombs were dropped on Hiroshima and Nagasaki in 1945 drove Japanese co-operatives to become strong peace campaigners at home and within the ICA. I do not remember the Japanese delegate's name but vividly recall her account of post-war chaos during which her two sons died of starvation. Ever since, she had campaigned for peace.

After the Worthing meetings I returned to Geneva and caught up with anecdotes of Saenger's increasing difficulties. An important event was a strong disagreement he had with Malte Jonsson, presumably on development in which Swedish co-operatives had strong interests. Up till then Malte had many times said that the secretariat should "keep behind" Saenger. He never said that again after the disagreement which I believed caused a fundamental shift among the Swedes who were still heavily involved in the Alliance's regional office in New Delhi and Moshi in Tanzania. Malte was also in the ICA's head office on their secondment He was therefore no charge on the Alliance.

Rumours grew of a Swedish candidate for the ICA presidency. The French Canadian Yvon Daneau was no longer having a clear run. Apparently he heard this at an official dinner given during a meeting of the ICA Executive. Peder Soiland, a

Norwegian member of the ICA executive was overheard to say to his neighbour "look at our new President" and nodded towards the Swede Lars Marcus. Apparently this was news to Daneau who went pale and shortly left. I came to have a high regard for Soiland. Although in his sixties he was tall, remained handsome and was believed to have fought bravely in the war. He also had a strong sense of humour which could sometimes be mischievous as perhaps on this occasion. It was a toss-up whether he was quietly letting Daneau know that he did not have a straight run; or whether he was supporting another Scandinavian. Certainly French influence began to decline, imperceptibly at first but was quite clear after 18 months.

The meeting of the Central Committee in Prague took me to that beautiful city for the first time and indeed anywhere behind the iron curtain. Czechoslovakia was still a communist state and differences became apparent on the flight. ICA staff flew together on a Czech 'plane and was intrigued when a large number of economy passengers were invited to move to the front section of the 'plane. Those who moved later told us that it had contained only one passenger who was obviously high ranking but insufficiently weighty for the 'plane's correct balance!

We stayed in the rear but were given VIP treatment on arrival. After receiving roses and glasses of wine we were ushered to waiting cars which were driven with a motor cycle escort to the recently opened Panorama Hotel. It was modern and stylish but its service was different from anything previously experienced. We were kept waiting at reception while staff behind the desk carried on with other jobs. I expected Saenger to lose his temper. Instead with devastating sarcasm he meekly attracted one of the receptionists by calling him "Sir". It worked!

ICA staff kept together for meals at which we could order but wait several hours for delivery. The second time this happened I walked out and ate biscuits in my room. We also had difficulties contacting our colleague Vladimir Kousmine who had a room with the Soviet delegation. One evening we decided to eat somewhere else and I tried to ring his room to see if he would care to join us. Not having his room number I rang reception and asked to be put through but they told me he was not staying at the hotel. We knew he was but they refused to connect whether from orders or cussedness.

Despite apparent restrictions Vladimir retained an even temper and humour and was discreet and tactful. Heavy smokers, he and Malte often joined in each other's office for a cigarette and chat. He told Malte that he and his son sent hidden messages to each other in the type and the way they placed postage stamps on the letters they sent each other.

The main event at the meeting of the ICA Central Committee in Prague was Saenger's resignation. A few days later Francoise Baulier was appointed Interim Director. This was a big upset for all the staff but particularly for me. We were correct and polite but not friends. At this stage it was uncertain whether her position was temporary or whether she would become Saenger's successor. The big problem was preparing for the next congress in a year's time. Francoise quickly invited Robert Davis, the previous Deputy Director to become a consultant to head its arrangements. It was good to see him again for he was a good organiser and had much experience with previous congresses. He spent much time in Geneva and we enjoyed several dinners together.

Francoise was not an easy person to work with. She upset staff in silly ways such as placing a short chair in front of her desk so you looked up to her. Another was her decision to open each day's post so that she would see all that was coming in. It caused you to wonder did you see everything sent to you and raised issues to trust. A personal annoyance was her changing my desk. The original had drawers on both sides of a central seating area but she felt this appropriate for someone more senior and withdrew it. It was replaced by one with drawers on only one side.

A far bigger problem came when she appointed Trevor Bottomley as head of Education. This made him my senior and I was responsible to him. This was despite his remaining tutor at the UK Co-operative College and visiting Geneva only occasionally. All this was in the days before the internet. The telex was the fastest means of written communication and generally his appointment was a big upset.

Coincidentally Bernard was visiting and we talked about what to do late into the night. Before falling asleep I decided to give my notice but on waking found that I had unconsciously decided not to do so. It was to be the right decision. Francoise's hostility brought me growing sympathy and proved fertile ground for later job opportunities.

She might have hoped that I would refuse to work under such an arrangement and give my notice. I did not but received it a short time later. During one of Trevor's visits Francoise called me in to tell me that my two year contract would not be renewed. My main surprise was that I had been told six months early. There was also irony in that it had been Bernard and I who had suggested a two year contract in case of personal difficulties or Geneva proved too expensive.

I was tempted to give immediate notice but again decided to wait. It was a good decision. Several short-term contracts came my way from the Co-operative branch of the ILO involving drafting and editing. The latter was of a book written by that Liam Pickett that needed reduction. I did this work in the evenings and at weekends. These assignments were tax free and well paid. They also pointed to my literary skills having commercial potential.

Nevertheless I was on my way out of the International Co-operative Alliance. Francoise could have merely confirmed non-renewal of my contract in writing but she wanted to have its receipt recorded so sent it by registered post. That necessitated my going to a post office to collect and sign an official receipt which I felt added insult to injury. Acknowledging, I observed that one past ICA director, Will Watkins had recommended me, a long-time director, Dr. Saxena had named me the runner up in an earlier education appointment, and the most recent director, Saenger had actually appointed me. How and why therefore should an interim director think differently?

The big question for everyone else though was whether Francoise would be confirmed as director. She was not and to great surprise an American, Robert Beasley, was appointed thus becoming the first trans-Atlantic director. This was as surprising because of the delicacy of relations between American and Soviet affiliates. Rumours of wheat deals between the USA and the USSR were reported to have influenced Beasley's appointment. He had strong agricultural and co-operative records. For 30 years he had worked in Farmland a large regional agricultural co-operative and became its chief executive. He had also been elected chair of the Co-operative League of the USA (CLUSA) and served on its Overseas Co-operative Development Committee.

He and his wife moved to Geneva in the late summer of 1984. Although he would not officially take over until the beginning of November he spent much time in the office. Francoise was still in post leading the organisation of the congress to be held in Hamburg in October after which she would leave. In the meantime she and Beasley had separate offices and I had little to do with either. I was hardly on speaking terms with Francoise and as Beasley and I would not be working together in future there was also little occasion to speak to him. The only real exchange we had was when I went into his office to give him copies of the papers for the meeting of the Women's Committee in Hamburg at the coming Congress and he gave me a big smile.

Beasley was very tall, with glasses but little hair. He was genial and one felt a more relaxed atmosphere developing. I believe he, and his wife found European life somewhat difficult because of its differences with the USA. They had been used to

144

shops staying open all hours rather than closing in the early evening. Shortly after taking over Beasley recruited Martha McCabe from the Co-operative League of the USA as a personal assistant. Together they introduced a number of American practices in the ICA.

Before that however there was the Congress in Hamburg and final days in the ICA for Francoise and myself. My contract ended at the beginning of November and before going to Hamburg I had already booked my flight home. For all my disappointments I looked forward to the congress having attended and enjoyed many of those of the British Co-operative Movement They gave a sense of being part of a movement, of seeing leaders and notables with whom one was familiar through the *Co-operative News* and the cut and thrust of debate including occasional oratory.

I assumed that ICA congresses would be even more exciting. Instead that at Hamburg was disappointing with no prior music or opening hymn as in British congresses.

Besides its disappointing opening I was set to see little of the Hamburg congress. Francoise had decided I should return to Geneva immediately after the meeting of the Women's Committee. She had scheduled this at the same time as the meeting of AGITCOOP which I could not therefore attend but Trevor Bottomley could.

After it I learned that Francoise had been elected chair of AGITCOOP. Alf Carlsson had resigned that position as he had succeeded Malte Jonsson as the ICA's Head of Development. I touched rock bottom. I was aghast at Francoise's election and also of people crowding round to wish her well headed by Trevor Bottomley. To make matters worse I walked back to the hotel in the pouring rain during which the handle of my heavy brief case broke. I struggled to hold it under my arm. At the hotel I took a solitary early evening meal but Jean Fracois Kister, head of ICA Communications, asked if he could join me. Although well-meaning he was a bore and despite agreeing I said very little while he spoke at great length about his difficulties with Francoise and his job.

It was a bleak meal followed by a bleak evening. Unbeknown though, things were about to improve. A party of around 30 British observers were attending the Hamburg congress and among them were a number of Scottish co-operative friends. Most ICA congresses had British observers and George Brown had organised this group. He and I had worked in the Scottish Sectional Office of the Co-operative Union, the Scottish Co-operatives Development Committee and the national Co-operative Development Agency. He and others were sympathetic to my difficulties and when learning that I was returning early to Geneva invited me to join them as their guest, they meeting my additional costs. I happily accepted and laughed when ICA staff told me that they had had to dissuade Francoise from charging me for a visitor's ticket

All this was confusing for poor Robert Davis who had been responsible for much of the congress's documentation. He wondered why I was not working with other staff when he saw me sitting in the visitors' gallery.

Among the British observers was a Scot. Dr. Ray Donnelly. We had long known one another, as past students of the UK Co-operative College and in various capacities in Scotland. Ray was now head of a recently created a Co-operative Studies Unit at the University of Ulster funded by the European Union. Hearing that I was leaving the ICA Ray had asked Bernard if he thought I might be interested in joining it as a lecturer in Co-operative Studies, although without tenure. The position had not yet been advertised because negotiations were taking place as to whether the unit should be moved from the university's Department of Education to its Department of Business, Economics and Management. Generous EU funding had prompted some competition between the two departments. The big question for Bernard and I was should I go to Northern Ireland. It was a very troubled place in the mid 1980s and the opportunity to discuss the possibility with Ray in Hamburg was welcome.

Another turning point also appeared and was quite unexpected. At the very large and formal congress dinner ICA staff sat at one of the outer tables. Lights were lowered during entertainment and I sensed a figure close behind me. It was Beasley and he bent low to whisper that he wanted to see me when we returned to Geneva to discuss the possibility of my contract being temporarily extended.

ICA LIBRARY AND ARCHIVES

When we met Beasley proposed that I should continue my job description functions but also try to trace lost parts of the ICA Library. Immediately after the move to Geneva doubts had arisen whether the full library had been transported but it was decided to delay checking until we moved to our permanent accommodation and it could be fully unpacked.

The extension to my contract would be limited to settling the library issue but I was happy to accept. The job in Northern Ireland was firming up but advertising it delayed by internal university politics. In any event I was interested to see what had happened to the library but soon perceived technical and political issues. The first arose from there being no complete inventory. Post war acquisitions had been catalogued but earlier ones had not. Identifying missing volumes would therefore be complicated. Political issues seemed to be an attempt to prove that Saenger had kept inadequate control of an asset so adding reasons for his dismissal.

Checking the existing catalogue against surviving books was a massive job. Consequently one of the local universities was contacted to see if two or three students could do this as part time income earning activities. Notable among them was Jan Pawlowski, a Polish student who later brought along his wife

Alina. Both played an important part in subsequent developments.

Centrosoyus, the Soviet central co-operative organisation and several east European co-operative affiliates queried whether any of the archives had also been lost. Enterprisingly Jan and Alina quickly studied the archives of other international organisations in Geneva to see how they were organised and from their lessons proposed a project to check and assemble the ICA archives. Their proposal was so well thought out that Alina was recruited to undertake that project. In the meantime, having married the surviving books with the catalogue we had a better idea of the number missing. Anne Lamming the ICA's last librarian reckoned the financial loss in 1980s values of around £350,000. She also urged that loss assessors be brought in but this was not approved.

Early enquiries pointed to possible mismanagement by Saenger and Davis but no evidence of this was found. Memos from Saenger showed that he had instructed that where a volume had a number of copies superfluous ones could be offered to UK co-operative libraries. One of my first jobs was to check on this. Each told me no such offer had been made and that they had received no ICA books.

The mystery deepened when the architecture of the London office was recalled. Entrance to the library was on the ground floor, to the left of the front door of 11 Upper Grosvenor Street. It was housed in two large salons with a number of smaller work rooms behind leading to a rear exit. That could not be seen from the front of the building or the main library salons. A lift and its shaft rose from the stair well on the ground floor making it impossible for staff on higher floors to see the front entrance unless they were on the lower flight of the stairs. Moreover the ground floor contained a large reception desk and the last receptionist confirmed having seen only the occasional single volume taken through the front door. It was now becoming clear that hundreds of volumes were missing and that it was probable that they had been removed through the small rear entrance. In olden days this would have been a kitchen entrance and off of it was a small yard leading to a back lane.

Evidence pointed to unofficial action but by whom and to where? Rumours flew around and surprisingly included the name of a professor at Aston University in Birmingham. I say "surprisingly" because he was not known in co-operative circles. I contacted him and the case blew open.

We first spoke on the telephone. He confirmed that he had hundreds of books from the ICA library. After a good look through them he had decided he did not want them and would be glad for us to take them back. He also offered to photocopy correspondence which revealed that two retired ICA's officials, so incensed by the ICA's move to Geneva, tried to keep back as much of the library as they could, believing that the new staff would insufficiently appreciate it.

The copied correspondence made no reference to British co-operative libraries thus confirming their claims they had received nothing. All letters concerned Aston University library and how to transport the books there. That had involved considerable organisation. The fact that this could go unnoticed was due in large part to the library having no librarian since Anne Lamming being made redundant several years earlier because of the alliance's financial difficulties. .

Vans from a local co-operative society had been used to collect and take books to two locations. One was a Fulham bookshop which raised the question of whether any had been sold. The other was to a staging post in the basement of a national co-operative organisation. There was no evidence that its officials had been aware of this. Their building was similar to that of the ICA in Upper Grosvenor Street. Little could be seen from the front and a rear entrance was largely hidden and accessed through a back lane. Aston University vans could therefore easily make collections although they were warned of a police presence because of IRA bomb threats!

After noting all this Beasley asked me to visit Aston University. When I did so and met the professor he made clear that they did not wish to keep the books and would like the ICA to remove them. The question then arose as to who would pay. I could not say and recognised this would have to be settled at a higher level. The alliance had already paid once in its move from London to Geneva.

Worse was still to come. I asked to see the books to assess their number and condition. I had expected them to be on shelves in some part of the university library. Instead I was taken to a basement and found hundreds of ICA volumes lying on its floor. They had just been tipped and many lay open with possible broken spines. I was uncertain what to do and was tempted to go to the police. Instead I returned to my hotel to telephone Beasley in Geneva. He quickly realised this was a bad situation and said he would call me back. When he did he said he needed to report to the ICA president and Executive. In the meantime I should return to Geneva after advising the professor of this move.

I spent that night in Birmingham and had dinner with Irfon Thomas. He was Secretary to the Midland Section of the Co-operative Union and a colleague of Bernard's. Irfon helped cheer me but I was still very upset at the state of the missing ICA books. However the matter was now out of my hands.

After I had left the alliance I heard that the ICA executive decided that the Aston volumes should be sent to the Co-operative Union's library in Manchester rather than be restored to the ICA library. . I do not know the terms. In anger I wished that I had gone straight to the police although that would have meant a public scandal embarrassing the ICA, those responsible and British co-operative organisations that had become accessories. The photocopies Aston University had sent me and I had passed to Beasley showed clearly what had been proposed, what had happened and who had been involved. The fact that the ICA had decided not to prosecute pointed to continuing tensions in relations between it and its British affiliates following the move to Geneva. I remain angry to this day that the books were not returned to their original library. Its back had been broken and haphazardly international co-operative history had landed in a national co-operative setting changing access and possibly even security.

Nevertheless there had been a silver lining. While I had been preoccupied with the library Alina Pawlowska been working on the ICA archives. They had been unearthed following Centrosoyus's request that they should also be checked to see whether any of them had been lost. It was difficult to prove what should be there. No inventory had ever been made. Past documents had been wrapped in hundreds of brown paper parcels which were tied with string. Brief details of dates and contents were written on each pack.

Having studied the archives of other international organisations, Jan and Alina Pawlowski had proposed a project to resuscitate those of the ICA. Alina had a temporary appointment to categorise and make an inventory but this would require space and time. Happily funding was found. I recall her working with piles of archive boxes which she filled having itemised and listed the contents of the brown paper parcels. She made such a good job of this and became so well-versed in ICA history that she was afterwards appointed the alliance's librarian and archivist.

Her inventory thrilled me. On a personal level it revealed the excellent sources that existed in the ICA archives for the Ph.D thesis that Anne Lamming had suggested some years ago. This had stayed in my mind but now became an objective. I had no idea though when I might be able to attempt it.

Happily by the time I left the ICA the job at the University of Ulster had been advertised and I had been appointed a temporary lecturer in Co-operative Studies. It was temporary in the sense that it was not tenured. It would be at Magee College in Londonderry.

Bernard had endorsed me applying although some friends urged me to not do so. This was in 1985 with considerable conflict in Northern Ireland. Dr. Marshall, past principal at the Co-operative warned me strongly not to go. However Prof. Tom Carbery, his close friend and ours from our Scottish days urged me to apply: he reported that "our old friend Ray Donnelly is awash with EU money".

I went and despite moving into a troubled area I welcomed the change despite sadness at leaving the ICA. Geneva had been an attractive place and I had enjoyed being there. However, I had found it generated emotional violence. Quite a few families of the friends I made there split confirming that wealth did not automatically bring happiness. Physically I also came to like the paler and gentler skies of the Foyle estuary rather than the stronger southerly sunlight of Geneva. Strangely in view of Northern Ireland struggles I found Londonderry a gentler place. Geneva had been a rich city whereas Derry was poor but family life was much firmer. Differences became apparent in Heathrow departure lounges. Passengers in that for Geneva were expensively dressed with Jaeger and Aquascutum much in evidence along with classy shoes and handbags. Those in that for Belfast were dressed in more functional and less stylish clothes and carried cheaper hand luggage. The change was salutary.

In the meantime Bernard had been promoted into a notable position in the British Co-operative Union. We were both happy for he was eminently suited for it. It was also the one in which he would be the most happy. We were also able to move back to Rayleigh from where he would commute.

Chapter Eight

LONDON AND NORTHERN IRELAND

INTRODUCTION

Bernard became Parliamentary Secretary to the Co-operative Union and the Co-operative Wholesale Society in May 1983. It was a happy move and one we could celebrate while I was still in Britain following the meeting of the ICA Women's Committee in Worthing. It was also a promotion as Bernard became a departmental head of the Co-operative Union. He was also moving into a historic role created in 1881. The secretary of the Southern Section Committee of the Co-operative Union had then been asked to observe and report on parliamentary actions affecting co-operatives. As the movement grew in membership and turnover, parliament became more significant to it and it to politicians locally and nationally. Eventually the Co-operative Union created a distinct Parliamentary Department with its own secretary and committee which were elected from the movement's main organs.

There had been some notable Parliamentary Secretaries. Henry May left to become General Secretary of the International Co-operative Alliance while A.V. Alexander was elected to parliament several times during the inter-war years. When defeated he returned to the parliamentary office and during the Second World War served as First Lord of the Admiralty. He became Earl Alexander and Churchill dubbed him his "favourite socialist". The most recent holder was John Gallagher and he had also joined the House of Lords as a Life Peer thus justifying Bernard calling him a "Wily Bird".

Bernard's appointment allowed us to move to Rayleigh and to my parents' cottage which for some strange reason we had not yet sold. It was not perfect because it was small and we had to jettison some furniture; but we could move in straight away and Bernard could commute from Rayleigh.

PARLIAMENTARY OFFICE

The Parliamentary Office was in Buckingham Palace Road near Victoria Station in London. It was in a large building which could have been labelled a mini Holyoake House, the headquarters of the Co-operative Union in Manchester. Its ground floor held the offices of the Co-operative Party while those of the Parliamentary office were a floor above. The one above that contained the offices of the Co-operative Press and the Southern Section of the Co-operative Union.

Major areas in Bernard's new work were politics and research for which he was well able and had held long interest. He was familiar with the distinctions between the Parliamentary Office and the Co-operative Party with the latter being party political and the former concerned with lobbying and representation.

It pre-dated the Co-operative Party the creation of which had aroused strong debate in co-operative congresses in the late 19th and early 20th century. The call to actually establish it in 1917 came from the Parliamentary Office following failure to redress perceived grievances These centred on issues such as short supplies of merchandise, excessive mobilisation of co-operative staff and the requisition of horses and co-operative halls. Evidence collected pointed to private traders using political means to gain competitive advantage. When the Prime Minister Lloyd George refused to meet a co-operative delegation but supposedly met one instead from the Jockey Club, British co-operatives decided to take direct political action.

From 1917 the Co-operative Movement had a political party and a Parliamentary Committee. The former fought local and parliamentary elections. Through later electoral agreements with the Labour Party these were Labour and Co-operative candidates. Alliance with the Labour Party and trade unions stemmed from shared historical roots also membership of the National Council of Labour. However co-operatives held that they constituted a distinct from of social ownership as distinct from state enterprises. Their electoral agreements were therefore between the Co-operative Union and the Labo0ur Party and did not include affiliation. Only one co-operative society affiliated directly to the Labour Party and that was the Royal Arsenal Society in south London. There were however close relations with the Trades Union Congress and the Labour Party. Both sent fraternal delegates to co-operative congresses and the Co-operative Union reciprocated at their Congress and Annual Conference.

Labour/Co-operative candidates elected to Parliament and those in the House of Lords formed the Co-operative Parliamentary Group. Bernard had had close relations with this when Research Officer to the Co-operative Party in the mid 1950s and would now resume with the objectives of the Parliamentary Committee rather than those of the Co-operative Party. Members of the Co-operative Parliamentary Group helped Bernard gain copies of parliamentary papers, seek information or raise questions on co-operative issues in either house.

Bernard's role as Parliamentary Secretary was not party political and was more heavily based on research so building on skills he had developed in earlier positions. Additionally he would represent for and lobby on behalf of the co-operative movement with governmental bodies, other trade associations and various interest groups as was seen when a proposal was made to introduce legislation to allow Sunday trading. The Co-op joined others in opposition. Together with churches, trade unions and other groups it successfully campaigned to Keep Sunday Special with the proposal being defeated in Parliament. Sadly it was only a temporary victory.

Bernard's new position also brought many personal pleasures. He enjoyed working in a mini Holyoake House in Buckingham Palace Road and to renewing earlier work friendships, several in the Co-operative Party from the 1950s. One was David Wise now the Party's General Secretary as well as a director of the Co-operative Wholesale Society and chairman of the Co-operative Insurance Society/ Another was Les Goodrum now the Party's Assistant General Secretary. A particularly valued friend was Marion Rilstone who as Marion Richards had been Bernard's Secretary in the 1950s. Tragically her husband died young and Marion raised their two children by herself. When she could return to work the Party had a job waiting for her and she was warmly welcomed back. As the party's offices were on the ground floor Bernard often called to speak to these friends when arriving or leaving the building.

He knew the staff of the Parliamentary office less well but soon developed good working relations and several strong friendships. Their work was growing particularly with European business. The position of senior European assistant was therefore advertised and almost 300 applied. Bernard short-listed and interviewed six but remained undecided about the two front runners. One had just completed a Master's degree and to help him decide he asked if he could read it. He was impressed and appointed her. She was Pauline Green who was later elected a Labour/Co-operative Member of the European Parliament where she became the leader of its Socialist Group. After that she became Chief Executive of Co-operatives UK, the organisation that succeeded the Co-operative Union. She also became a Dame. By then Bernard had retired but he laughed when recalling her joking with friends in the Co-operative Party that as Bernard's European assistant she would now need to learn more about the Co-operative Movement and the European Union. She proved a good learner!

Several warm moments came from Bernard's representational work. One was with Inland Revenue when he realised that a senior civil servant on the other side of the table was his niece Angela, the daughter of his brother Kenneth. They warmly greeted each other and then resumed negotiating positions.

A particularly warm moment for me came after the success of the campaign to Keep Sunday Special which was reported to the Co-operative Congress in Llandudno 1987. As Parliamentary Secretary Bernard would present the report which was the first business after lunch. He and I but no one else knew that he planned to retire at the end of the year which meant that this would be his last congress. For that reason I decided to photograph him at the rostrum preparing his papers before congress resumed. I hardly noticed the taped music but he did. It was from *My Fair Lady*.

Rising to present his report Bernard first said:

"When you returned from lunch just now you may have seen me preparing my papers and Mrs. Rhodes taking my photograph with music from "My Far Lady" being played in the background." Then pointing to me he added: "Well she is my fair lady and when we defeated the bill and can now Keep Sunday Special "I could have danced all night"

Laughter and applause all round plus warm smiles for me. I was very touched. We were a well-known co-operative couple but Bernard was inherently shy and seldom made personal comments. That he did so at such a large public co-operative occasion was heart-warming and also reflected Bernard's quick wit.

BERNARD'S RETIREMENT

Bernard retired shortly before Christmas 1987 almost two years before his due retirement at 65. Several factors shaped the decision. One was the demands of the job against age. Commuting to and from Rayleigh wearied him and he had begun to fear that his memory was not as good as it should be, Retirement attracted and Bernard hoped it might allow him to attempt a post-war history of the British co-operative movement.

A number of co-operative organisations marked his retirement by hosting special events and presenting retirement gifts. I particularly remember that at the Co-operative Union. We travelled to Manchester by train and I saw for the first time a public telephone at the end of the carriage. I spent much of the journey wondering how it was technically possible. Of course this was in the days before mobile telephones.

Arriving at the Co-operative Union we first met Irfon Thomas whom I had met in Birmingham during my visit to Aston University in search of lost ICA library volumes. He had since moved to Union headquarters where among other things, he headed the management of the election of the next Congress President. Much to our delight Bernard had been nominated, no doubt as a retirement tribute. He was not elected but Ifon was assiduous in not letting slip any information on how the election might be going.

We also renewed contact with Roy Garrett, the Union's Librarian and Archivist for whom we had great respect and affection. This gave Bernard the opportunity to discuss availability of Co-operative Union sources for his post-war co-operative history. I was also able to speak to Roy about a possible subject for my Ph.D thesis. A few months earlier at the Llandudno congress he had urged me to consider basing it on the 3,000 or so letters Robert Owen had written which the Co-operative Union held in its archives. Speaking of this again at Bernard's retirement I hardly liked to admit that I was not over keen. Instead I blurted out my long held interest in Anne Lamming's suggestion of basing a thesis on how and why the International Co-operative Alliance survived the two world wars and the Cold War when similar organisations espousing peace and the international brotherhood of man split. Roy was immediately enthusiastic. His face lit up and with a great big smile he exclaimed: "How exciting!" That became the deciding factor although sadly Roy would not live to read the result.

RITA IN NORTHERN IRELAND

Thought of tackling a Ph.D had returned because of problems I was experiencing in Ulster University where two years earlier I had been appointed a Lecturer in Co-operative Studies. Whereas I had wanted my two previous jobs, I had had little ambition for this. As much as anything I was at a loose end and too young to retire. Teaching Co-operative Studies in a university pleased but the location and internal politics were not easy.

Those in the university stemmed from uncertainty in which department to base the Co-operative Education, Research and Training Unit (CERTU) and the Certificate in Co-operative Studies together with research into the viability of community co-operatives within the Northern Ireland economy. Initially CERTU comprising Dr Ray Donnelly and a research assistant had been based in the Department of Adult Education but shortly before I joined it had been moved to the Northern Ireland Small Business Unit (NISBI) within the Department of Management and Economy. Ray's contract, and that of his research assistant had not been renewed and I another lecturer therefore had no one to introduce or guide us. My new colleague was Paddy Bolger, a renowned Irish co-operator and academic and author of notable history of Irish co-operation. Previously employed by the Irish government's economic ministry, Paddy had gained two years' leave of absence being uncertain how the university appointment might work out. Shrewd man! He lived with his family in Lifford just across the border in Donegal and each day drove to Magee College where we would be based although we also had classes in Belfast. I was relieved when Paddy agreed to take these while I would take those at Magee

There was also a new Research Assistant but he would be based in the Northern Ireland Small Business Institute, our parent body in the university's Jordanstown campus on the outskirts of Belfast. The university had a further campus at Coleraine and another in central Belfast but Prof. Gavin, Provost of Magee

College, Derry had successfully bid for CERTU to be based there.

Tensions soon emerged between CERTU and the Northern Ireland Small Business Institute (NISBI) to whom we reported and who had ultimate control. CERTU had apparently been moved there because new co-operatives were likely to be small businesses. Nevertheless the syllabus for Co-operative Studies related also to larger co-operatives at other stages of development. In the mid 1980s Northern Ireland had only one significant retail society, namely the large Belfast society and a greater number of agricultural co-operatives, some big. A young credit union movement was growing and was highly relevant to Northern Ireland's needs.

Another difficulty was that NISBI disliked examinable subjects as was the Certificate in Co-operative studies. At first Paddy and I were amused: how could you be in a university but against exams. Nevertheless NISBI'S position hardened. It derived from its focus on business start-ups for their job creation potential and training for these was more relevant than longer term education.

Ideological tension also arose. NISBI's director and his assistant director came from big business and had little sympathy or knowledge of co-operatives. Tension surfaced in various ways. One was at a meeting of CERTU's advisory committee which comprised representatives of a variety of co-operative and two of the lecturers who had successfully gained generous EU funding for the Certificate. That funding was one factor in the competition between university departments to house the Co-operative Education, Research and Training Unit. At one of the committee's meetings the NISBI director told Paddy and I to forget about teaching co-operative principles which so roused one member that he shouted that that was "risible".

Other tensions were organisational. Our research assistant was increasingly given NISBI work and that for CERTU suffered.

Another difficulty arose when Paddy suffered a slight stroke and I was asked if I would agree to his contract being terminated and I move from Magee to NISBI on the Jordansstown campus. I rejected both proposals. We were also had doubts about how NISBI was handling CERTU's EU funding. Statements did not fully explain and trying to clarify proved difficult as well as delicate illustrating the internecine nature of university politics. One of Bernard's Yorkshire sayings came to mind: it was 'Keep band in nick' and I did not pursue the issue but doubts remained. Fortunately we had strong support at Magee with its provost, Prof. Gavin who wished us to remain there as a distinct co-operative studies unit.

When our research assistant was fully taken into NISBI we were given permission to advertise for a replacement to be based with us at Magee. Prof. Gavin had strongly supported this. Pauline McLennaghan was appointed and became a great asset. An agreeable personality she made effective contributions but her interview showed me how careful I needed to be of political divisions. Her appointment was opposed by a much respected local businessman but she had impressed me in a number of ways. She was in the final year of a Ph.D thesis in Dublin which was on Derry enterprises. She had been born and raised in the city and was sympathetic to co-operatives. I later learned that the businessman who opposed her was Unionist while she was a nationalist. Qualifications, temperament and ability were what I looked for but in Northern Ireland other issues became involved. They brought home to me that Paddy and I had probably been appointed because he was Irish, catholic and nationalist and I was British with presumably unionist sympathies. We cancelled out each other.

Pauline and I became close but she and Paddy even closer. His health was not good and she became a close family friend who gave him much help with early computers. Paddy had a co-operative personality as well as co-operative convictions. He smoothed awkward moments but enjoyed raising a laugh. Each day he crossed the border from Donegal and on one occasion wore a black beret and sunglasses, well known IRA garb. He gave a great big smile and was waved on, possibly because the border guards knew him or recognised he was making a joke.

Our students came from old and new co-operatives and I was pleased to teach once more. I needed to quickly learn about their co-operatives. Paddy introduced me to some and representatives from co-operatives on CERTU's advisory committee took me to others. A new member was Paddy Devlin, Chair of the recently created Northern Ireland Co-operative Development Agency (NICDA). He was a well-known Northern Ireland politician. Along with John Hume and Gerry Fitt he had been a founder member of the Social Democratic and Labour Party but had moved away when its catholic emphasis grew stronger than its Labour one.

I first met Paddy Devlin at Magee when he visited CERTU. A university caretaker warned me to not be alarmed if I saw the pistol he was allowed to carry for personal protection. I did not see it but soon realised he never hung back from making a point. He strongly objected when at a meeting of the CERTU Committee I referred to Northern Island as a "province". Instead of asking him for an alternative I floundered trying to find a synonym Nevertheless he invited me to join the board of the Northern Ireland Co-operative Development Agency, an irony having been a staff member of the national Co-operative Development Agency. I happily accepted but I should have had my wits about me. Accepting a position by invitation confers less legitimacy than one gained by election. Patronage is involved and in later struggles I found myself out of favour and off the board.

LIVING AND WORKING IN THE TROUBLES

It was not only the job I needed to learn but also its location. Settling down in Geneva had been easy. Moreover Bernard and I had moved much for his work and I reckoned I knew how to move. Derry though was something different including what you

162

called the place. Early on I said Derry or Londonderry according to the company I was in. Wishing everyone well I finally decided to alternate as I do in this account.

I also learned quite early that if something untoward happened 500 yards or so away, you were safe and not affected. Nevertheless, heavily fortified and guarded police stations were a shock. One along a nearby street was bombed, causing the street to be closed and traffic redirected into the nearby city centre. Some areas were not safe for buses to pass through and Sinn Fein instituted a community taxis service. At one time I needed to use these to reach Magee College. Each carried a number of passengers who told the driver where they wanted to get off and then paying the fare he requested. They spoke little to each other and certainly not to me.

I also quickly learned where and not where to go. I was advised not to visit an estate on the hill overlooking the bombed police station mentioned above. A young woman had conducted a genuine census survey there but had aroused suspicion and was murdered. You also learned to whom you could or could not speak. I felt awkward the first time I was passed by a military patrol. A cheeky young soldier smiled and said something to which I would normally have replied but suddenly thought that that might be unwise. It was unwise to be seen talking to the army or the police as Bernard learned when a route we were driving on was changed. He leaned from the passenger seat and called to a nearby policeman for directions. I snapped that you only spoke to the police after they stopped and spoke to you. You should not call out or ask them anything for fear of raising the suspicions of those nearby.

Because of the badly damaged traffic system I had to learn to drive and to buy a car. Its British number plate made it distinctive and on several occasions I saw the military or police closely inspecting it. It also received close attention at ferry ports when heavily loaded.

I had never wanted to drive and had dissuaded Bernard from doing so many years earlier but Northern Ireland changed all that. Although Paddy took the Belfast classes we both had meetings in Belfast and the train service took over two hours and even longer if there was trouble. I needed to drive to Belfast and other places but had to first pass the driving test. That was an experience.

My driving instructor was Eddie McDonagh who was recommended by several at Magee. He was excellent because he spoke little except when correcting or giving advice. Driving around Londonderry was a special experience. Eddie never spoke of the troubles or of his own views but he kept a sharp eye. I suspect this was to avoid danger but also to see what was happening suggesting that driving instructors, taxi and bus drivers become very familiar with their home territories.

I learned in my car, bought second hand with 6,000 miles on the clock. It was a 1979 Ford Popular Plus and Bernard nick-named her Poppy (Popular) Excalibur (magic). I drove it until 2005 and never had another car. It failed its MOT only twice: once when its original shock absorbers had weakened; and when the passenger seat belt had got badly twisted. At the beginning it looked as if it would have a short life. I failed three driving tests and for the fourth Eddie suggested I drive his car which was "lighter" and perhaps easier to control on three point turns etc. The examiner got in and told me to drive off. I turned the key and believed I had ignited for although I could not hear anything, I knew it was a much quieter car than Poppy Excalibur. Imagine my shame when he pointed out I had not ignited at which I had a temperamental tantrum, got out saying that I gave up. Amazingly the examiner persuaded me back and told me to try again. I was in such a temper that I drove certain I had failed and swearing under my breath. Amazingly I had passed and for years after years I remained grateful to that examiner; also somewhat mystified.

There was a sequel. Afterwards I said to Eddie that I would still be scared driving in icy conditions. He suggested I try out the skid pans or even take an advanced drivers' course. I did both possibly out of a sense of false bravado. Eddie was again my instructor and I was amused to be examined by a Royal Ulster Constabulary (RUC) Traffic Inspector; you kept your distance from the RUC. He was pleasant and relaxed and we had a good chat. Amazingly I passed and automatically became a member of the Advanced Drivers' Institute. That caused much hilarity when we recalled how long it had taken to pass my first driving test.

Although I became an advanced driver I was never an enthusiastic one. A foot operation in 2005 led me to give up driving. I was quite relieved although I was sorry to part with Poppy Excalibur which I had had for 19 years. I placed the annual amount I spent on running her into a taxi fund and have not felt extravagant in doing so. Not once have I exceeded the money I spent each year on running the car.

Ironically Northern Ireland's troubles made it easier to learn to drive than the mainland roads because there was far less traffic. In those days there was little motor way. The few garages there were opened only during the day and on one occasion that caused a nasty incident. Paddy, CERTU's two secretaries and I went to Belfast for an evening farewell function for one of the four lecturers who had proposed the Certificate in Co-operative Studies and who was leaving to take an overseas appointment. En route we passed the garage where I normally stopped to refuel but on this occasion for some reason I did not and it was closed when we returned some hours later. It was a two hour drive to Londonderry and I immediately feared I had insufficient petrol. Paddy and I watched the gauge with increasing desperation that eventually caused me to stop at the police station in Dungiven. Never mind about not talking to the police here was I going to them through fortified defences and asking for help. My British accent no doubt helped as I explained the situation, hoping that Paddy who had come in with me would not open his mouth.

165

Fair dues, the police were helpful although one had his gun trained on us. They let us have a can of petrol which they took out to the car. Poor Poppy Excalibur and the two girls inside! Bright lights shone on them while two police, one crouched behind and another standing in front watched as a third emptied the can into the petrol tank. No doubt we paid but I cannot remember what it might have been. What I do remember is the gratitude, the warm thanks and the big smiles we gave Dungiven police.

I usually enjoyed the drive between Londonderry and Belfast. We drove between small towns and villages and through wild and hilly countryside. Shortly after leaving Derry we passed Burntollet and Paddy told how some believed the troubles started there. Apparently, the RUC had been unusually violent in dispersing a student march from Belfast. Many students were injured and their parents, who were predominantly middleclass, objected in greater numbers than previously and protest widened.

Returning to Derry we drove up hill from of the top of which you got your first sight of the city. To the right was the large Altnegelvin hospital. You knew you were nearing Derry because for the first time you saw the helicopter that circled over it 24 hours a day. In the town itself you hardly noticed it and quickly became used to it except at night when its lights might shine through your windows.

Despite the struggles Londonderry was a beautiful place. Physically it was unusual in that a large part of its city wall survived and the office of the housing association from which I rented my flat was in Magazine Street right beside the lower part of the wall. Higher up was the Diamond which elsewhere would have been the town square. On one corner was the Austins department store in which Bernard had one adventure. After coffee there one morning he found police barring exit because of a bomb scare around the corner in the Diamond. A bomb had been thrown from an upper window further along the street as police cars passed. It fell in the roof of one but, thank God had not exploded as Bernard and other customers might have been injured. I think that was the nearest he came to direct violence.

I had been surprised at how much normal life there was in the town. It had high levels in music, arts and design. I enjoyed concerts in the Guild Hall, learnt of various choirs and admired Derry women's distinctive fashion sense. A strong tradition of embroidery survived perhaps best seen in the individually designed Irish dancing dresses. Derry was beautiful whichever way you approached it.

Sadly place names caused problems. One evening I was giving a tutorial and sitting by a window overlooking a main road. We were distracted when a young man was stopped and roughed up by a military patrol. Such scenes always distressed but this one led to a joke. The student with me told me how a friend was driving to Londonderry from Limavady and was stopped by the police. After his driving licence etc had been examined he was asked where he was going and he answered "Derry". The policeman told him that there was no such place and that he should move his car over to the hard shoulder and stay until he could remember where he was going. An hour passed and again the police asked where he was going to which again he replied Derry. Once more he was told to remain on the hard shoulder but the third time he was asked he barked "Strabane". That town's name was not disputed and he had to be let go. The joke was that to reach Strabane he had to pass through Londonderry and of course, he stopped there.

The troubles affected driving and transport and of course also housing. Initially I rented a terrace cottage near Magee from a professor who was to lecture in India for a year. This was on the catholic or nationalist side of the town but when he returned I needed alternative accommodation. I was lucky in being able to rent a flat from the Derry Housing Association. It was across the river in a protestant and unionist stronghold. Ebbrington barracks were just down the road, which helped explain why my car with its British number plate so easily caught military attention.

167

The flat was in Melrose Terrace in one of two large semi-detached houses that had been modernised. It contained a living room, bedroom, kitchen and bathroom and was on the top of a hill overlooking the Foyle. I had beautiful views particularly in summer months when the sunset was later than on the mainland because of Derry's north westerly position. I also enjoyed a panoramic view of the town.

At night I took a tip of one of Magee secretaries to place jewellery I was removing in the case used to carry lipsticks and to place it on my bedside table. If there was an alarm you quickly grabbed it and put in a pocket.

Although I remained safe violence was near. The worst incident for me was at Magee where a prison officer had attended an evening class. As he left the building and was getting into his car he was shot dead by a jogger who was never identified. Police were soon present but then the prison officer's car with his body still in it was blown up. Another policeman standing near it was also killed and much damage was done to the front of Magee College as well as to parked cars facing it. I had lent my car to a friend and it happened to be there. The car next to it was damaged but amazingly Poppy Excalibur was not.

Another incident occurred the night after Bernard and I had been to a pizza restaurant. We had parked "Poppy Excalibur" nearby on waste land just off the Strand, the main street. Late next night we were suddenly lit up by what I thought it was heavy traffic but a second later we heard a loud explosion. We looked out of the window and saw that it was in the area we had parked the car the previous evening.

Troubles came close to our staff. Nearby was the office of the Workers Education Association and its secretary lived in a largely protestant area on the Waterside although they were catholic. Despite having lived there some years they moved because of increasing hostility and threats against them. One of our cleaners had more immediate problems. Her son had been arrested for alleged murder. He was tried and convicted after I had left but I suspect that he was guilty. Apparently his mother, our cleaner had taken him as a child to the grave of her brother who had been murdered by Ulster Volunteers. The previous night the RUC had come to her house to search for weapons which she denied having. They caused considerable damage particularly in the bathroom which was ripped apart and left unusable. She could not afford to repair it.

The troubles also came close to home elsewhere. When renting the professor's terrace house I used a nearby small corner shop and got chatting with a woman who served there. On one occasion she told me how she supported the peace campaign of two Northern Ireland women after which she was visited by someone from the IRA. He demanded that her daughter join one of the IRA children's events to which she jauntily replied, "Over my dead body". He told her, "That can be arranged". She left the women's peace movement.

As much as one was torn by the troubles others arose at the university when we sensed that the future of the Co-operative Education, Research and Training Unit was in doubt.

END OF THE CO-OPERATIVE EDUCATION, RESEARCH AND TRAINING UNIT

We already knew that the Northern Ireland Small Business Institute was unhappy with the Certificate of Co-operative Studies because it was educational rather than training and was examinable. Additional trouble arose from competition for funding.

The European Union put much money into Northern Ireland to try to heal its problems. Funding the certificate was an example but bigger ones could be seen in improving infrastructure and in grants to economic and social projects. These were often run by volunteers or those who were poorly paid. Competition between projects and their organisers roused strong feelings and peace loving groups with good intentions often fell out with each other.

We were dismayed to find CERTU was threatened by, of all organisations, the Northern Ireland Co-operative Development Agency. It was one with which we had affinity and from whom we would have expected support. Even more to the point, two of its Belfast staff were students of the Certificate in Co-operative Studies.

The trigger had been the appointment of its chief official, its organiser. Although not on the appointments committee I had been happy to endorse this. Paddy knew him from past experience however and had reservations but did not explain; always charitable Paddy felt he might also be mistaken, sadly he was not. It was some time before I heard of NICDA's growing antagonism to the Certificate in Co-operative Studies and to education rather than training. To some extent I could agree because co-operative start-ups needed training but the certificate was also for well-established co-operatives. The matter became heated over competition for EU funds. NICDA began a campaign to gain greater EU funding and argued it was more relevant to Northern Ireland needs than CERTU. Paddy Devlin, NICDAS chair led negotiations with NISBI to discontinue the Certificate in Co-operative Studies and to provide training programmes for NICDA.

Hindsight allows me to describe this simply but at the time much was unclear and we came to know the full position too late. We sought help through the Northern Ireland office which was the organ through which EU applications were made. Bernard also suggested that Lord Graham of Edmonton who at that time had shadow responsibility for Northern Ireland could diplomatically seek answers to some of the questions we were raising. Both Bernard and I had long links with Ted who had followed Harold Campbell as General Secretary of the Co-operative Party and was then elected to the House of Commons. When he lost his seat he became a life peer and joined the Co-operative Parliamentary Group from where he now gave Bernard much help. My links stemmed from Ted and I both having been students of the Co-operative College. Several times he also reminded me he had been on the committee that interviewed me for the position of Secretary/Organiser of the Enfield Co-operative Society's Co-operative Party many years earlier.

I agreed with Bernard's suggestion but we had badly misjudged. Instead of discreet enquiries Ted raised a parliamentary question for which there was much publicity and uproar in Ulster University and the Co-op with the *Co-op News* giving it headlines. I spoke on the 'phone to Ted and he admitted his move was likely to cause me 'flack'. He got headlines; I was expendable, another hard political lesson.

There were others in the Ulster University that played on the side of cautious. CERTU staff was given the option of moving into the Community Studies Unit which was offering a new Certificate in Community Studies and which could contain a co-operative element. Paddy declined immediately and returned to his position in the Irish Civil Service. Pauline McClennaghan and I agreed to the shift along with Amanda Fullerton who had been our chief secretary and now became that of the Community Studies Unit.

The university could claim it was retaining co-operative studies although in a reduced form. This drew sharp contrast for me with the successful Co-operative Studies Unit at University College, Cork which Paddy and I had visited and with which we had developed good relations. It was funded by the Bank of Ireland and we had wondered whether we might make a similar application to the Co-operative Bank. The Co-operative Wholesale Society (CWS) was already involved in Derry with the Galliagh Co-operative Society on its outskirts. This was a retail society established by the local community and had an impressive single store which the CWS helped stock. It was run by a rota of volunteers although a full time paid manager had recently been appointed.

We wondered if the Co-operative Bank might be persuaded to do to join the CWS. This was a year before Terry Thomas, later Lord Thomas became the bank's managing director. As its marketing manager though, he had already successfully argued the case for environmental and ethical issues to be included in the bank's business strategies.

CERTU's demise rendered such an approach null and void. I still had employment but was at something of a loss. I was disillusioned about the Ulster University, the Northern Ireland Small Business Institute and the Northern Ireland Co-operative Development Agency. But I was only 53 and too young to retire, despite having no further ambitions. Despite all this and most ironically Bernard and I were considering settling in Northern Ireland near Derry. His retirement loomed and we were attracted by beautiful scenery and low house prices. This remained an option for several years. What finally decided us against it was the hour's flight to Heathrow before travelling anywhere else. We planned various holidays for when we had both retired.

Despite all this disillusionment work in the Community Studies Unit proved interesting. An objective of its certificate was to bring nationalists and unionists together so students were recruited from both sides of the Foyle. This made for a lively environment. Its staff included two other women, one of whom had come to Londonderry a decade or so earlier and was a Quaker. A lively character, she was a single mother and had the over-riding objective of peace as did our other feminine colleague. She was a women's right campaigner although she had married a younger man, already had a baby son and another baby on the way. The men staff included an IRA man who I have to admit I came to respect. He was honest and decent and had spent time in prison productively furthering his education by gaining a degree. He recalled our Quaker colleague settling in Londonderry which suggested that Sinn Fein and the IRA kept tabs on newcomers. I wondered if they had with me and my British car number plate.

My co-operative role continued. I taught about co-operatives and continued close contact with emerging co-operatives. Sadly too often these sprung up on hope rather than viability. Viability could cut across human elements as with a women's co-operative producing hand embroidered Irish dance dresses. Their skill and artistry was a joy to behold but hand embroidery took longer than that produced by machines. They would have had greater chance of success had they registered as a marketing co-operative rather than a productive society selling dresses embroidered at home. Instead, its members wanted to sit and chat while they sewed. Technology also influenced viability as we found with a number of our students exploring setting up an incinerating business.

Teaching adults brought some heart-warming moments. For some the community studies course was a first experience of adult education and they were generous in their post exam thank you gifts. They also triggered adventures as when we joined a cross border community studies event in Donegal.

Five members of the potential incinerating business decided to hire a car and drive themselves. I was therefore surprised when I found that they had left earlier than planned and had left one of their colleagues behind. He was now asking if he could come with me and I immediately realised why. An ex prisoner and IRA man he would be well logged at border posts. They had calculated he would stand a better chance of getting through with me and my British number plate car. His friends obviously wanted to live it up before the start of the course. It was a two day event with an overnight stay and afterwards produced a very delicate situation. The Donegal people said that a duvet and a valuable vase were missing and asked if we would check with our students. They were particularly worried about the loss of the vase. Confirmation gradually emerged that one of our students had taken them. It was hard to believe because she was popular and believed to be honest. Difficulties arose from her boyfriend being a well-known IRA member. Very quietly she was persuaded to hand the stolen items over and again very quietly they were returned to our Donegal hosts.

Life was lively in community studies but I was preparing to leave. Bernard had retired and we wanted to be together. He spent quite some time with me in Derry. As I said earlier we even considered settling down there but eventually decided to make Rayleigh our retirement home. We had already moved from my parents' cottage into a larger house a short distance away.

I was uncertain what to do as far as work was concerned. No ambitions remained and I was generally disillusioned. Ideas emerged but took time. One began during the summer break between CERTU's closure and my joining the community students unit. Materials and Techniques of Co-operative Management (MATCOM) invited me to lead one of their Worker Co-operative programmes at the Co-operative College in Malaysia. The Plunkett Foundation also asked me to jointly lead in Cairo a training of trainers programme for women in Agricultural Co-operatives. One could follow the other and I would be away for around six weeks. The MATCOM programme arose from a conference in Santarem, Portugal that I had joined in Easter when I had been asked to present a paper about the Certificate of Co-operative Studies and the Co-operative Education, Research and Training Unit. MATCOM's director, Lennart Skarret had also participated along with two colleagues from the Co-operative Branch of the International Labour Organisation. It was good to renew contact. During the conference Lennart broached the question of whether I would be available to work in the development of national workers' co-operatives programmes. Two coming up were in Tanzania and Malaysia. He thought the latter would be better because Tanzanian conditions were harsh. The Plunkett invitation had come through the ICA Women's Committee who still wished me well.

174

Both events were well paid and prompted the idea that perhaps I could attract others and fund an attempt at a Ph.D thesis. The idea took strength when the ILO Co-op. Branch invited me to do a month's research in Geneva and the Community Studies Unit gave me leave of absence if I paid my salary to a locum. I readily agreed. Four weeks in Geneva gave me the opportunity to renew links with the ICA and to learn more about their updated archives. These showed a wealth of sources for my proposed subject and Robert Beasley expressed interest and approved my future access to the archives.

When I returned to Derry I contacted the Co-operative Research Unit of the Open University and registered with them to do my thesis. Alan Thomas, later Prof. Thomas agreed to be my internal supervisor. Thus by the time I left Ulster University some kind of future path existed.

LONDONERRY POSTCRIPT

I left Derry but it never fully left me. It returned graphically and tragically. Amanda Fullerton had been CERTU's secretary and moved with Pauline and me to the Community Studies Unit. She had recently graduated and a lovely photograph of her in graduation gown standing between her parents appeared in a local paper. I was struck by their good looks. Her father appeared to have charisma with a beard and a great big smile. Nevertheless he was a controversial figure as a Sinn Fein councillor on Buncrana Council across the border.

Their daughter Amanda was one of life's enhancer. Attractive and good fun she had a lively sense of humour and was kind and charitable. I later grieved for her when it was announced on TV news that her father had been murdered and in the most dastardly way. He and his wife had been in bed when members of the Ulster Volunteer Force entered his house and shot him dead as he got to the head of the stairs. There were vicious killings on either side in the Northern Ireland troubles and this was certainly one of the most notable. I wondered how on earth his wife could

175

ever recover from such sudden horror or how his family ever came to terms with it. One of his sons was interviewed on television news and the family likeness was clear. I wrote to Amanda through a mutual friend but had no reply, the horror and shock probably still being too great.

Mr. Fullerton's murder brought home to me all over again how difficult it must be to get over such atrocities and to wonder whether it can ever be possible. With humility I can only say that my four years in Northern Ireland taught me much.

Chapter Nine

MONGOLIA

INTRODUCTION

The first years of the 1990s were eventful although neither of us was in full time employment. We each continued various co-operative activities, Bernard in the early stages of his post-war xo-operative history and as Chair of the UK Society of Co-operative Studies; while I began research for a Ph.D thesis. I also undertook short-term overseas assignments to pay for this. One in Mongolia would become my biggest adventure.

BERNARD'S ACTIVITIES

Bernard began his research into British post-war co-operative history in the late 1980s. Sadly his request to use the archives of the Co-operative Wholesale Society was turned down so he concentrated on two main sources: historical editions of the *Co-operative News* held in the British Library's Newspaper archive at Colindale in north London; and Congress Reports of the Co-operative Union. Bernard sought no grant and paid his own expenses.

His other main activity was in the Society for Co-operative Studies whose governance attempted to bring co-operative leaders and activists together with academics interested in and working with co-operatives. Elections to its committee reflected this balance. It elected the society's officers who comprised a junior and a senior vice chair, chair and past chair. Each held that position for a year before rising to the next position but once that of past chair had been completed the holder left the committee and could not seek re-election for at least another year. The point being made is that when Bernard was elected junior vice chair he made a four year commitment. For him and other office holders this process meant that they became well versed in issues facing the society. Bernard also became convenor of SCS meetings in London, a position similar to that which I had held in Scotland a decade earlier.

Sadly in late 1992 he became seriously ill. A firm diagnosis was long delayed so we eventually sought a private consultation. We were then told he needed surgery and he was immediately admitted to hospital on the NHS. It was agreed that an operation was necessary but was thought that it could be delayed until the New Year.

Bernard was sent home and a fraught period followed during which he became very ill. We could not get a return hospital appointment and his doctor made no emergency appeal. Worsening pain led him to eat less and less and to sit up many nights because that was easier than lying down. Finally I managed to contact his consultant's secretary and appealed to her for help. The appointment she arranged was on 21 December and the consultant, Mark Phillips immediately said Bernard was seriously ill, admitted him to hospital and arranged for a major operation on 23rd December. Afterwards I was told that had it been delayed just yet another day his bowel could have burst. Although that had been avoided I feared the worst when asked to see the doctors the next day.

A Chinese woman doctor spoke to me in the main corridor. With people passing she told me that Bernard was terminally ill. He had cancer as his weight loss indicated. I was looking down and the floor swam but I managed to suggest that perhaps that was due to his not eating because of pain. I also asked if or how he should be told and the Dr. suggested we wait until he was stronger.

This was Christmas Eve. The next week was hell as I tried to convince Bernard he was getting better and begin to discuss where we might go for our summer holiday. Then something else bad happened. On 30th December Bernard telephoned from a public telephone to tell me he had just been told that he did not have cancer. He was over the moon and I had to pretend equal joy. But I knew differently and I was furious that I had not first been consulted about his being falsely reassured.

Next day, Year's Eve I visited and a male charge nurse told me how pleased they all were at the good news. I exploded. He tried to assure me but seeing my disbelief took me to a filing cabinet from which he showed me Bernard's file. Its histology report showed that he had diverticulitis and not cancer. Not only was the lady Chinese doctor wrong in diagnosis but also wrong to have proclaimed terminal illness before the histology report was available.

Although Bernard was not terminally ill it took a long time for him to recover. His life had been changed by a permanent stoma following his colostomy. Initially he accepted this well with support through a stoma clinic and a key that gave quick access to toilets for the disabled. After several accidents though, Bernard became less sanguine and began to withdraw. Although he remained active in the Society for Co-operative Studies he did not continue with his post-war co-operative history. Quick access to toilets became a priority. We still took holidays but air journeys became fewer. Christmas 1994 was spent in Lisbon, one of our three favourite cities. I fondly recall our mutual pleasure on the long walk to church on a cold frosty Christmas morning but on the flight home he had difficulties and decided not to fly again.

Fortunately all this happened *after* the biggest adventure of my life, an assignment in Mongolia.

RITA IN MONGOLIA

This had arisen from visits I made to the International Co-operative Alliance in Geneva to access sources for my Ph.D thesis. Robert Beasley, director, had given me permission to use their archives which had rich sources on war and peace. During

179

these visits I also caught up with past colleagues in the nearby Co-operative Branch of the International Labour Organisation.

During one of these visits its head of education and training, Pekka Pilvio asked if I might be interested in an assignment in Mongolia which was beginning to liberalise its economy. Its communist system was in decline as it, like other Soviet states was becoming more independent. Consequently Soviet consultants and experts were leaving and new programmes were being mounted by the United Nations and its Agencies. UNIFEM, the UN agency for women had proposed a project for Mongolian women, many of whom were becoming unemployed as state industries were privatised. The project would aim to create new jobs through the development of workers' co-operatives and mounted through the Mongolian Federation of Women. This was a nationwide organisation similar to Britain's Co-operative Women's Guild or the Women's Institute but it was state run organisation rather than a voluntary one.

The project had two main elements: a revolving loan fund and a co-operative training programme for which the Co-operative Branch of the International Labour Organisation had been consulted. Pekka asked if I would be interested in the training programme which would use the ILO's Materials and Training for Co-operative Organisation and Management (MATCOM). I must have looked a bit bemused as he reminded me that Mongolia was "behind India and on the way to China".

The assignment would be for six months and this raised two important questions. Could I spare that time from my Ph.D research which I hoped to complete in time for the centenary celebrations of the International Co-operative Alliance in 1995: and if I did accept would Bernard come with me. Neither of us wanted to be apart that long in a situation particularly with difficult communications. It would pay well and help finance my studies so we eventually decided I should accept and go by myself.

It would be a harsh assignment during the Mongolian winter; also in a country the United Nations designated least developed and one that was also experiencing political upheaval. The People's Mongolian Revolutionary Party had come to power in 1921 and three years later declared the country to be the Mongolian People's Republic. It then became a Soviet satellite state but the USSR did little to develop it and used it mainly as a buffer state between itself and China.

The collapse of communist regimes in Eastern Europe prompted unrest in Mongolia and the grip of then ruling party had been broken in an election in 1990. Liberalisation began and earlier Soviet assistance was being replaced with new forms channelled through a variety of organisations including the World Bank, the International Monetary Fund, and the United Nations. Various voluntary organisations such as the American Peace corps, British Overseas Volunteers and United Nations Volunteers were also working in Mongolia.

The UNIFEM project aimed to encourage self-help among women in general and equip the Mongolian Women's Federation to adapt from being a privileged and state funded organisation to one that was voluntary.

The project would begin in November 1991, two years after the atrocities in Tiananmen Square, Beijing. In neighbouring Mongolia upset had subsided although great uncertainty and unease persisted. On the one hand it was generally accepted that the previous political system had collapsed but on the other there was no clear idea of what should replace it. A market economy was thought to be an option but was little understood. This would create problems in developing a training programme in language that could be easily understood. How to define and translate its underlying concepts, terms and mechanisms for trainees who knew only Marxist economics? The translators and interpreters I was accorded had studied English in Moscow universities and had never been to the west

Underlying mounting the training programme were economic problems that compounded the country's political transition. For many years basic food items, rents and bus fares had been subsidised. These were now being withdrawn but led to raising costs for ordinary people. Only two items were in reasonable supply, namely flour and meat. The latter came from Mongolia's huge livestock population of 25 million but collapsing systems of procurement and distribution caused problems. Seasonal goods such as milk, butter and eggs were in short supply because means of processing and storing were little developed. In the past shortages had been easily met with imports from the Soviet Union but these were now drying up.

In any event imports became difficult because of the depreciation of the Mongolian currency, the Tugrik. When I arrived it was seven to the US$ but when I left it had risen to just over 200 to the US$. I would learn that the highest paid staff in the Mongolian Women's Federation received 1,200 Tugriks a month but for those who became unemployed the benefit was only 200 Tugriks a month.

To recruit trainees we needed to identify those needing work but unemployment levels were difficult to establish for a number of reasons. Government statistical services were little developed because they had not been needed. New methods were urgent but proved difficult to implement because of a shortage of paper. To save it a Labour Market I visited placed the details of five or six unemployed people to each card; there were not enough cards for each claimant to have one. Consequently indexing and cross referencing let alone the compilation of statistics became very difficult for the Ministry of Labour.

Before arriving to face these problems I was well briefed by UN documentation, the Co-operative Branch of the International Labour Organisation in Geneva and MATCOM in Vienna. A large medical kit and a diplomatic passport were given along with travel details. These had been difficult to arrange. It had been thought wise to avoid Moscow because of the high rate of baggage loss at its airport but Beijing had only two or three flights a week to Ulan Bator in Mongolia. Train was a possibility but I would have to be accompanied in China but a Chinese national would not then be allowed into Mongolia and I would have to be met at its border.

There were also problems arriving in Beijing. Bernard had accompanied me to Vienna but we bid emotional farewells when I flew from there to Beijing on 2nd November, via Copenhagen. By contrast with other airports and what it later became, Beijing airport was small and shabby. I had been warned during briefing not to leave the airport until I was officially met which was the custom with such assignments. But no one came to meet me and making alternative arrangements was bedevilled by the fact that all public notices were in Chinese and with no translations. How then to identify an information office or even a bureau de change to get local money to telephone the International Labour Organisation through whose regional office I would be working when in Mongolia. It would be closed because it was Sunday.

Eventually I teamed up with another passenger who had also not been met. He managed to change some money to pay for a taxi and we agreed the US$ I should give him to cover my half. We showed the driver the names of our hotels and indicated I should be dropped first. Unfortunately we landed first at my fellow passenger's hotel. He was somewhat somnolent and confused and tumbled out of the taxi, leaving me to pay the full fare. The trouble was I only US$ and at my hotel the driver charged US$41. Two bell boys who had come to take my luggage gasped and I knew I was being over-charged. I asked for a receipt which gave me no scope for argument because it was in Chinese and I could not understand it or the rate of exchange from the Yuan indicated. I presented it to the ILO the next day along with a complaint at not being met at the airport.

I later learned that the driver had not done so because it was his final day working for the ILO. He assumed that because it was Sunday I could not make a complaint until the next day by when he would have left and could no longer be disciplined.

The regional briefing went well and I also had opportunities to see a little of central Beijing. It seemed to combine old and new. An example was the elderly lady I saw outside a modern department store. She had bound feet that looked almost like hooves. But she seemed happy as she trotted along.

The problem of how to travel to Mongolia had been solved when a seat one of the few weekly flights had been purchased. I arrived in Ulan Bator on 6 November. The temperature was minus 6 degrees and would not rise beyond freezing until the following 24th February. I soon learned ways to keep warm.

This time I was met and by someone with whom I would work in the office of the United Nations Development Programme. That co-ordinated, managed and supervised UN projects in Mongolia. Besides handling experts and consultants UNDP also fostered good relations with Mongolian government departments and various national bodies like the Mongolian Women's Federation with whom I would be working.

We covered miles as we drove from the airport but as we came to the outskirts of Ulan Bator I saw a number of schools. Children seemed to be well looked after. Arriving at UNDP offices I was met by two officials from the Women's Federation. One was my counterpart, the Federation's Education Officer while other would be my interpreter and translator. An UNDP assistant who would handle my UNDP links also joined us.

It was explained that Mongolian women went by their father's name and did not use first names but they agreed that I could. So Uranchimeg became Urnaa, Ghanbattaa became Ujmaa but my UNDP assistant remained Narantoya. Urnaa became a great help and proved a lively character. She was in her late 30s and her command of English, learned in a Moscow university, was superb. She had never been to Britain. Her colleague and my counterpart, Ujmaa spoke no English but we became good friends, skilled in smiling and gesticulation. From the deference paid to her I quickly gathered she had some place in the party hierarchy.

Becoming familiar with Mongolian names was a language difficulty but there were other language problems. A major one was the management of money. A bank account was not feasible because I could not understand spoken or written Mongolian: and the State Bank was the only bank. My salary was paid into my Co-op bank account at home but a generous daily subsistence allowance was paid by UNDP. This was regularly paid in US$ and quickly mounted. A money belt was the only solution but made me feel like a walking money bomb, particularly as inflation rose and US$ became widely sought.

Subsistence payments were high because of Mongolia's harsh conditions. Ulan Bator had only two hotels of European standard which were very expensive and whose tariffs were in US$. Surplus cash would not have been a problem had I moved into one of these but I was manoeuvred into cheaper alternative private accommodation.

Hotels proved a danger. We travelled widely and stayed in state hotels of similar architecture. In their public areas one stood out as a foreigner and a likely dollar holder. The risk was in being followed to your room and attempts then being made to get you to open its door. I had been warned never to do that unless I knew who was on the other side. Fortunately doors in state hotels were strong.

Western consultants and experts were ready targets. We had to carry US$ because we were not allowed to use the Tugrik. That meant we could not use local shops and had passes to obtain goods at the diplomatic store which only took US$. Mongolians were not allowed to use it although Urnaa could come with me as my interpreter. The store had a single check out but if there was a power cut an abacus was used to tally our bills. The speed at which it was used fascinated although I sometimes wondered if I was being overcharged. I could not check and there were no receipts.

The store provided no bags. You had to take your own to carry your shopping and pointed up a big difference with the west. Mongolia was not a consumerist society. Shops sold basic Mongolian foodstuffs carried in hard wearing personal bags. No imported goods were available. The Diplomatic shop occasionally had some but their procurement was haphazard. This was underlined by the fact that a few months before my arrival the Diplomatic shop had completely ran out of goods and had had bare shelves. There had then been bad food shortages throughout Mongolia.

Generally speaking there were few ways to spend money in Ulan Bator. Mirth rose in UNDP when a volunteer Indian worker arrived one evening and asked for directions to the nearest Indian restaurant. He had to be told that there were no other restaurants or cafes apart from those in the two hotels. Consequently one could not spend one's dollars on a social life. Finding accommodation also proved difficult and competition arose for my rent because it would be paid in US$.

Staff in UNDP's general office guided me to a "private" hotel which Urnaa, my interpreter took me to see. The accommodation was a large L shaped bedsit with a small kitchen and bathroom. The charge was US$35 per day. I had reservations because it appeared to be the home of a young couple. They were prepared to move out and I imagined they would do almost anything for US$35 per day. I reluctantly agreed. Fortunately for me but unhappily for them, the decision was soon overturned.

Immediately afterwards I had an appointment with the Vice President of the Mongolian Women's Federation, a Mrs. Dolramaa. She was well known and a Member of Parliament who had been a junior Finance Minister. Urnaa entered her office with some reverence and I followed behind in a long walk to

Mrs. Dolramaa's desk. For all the formality an interesting meeting followed. During it she asked where I would stay and Urnaa explained the tenancy we had just agreed. Mrs. Dolramaa appeared unhappy and said that had she been given first option she could have offered similar accommodation at only US$25 per day. Moreover she would have given what I paid to the Mongolian Women's Federation so that they could import needlework materials from China. Deference to a senior figure in the Mongolian Women's Federation obviously coloured Urnaa's response and she quietly urged me to agree to Mrs. Dolramaa's offer. I did and experience proved I had been right to do so. The flat was the same design as the one I had seen earlier that morning but it was nearer to the centre of town and the office.

Despite her privileged position Mrs. Dolramaa and her husband had previously lived in the flat but he had since died. She had then moved into the flat next door that belonged to a son who was in the Mongolian embassy in Washington. Mrs. Dolramaa and her family were keen to maintain and protect the larger flat against his return. This new arrangement was obviously better and Urnaa arranged my withdrawal from the earlier tenancy.

As Mrs. Dolramma's tenant I also had increased protection. Even so she urged me not to open my door unless I was certain I knew who was outside. If in any doubt I should quickly check with her or a daughter-in- law who often stayed with her. Her name was Chimge. We became good friends. She wanted to improve her English and her husband was frequently away on work in the USSR.

I settled well into Mrs. Dolramaa's small flat. The only issue of potential disagreement was the radio receiver in the hall. It played continuously and I could not switch it off although I turned it to its lowest level. Each time Dolramaa visited though she increased its volume. Such receivers were everywhere in Mongolia, including our office. They had two main functions:

propaganda and safety, the latter appropriate in Mongolia's sub-zero temperatures.

Accommodation was reasonably settled but I had problems with food that I had never previously experienced, even as a child during the war. I had been warned of shortages and vowed I would eat everything I was given. That was broken at my first meal of cold white tripe. The federation had booked me into a Mongolian hotel far below European standards. It had a wide central staircase with no banisters to protect against falls into a large central stairwell. My room was one of two that shared a toilet which had a deep, deep hole, but no flush. Fortunately the other room remained empty. There was no lock on my door or on that from the corridor into the two rooms. I placed a case against it to be warned if someone was coming in.

Nevertheless staff smiled and helped. My room was clean and reasonably comfortable. Windows were double glazed but one had a broken panel. I was about to tell reception when I realised they probably knew but had no glass to repair. The room had a television and although I could not understand what was said. Pictures conveyed some news including the drowning of newspaper tycoon Robert Maxwell when he fell from his yacht. Meals were served in my room despite there being a hotel restaurant. When I tried to use it I was not welcomed or given a table. In high dudgeon I went to the front desk to complain: they suggested I had not been served because I was thought to be Russian.

After that I had meals in my room and fortunately could eat most of the food served. Five days later I moved into Mrs. Dolramaa's flat when different food problems arose. Bernard and I had moved many times and I knew how to organise a new larder. In Mongolia food shortages made that all quite different and led to an amusing incident.

Ulan Bator still had a Soviet garrison which contained families as well as soldiers. For their benefit it had a shop from which Urnaa thought we might be able to buy something. So she took me to one of the garrison gates and asked the sentry if he could help us. He agreed and she asked me to give him US$1. In Russian she then asked him to bring anything he could get from the garrison shop. I gave him a great big smile when he returned with a loaf of bread and six eggs. He had change! Urnaa suggested she ask him to keep it which he did with a big smile. Now I could enjoy a boiled egg with dry toast 'soldiers'. No salt and pepper yet or butter. By then I had learned how to use the cooker which, like the sink was identical with those in many other Mongolian flats. Standardisation and mass production was obviously economic.

Ulan Bator has of course since changed but in 1991 it had a population of around 500,000 in what was a relatively small area. There were many high rise flats built in a rush of urbanisation in the shift from feudalism to socialism. As in the USSR it was hoped to by-pass capitalism. Nevertheless some old traditions survived and between blocks of flats were groups of round Gers. Highly decorated and tent like these were made of felt and camel wool and appropriate for Mongolia's dry climate. They were also surprisingly warm. Although we had minus temperatures little snow fell that winter. Each fall was covered with ash from the one surviving power station. When broken up slabs of frozen snow resembled divided Liquorice All Sorts. "Babushkas" kept roads and pavements clear using man-handling large shovels.

Mongolia was about four times the size of France and Ulan Bator accommodated approximately a quarter of its 2,000,000 population. There were few other centres of population so few roads were required. Only around 1,300 kilometres of road then existed running mainly from north to south with very little between east and west.

I travelled by road, rail and 'plane. The Women's Federation had three cars, each with a chauffeur. They ferried me around Ulan Bator but there was only one long car journey. Several were by train and two were flights, one of which was memorable.

While Urnaa and I waited for it to be called I heard English spoken. Opposite sat a man wearing a beige flat pancake hat of the type warn by Muslim clerics in some countries. We got speaking and I found he came from the Isle of Dogs in London. He was en route to a western Mongolian province and was accompanied by a Mongolian Member of Parliament. Religious freedom was spreading My new found friend brought me up to date with news from home including the release of Terry Waite following his kidnap and years in solitary confinement.

Another reason the flight was memorable arose from it being delayed. Twice we were taken out to the 'plane but brought back because weather conditions had worsened. Bernard was frightened of me flying and urged me not to. He was worried about maintenance and I remembered this when walking to our plane and one standing nearby seemed to lose a wheel. Laughingly a mechanic chased after it and returned spinning it like a child with a hoop.

One return to the main building led to the third reason why the eventual flight was memorable. We spent the whole day waiting with little warmth and no food. There were no cafes or restaurants. Nevertheless I saw people going into what could have been a café. Much to Urnaa's embarrassment I entered and found it to be a low level staff canteen. In pity, and accepting Urnaa's explanation of my misunderstanding, they gave us both something to eat and drink. I was learning though that rules were kept in Mongolia, even by those in the Communist hierarchy. Another example sadly occurred with a puppy abandoned in freezing conditions.

We were staying in a college when visiting a rural area. Bad weather with recurring blizzards taught me the value of continuous radio broadcasts that included weather forecasts. We were due to walk across country around 600 yards to the nearby village. Urnaa and another person with us repeatedly checked to see if snow or winds were changing direction so forcing us to retrace our steps.

On leaving the college we heard whining and found a stray mother dog trying to shelter her puppies in the snow. Nearby was one she had apparently abandoned. We picked it up although I think we had no idea what we might do with it apart from taking it in and giving it some food. As we returned to the college Urnaa was carrying the puppy but cleanly dropped it when college principal opened the main the door. Urnaa walked in as if she had nothing to do with the puppy. For a fraction of a second I hesitated before deciding I had also better leave the puppy in the cold. By this time I knew that rules had to be kept. Moreover there was little I could have done: Mongolia lacked kennel or domestic vet facilities although there must have been vets for the herders and their flocks. Later from my flat in Ulan Bator I saw a dog hobbling with probably a broken leg. It followed a group of children but instead of helping they began to stone. It got away but I could not know for how long it would survive. One of the American Peace Corp girls I met did adopt a cat but when it became ill there was no domestic vet to whom she could take it. Instead she asked a hospital doctor with whom she had become friends to treat it and reluctantly he did.

Besides vestiges of discipline other parts of the communist state also survived. Most public buildings in Ulan Bator were low apart from a tower block that included the offices of the Mongolian Women's Federation and other state related bodies such as that for music composers and performers. The tower stood to one side of what I called Ulan Bator's Red Square and had a pagoda style roof below which was a massive display sign showing time and temperature. Returning early one morning after an overnight train journey I automatically looked towards it to see how cold it was. I learned that it was minus 19 degrees.

I gradually realised that I was not left alone in the office. Someone was always with me. Initially I shared an office with three officials of the women's federation. Our four desks faced each other and formed a block in the middle of the room. The ubiquitous loud speaker relayed continuous music or information. I travelled much in the early days but later settled down to more desk work. I then found I had too little space and asked for and was given another office which I shared with Ujmaa my counterpart and Urnaa my interpreter.

If both were out of the office Yagaan, the cleaner called to see me. Again I had no objection for with smiles and hand gestures we had become good friends. Each morning she greeted me and emphasised that outside I needed to keep my neck and mouth covered with a big scarf. She even knitted me one in camel wool!

Although I gradually learned to work in a setting quite different from anything previously experienced an incident irritated and amused. It showed that the communist respect for books was true and not a myth. The International Labour Organisation was to send me a set of 40 training manuals to help devise a Mongolian training programme. In English they would be sent to the UNDP office and come in a large box.

This they did and I saw them as I was leaving UNDP one evening before travelling to Sainchand in south Mongolia the next day. I saw them and asked for them to be sent to the Women's Federation office. When I returned a few days later I found that not merely had the manuals not been delivered, they had completely disappeared. Their existence was even denied and suggestions made that I had imagined seeing them. Denial remained firm and I had to request a new set which of course took time to arrive. But when it did Urnaa immediately took it and wheeled the large box to the office of Mrs. Munho, the federation's president. I hurried behind protesting they were for me and were working materials. I lost them again when the president graciously accepted the manuals and asked Urnaa to place them in her bookcase. She invited me to request any as and when I might need them.

The President was a Member of Parliament and of some repute, so was not someone to cross. Urnaa accompanied her on many visits to other communist states and particularly recalled meeting the Romanian leader Nicolas Ceausescu and his wife

Elena. She had been horrified to later see their unofficial trial and execution on television.

The disappearance of the first set MATCOM manuals and the preferential placing of the second set illustrated Mongolians wish for books even in unknown languages. I was told many times that Mongolia had high levels of numeracy and literacy. These were each over 90 per cent and higher than in the UK. I was sceptical although I had been impressed with seeing many well-kept schools. Children seemed to be well cared for and enjoyed numerous playgrounds on street corners and between blocks of flats. Later in the economic turmoil after my visit news broadcasts reported savage deterioration. Children were being abandoned and becoming homeless. I dreaded to think how they survived in such a climate. Under the communist regime children even had their own palace. This and one for women along with several other public buildings had been donated by other communist regimes.

My main memory of the Women's Palace in Ulan Bator came on Women's Day in March 1992. It was packed, particularly the theatre where presentations were made to notable women. I admired the mother of the country's largest family walk across the stage with her bosom festooned with medals to collect yet another medal. A famous film actress currently starring in a saga of Genghis Khan was also saluted. That evening the Women's Federation held a reception in the Ulan Bator hotel. I played a somewhat incongruous role alongside the federation's officials. A number of guests wondered who I was.

Amazingly I kept well apart from a few stomach upsets. The large medical pack I had been given contained treatments for those and so many other ailments. My main concern was not to slip on the ubiquitous ice. Somehow I managed not to fall but horror stories circulated from those who had been injured. The big problem was a shortage of drugs although the nearby hospital was modern and seemingly well-staffed. I needed to go there for two problems. One was an unfamiliar discomfort under my right arm and the other for corns caused by wearing thick socks in snow shoes.

Urnaa accompanied me but became distressed when passing a ward where her 12 year old nephew had recently died from appendicitis. He could not be adequately treated and Urnaa recalled his screams. Another upsetting case was that of the pregnant daughter of an official in the government's Labour Department. Pekka Pilvia in the International Labour Organisation in Geneva had recommended close contact with her and despite her high status she could not obtain the drugs to treat her daughter's dangerously high blood pressure.

I was in a far less dangerous condition. Given a notebook I was directed to an armchair outside a consultant's room. Another armchair provided a comfortable waiting area. After examining me the first consultant wrote his diagnosis in my notebook and told me to see another consultant who took on board the first one's views and then added his own. I was to keep the book but take it each time I visited the hospital. It became my health record. Neither consultant could decide what was causing the trouble.

A shortage of medicines was a problem when walking became painful through a number of corns forming in my left instep. I was directed to get to a pharmacy to see if they could give me some goose fat. Fortunately they could and wrapped in a sheet of paper folded into an envelope. For a week I had to soak my foot each night and then salve it with the goose fat. At the end of the week two nurses at the hospital tried to remove the corns without any pain killer. It was a miserable experience and occurred in mid February. I was feeling sorry for myself with some degree of homesickness. I lay back, tried to ignore what was happening and "thought of England".

Conditions were hard and while I had much to engage me Bernard would not. As much as I missed him I was relieved that he had not come with me. Keeping in touch with him was difficult. There were no e-mails in those days and letters were sent through the United Nations' postal system either through Vienna or New York. We also telephoned every second Monday, arranged through the UNDP office. It was 4pm in Ulan Bator and 8am at home. This arrangement worked well although there could be telephone difficulties. One of the British Overseas Volunteers was Nick Guyler, an agricultural expert who had recently retired from farming in Norfolk. He had booked a telephone call to the British Ministry of Agriculture in London and was taking it in UNDPs general office. Repeated disconnections raised his tempter till in the end he slammed down the 'phone and let off a tirade at office staff. It was expressed in pure Essex so as he passed I asked where he came from, a silly question at the wrong time. He snapped "Norfolk" and stormed out of the office. Some weeks later we sat opposite each other at a dinner party and the question arose in reverse when he asked where I came from. I replied, "Rayleigh in South East Essex". He laughed and said he was born in Hockley, the next small town to Rayleigh. We had been born six miles apart and were now meeting up 6,000 miles away. Good chat and much laughter followed during which we recalled every pub between Rayleigh and Hockley.

All this is background to the project whose aim was to encourage self-help in the form of workers' co-operatives among women. Many were becoming unemployed as the Mongolian economy moved from a centralised command form to a market economy. The project was to be channelled through the Mongolian Women's Federation which should become a voluntary organisation rather than a party subsidiary. That and the job creation part of the project would be underpinned by a revolving loan fund of US$3 million for which an American consultant, Barbara Devereux, would train the Women's Federation in its administration.

Barbara's role was shorter than mine but nonetheless memorable. There was a rush to borrow clothes for her suitable for the Mongolian winter. When she arrived she wore ordinary shoes, no hat and only a gilet over woollen trousers and jumper. Despite the resulting terrible cold she developed she was good company. She entertained with her account of visiting Tiananmen Square after being begged not to by the ILO Regional Office in Beijing. En route the taxi driver warned her not to drop a rose in respect for the protestors two years earlier. She managed to do so without being apprehended. A much more timid personality I had needed no such advice and in fact did not visit the square until some five years later when returning to Ulan Bator for a conference. Then the most moving experience was seeing a uniformed soldier smelling roses on a bush at the side at the side of the square. I photographed him photographing a rose.

Barbara and I enjoyed each other's company. We spent some pleasant evenings together during which she expressed doubts whether the Women's Federation would be able to manage the revolving loan fund. At that point my part of the project seemed on track but I later came to share her doubts. My main problem at that stage was language.

Urnaa had other responsibilities with the federation and it was therefore decided to recruit another interpreter/translator. She used only her patronym of Narantoya. Initially we got on well. Although agreeable and with good English I gradually realised she was a mischief maker. I could not always trust what she said about situations or other people or what she might have said to them about me and my wishes. Privately she also expressed doubts whether the Women's Federation were capable of managing the project. This as a judgement Barbara could legitimately make but not Narantoya.

Her time keeping deteriorated and after taking advice at UNDP I asked the Women's Federation to replace her. I was much relieved when Urnaa returned.

The project was a formal operation capable of measurement, monitoring and evaluation. It also provided opportunities for informal benefits. My briefings in Geneva had included advice on Mongolian figures who might be able to help me. One was the Ministry of Labour official whose pregnant daughter was in hospital, without drugs to treat her high blood pressure. Another was the President of a recently formed union of workers' co-operatives, Mr. Jasray who had earlier been a deputy Prime Minister but now concentrated on his co-operative union. The third was a Mrs. Tsoomaa who managed a young workers' co-operative that ran a US$ shop and was also Vice President of the Mongolian Union of Production and Service Co-operatives.

Each helped in different ways. When leaving I thanked Mr. Jasray for his help with a copy of Will Watkins' book *Co-operative Principles Today and Tomorrow.* He most kindly sent Bernard a pair of black leather gloves. Several years later I heard that he had had Will's book translated into Mongolian. This was significant in a situation where state co-operatives were discredited but little was known of voluntary western co-operatives.

Mrs. Oonon helped guide me round her own ministry and others while Mrs. Tsoomaa gave immediate practical help. Only one power station survived in Ulan Bator and power cuts occurred every day. During them I donned an anorak and was helped by the Mongolian practice of always having a thermos flask filled with hot water to provide a warm drink. Light was a problem though. I had taken torches but used them sparingly to save their batteries. Candles were so scarce they were on a black market but Urnaa persuaded Mrs. Tsommaa to let me have two.

Alongside the formal project there would be informal influences. Some, like these were favourable but others were not. These included the subsequent decline of the Women's Federation and its inability to implement what the project created. The federation's previous favoured status allied to government and the party changed. Women's membership became voluntary and with choice many women left. Reduced membership subscriptions led to a reduction of staff and moves to less prestigious central offices. It was therefore not surprising that the federation failed to administer both the training and the revolving loan fund elements of the project.

The political, economic and social environments contributed to the project's difficulties. They were changing but the past damned co-operatives. A recent government statement attributed the country's economic and social ills to "Central planners and co-operative leaders". Moreover Mongolians were split between those wishing to avoid responsibility, and those eager to become private entrepreneurs. I quickly saw how the latter, often members of the party's hierarchy were potential entrepreneurs. They included Mrs. Munho the president of the Women's Federation who kept our training manuals in her book case. She had ambitions to establish a private business producing health drinks from the juice of a Mongolian yellow berry.

On most visits we were accompanied by or met local members of the party hierarchy. I should not have been surprised that they were often friends who enjoyed an opportunity to meet. Sometimes the purpose of visits was forgotten. On one occasion we were visiting a textile factory and a group of women workers struck me as a cohesive group. They were becoming unemployed and I wanted to explore whether they might be interested in forming a workers' co-operative. When I suggested this to the accompanying dignitaries their leader immediately disagreed and walked off followed by others in our group including Urnaa my interpreter and translator. She was popular and had many long-standing friends pleased to meet up with her. I stayed with the women and their sewing machines and tried to communicate with smile and gesture. It was quite some time later that Urnaa and the others realised that I was not with them and came hurrying back to find me. This tine I made sure my questions were put and answers received. The machinists indicated no interest in a co-operative but I wondered whether they were inhibited by our leading dignitary having other designs on them.

It had become clear that the traditional MATCOM co-operative training programmes in third world countries were not immediately appropriate for the post-communist situation in Mongolia. Rather there needed to be a pre-training or proselytizing phase during which people became familiar with voluntary co-operatives as defined by the International Co-operative Alliance and the International Labour Organisation. A saving grace was the possible retrieval of the experiences of Mongolia's earliest co-operatives which had formed around 1913 and before the communist take-over. Mr. Jasray, president of the Workers' Co-operative Union was interested in them alongside his campaign to reintroduce the Mongolian script.

Developing understanding and commitment to voluntary co-operatives would take time and was made difficult by the lack of a suitable legal framework. I had no legal background and had never been strong on co-operative law. Yet I found myself discussing its main features with civil servants. I was grateful for having packed Bill Chapennden's guide to the British Industrial and Provident Societies legislation. Not that it was appropriate for the current Mongolian situation but it helped guide me on underlying principles. In any event I was happy to recall Bill who had been a fellow student with me at the UK Co-operative College.

Mongolia's Economic Body Law passed a few months earlier laid down the forms of business which could develop. My toes curled when it explained that co-operatives could be a sole proprietor such as a single stock breeder, or a partnership without limited liability or a company whose shares could be sold on the newly established bourse. Fortunately the Mongolian Union of Production and Service Co-operatives were already proposing changes but these would obviously take time to be accepted and introduced.

Competitive momentum in other directions was already developing. Several of the project's trainers seemed keen to learn business techniques for their own private businesses. Ujmaa, the Women's Federation Education Officer appeared complicit which caused tensions between us. Christmas day was no holiday and in the afternoon we visited a supposed co-op wanting one to one training on determining prices. I had strong doubts whether the business would ever be a co-operative and remonstrated with Ujmaa by the car in minus 33 degrees Urnaa interpreted for each of us and was obviously uncomfortable. Ujmaa reminded me that under the Economic Body Law a co-operative could have a single proprietor. I had to remind her of the project's aims. In the late afternoon sun everywhere looked slightly blue in the coldest temperatures I experienced.

The cold became a way of life. Those living in flats with balconies used them as additional refrigerators. Many had relatives living in the country who at the beginning of winter would slaughter and butcher an animal so its joints could be kept on the balcony of a relative in Ulan Bator. I soon learned to dress for the cold. One problem though was making a quick exit once dressed and muffled. You were at risk if you delayed and began to sweat. Moving then into sub-zero temperatures could be dangerous.

With hindsight I am amazed that I never fell on ice or snow and walked regularly to the office. On the way I passed over a modern bridge spanning a frozen river bed. At one end was a grand Soviet style statue but beneath the body of a horse lay frozen into the river bed. First sight horrified and raised questions of how could it have died alone with no one attempting to move it. It reminded me that there seemed to be no domestic veterinary service. Perhaps a frozen horse carcass caused little upset because so many kinds of animals walked around Ulan Bator. I got used to small flocks of sheep foraging outside my flat, or passing the lone cow as I walked through the town. I had a droll experience walking home one evening. On the other side of a rare set of traffic lights was an unsaddled and unbridled horse. Like me he seemed to be waiting for the light to turn green. When it did we passed in the middle and continued on our separate ways.

As we moved towards the end of the project language became a big problem. We had identified training needs, drafted a training manual to meet them, and were preparing to pilot through training trainers when Mr. Ghanbataa, personal assistant to Mr. Jasray warned that there was a Marxist tone in the draft manual's economics. Throughout he had maintained a watching brief on behalf of Mr. Jasray. The dilemma was how to correct. I could not read Mongolian and the Mongolians had difficulty grasping western economic concepts. We attempted to resolve it by forming a small group comprising Mr. Ghanbataa, Urnaa, myself and Suren. I was meeting him for the first time but he had been proposed as he had a high reputation as an interpreter/translator although he was now retired. We went through the Mongolian text word by word. Where misunderstandings arose I explained the theory and the other three negotiated appropriate Mongolian terms. Hopefully we ended with a more accurate translation but I could not be certain.

Four years later I returned to Ulan Bator for a conference organised by the International Labour Organisation and Mr. Ghanbataa met me at the airport. Life had moved on for him. He was now a business man and no longer worked for Mr. Jasray who had become Prime Minister. I was amused to hear the clanking of jars or bottles in the boot of his car. When he opened it I found bottles of Heinz Tomato Ketchup which he was selling wherever he could.

RETURN FROM MONGOLIA

I left Mongolia on 21 April and was first debriefed by the International Labour Organisation's office in Beijing. That went well but my happiest memory was being reunited with fresh fruit. There had been none in Mongolia apart from small apples given as a rare treat at one meeting. The climate allowed around only 120 growing days a year. Berries flourished but no other fruit apart from the small apple. The economic situation did not allow imports. A delight and honour on Women's Day in March had been to be presented with a red rose. This and a few others

201

had been grown in the only greenhouse in Ulan Bator that had no room for fruit. To cement my joy at being reunited I ordered a large plate of fresh fruit in my Beijing hotel. As I sat savouring the sight I photographed it to always remind me of the pleasure.

Then I flew home, first of all to Geneva for my main debriefing. Arrangements were made for Bernard to join me and our flights should have enabled him to meet me in. Yet, I who was travelling from Beijing arrived on time but he flying from Heathrow was delayed. Consequently I met him in. What a reunion! It was Friday afternoon which meant we had the weekend together before debriefing began on the Monday morning. We talked and talked and talked. Anecdotes flew around. Tonsils got cross threaded. I happily removed my money belt and invited Bernard to count the US$ I had saved. Next morning we deposited them in the Swiss bank account I still held from my days with the International Co-operative Alliance in Geneva. After the final debriefing we returned home.

MONGOLIAN POSTSCRIPT

We had had plans for representatives of the Mongolian Women's Federation to visit Britain and the Co-operative Women's Guild and the Women's Institute. Sadly they never materialised. The Federation lost its sheltered status and had to move to cheaper accommodation and reduce staff, Moreover contact was difficult because there was no personal address system in Mongolia and no postal service of the kind we know.

At home I had an amusing incident. The discomfort under my right arm for which I had gone to Ulan Bator's hospital recurred and I visited my own doctor. She feared TB because Mongolia had no distributive dairy system and sent me for a hospital appointment. I was told that should treatment be necessary I would be asked to remain and when that actually happened I panicked. When I returned to the consultant he apologised and with a big smile asked if I would tell him something about Mongolia. I happily obliged.

Chapter Ten

EGYPT, WRITINGS, AND TRANS SIBERIA

TANDEM RESEARCHERS

In the early 1990s both of us were busy writing, Bernard on his post-war history of British consumer co-operation and I on my Ph.D thesis undertaken with the Co-operative Research Unit of the Open University. Alan Thomas, later Professor, was my main supervisor. The dean of another faculty was the other supervisor although her seniority and other commitments meant she joined us less regularly.

In his history Bernard aimed to bring together written sources of various kinds and his own eye witness accounts. He had been central in a number as in his appointment in 1960 to the Co-operative Union as its first Development Officer. Later he was a member of the sub-committee that proposed organisational changes to the Scottish Co-operative Wholesale Society. In 1972 these led to its becoming the Scottish Co-operative Society. Only a year later, Bernard was a close observer of the collapse of its bank and the society's subsequent merger with the Co-operative Wholesale Society.

I could bring few eye witness accounts to my research, dated as it was between 1910 and 1950. Important among those I could were the memories of Will Watkins who had been employed by the International Co-operative Alliance during the inter-war years and was its director between 1951 and 1963. He had also written an authoritative history to mark the 75th anniversary of its founding. I taped a number of interviews with Will, and he commented on the draft of my first chapter, with quite a few criticisms.

Bernard and I developed easy working relations, he in his study and I in mine. We enjoyed flexible working time, going out when and where we felt like it and even modernising the house with a new kitchen and a downstairs cloakroom. In April 1991 we took two new cats. We were desolated when their predecessor died. The RSPCA persuaded us to take Ebony and Jasper, a brother and sister. They were about a year old and had been left in a flat when their owners moved. Neighbours saw them at windows and contacted the RSPCA, and with police they rescued them. Because of their trauma, the RSPCA said that they should be homed together. We agreed and took both but renamed them Sylvester and Winsome. Bernard suggested both names. Sylvester because he was a nervous cat with quick, quick, slow movements that reminded us of Victor Sylvester to whose band we had danced at Hammersmith Palace many years earlier. Winsome became she looked winsome. Whereas Sylvester spent most of his time indoors, Winsome was intrepid and roamed nearby gardens, chasing many birds. Her special friend was Barney the cat a few doors away. He often chased her although we believed she enticed him. Once away I swear Winsome ran in high heels, her steps being so dainty and provocative. For many years she and Barney remained close.

With our pets and house modernisation we were comfortable. Later we also extended our patio. This had a garden seat, my present to Bernard for his 70th birthday. We spent many pleasant hours on this. Home comforts provided a welcome backdrop to our research and writing but sadly Bernard's illness and lengthy convalescence meant his work lost momentum. He made several attempts to resume but eventually gave up. He had also been de moralised by the refusal of the CWS to grant him access to their archives.

Ph.D THESIS

I continued with considerable time at the Open University, grateful that I had belatedly learned to drive. The road between Rayleigh and Milton Keynes became quite familiar.

I had taken thousands of photocopies from the ICA's archives in Geneva, including correspondence, reports, agenda of various meetings and conferences, minutes of Executive and Central Committee meetings and verbatim reports of Congresses. I worked on the photocopies together with secondary sources on the two world wars and the cold war.

Initially Alan Thomas and I were unsure how to structure the research. Eventually we decided to study the Alliance's crises and responses to them to ascertain recurring features. Two emerged namely a heavy influence of co-operative ideology and organisation. We agreed to try to determine how far they explained the ICA's survival despite world conflict.

The first crisis studied was that of the 1914-1918 War. Whereas the ICA had remained united, both the Socialist International and the International Federation of Trade Unions had split. We gradually saw that the ICA had distanced itself from the war. It increasingly saw it as one between capitalists rather than co-operatives whose fraternity helped them maintain contact during the war. Despite censorship and shortages of paper, co-operative leaders maintained the monthly publication of the *Bulletin of International Co-operation*. Edited in the alliance's head office in London, it was sent to the Dutch consumer co-operative movement which sent it to German and French counterparts. They then translated, printed and distributed to their members. Personal messages were also sent, some about prisoners of war, others of sympathy as when the son of a German co-operative leader was killed in the battle of the Somme in July 1916.

Nevertheless the strains caused by the World War led the alliance to delay holding its first post-war congress until 1921 and then in Geneva in neutral Switzerland. Tensions between affiliates were easing and travel was becoming less difficult. Damaged rail systems were being repaired and improved coal supplies facilitated more regular train services.

Attempts were made to heal tensions between members. A particularly interesting one was their agreement to deliver reports on how the war had affected them; what measures they had taken to adapt and how the war had changed them and perhaps their status. New states like Finland and Poland had emerged. The frontiers of other states had changed. Some notably Russia had experienced revolution. The resulting congress report reflected these and can be seen as an early form of a statement of truth and reconciliation. It showed how global war impacted on voluntary co-operative movements and how they as democratic and non-governmental organisations responded. Frequent references were made to co-operative principles and expressions of regret given where these had had to be broken as when governments demanded trade with non-members. At that tine ICA membership included many consumer co-operative movements.

During the inter-war years it experienced mixed fortunes. On one hand its long-standing support for the settlement of disputes by mediation and arbitration led it to welcome the establishment of the League of Nations: it developed close working relations with it and its agencies, particularly the International Labour Organisation. On the other hand the rise of Fascism and Nazism in Europe and militarism in Japan posed a number of crises in the alliance besides threatening a new war.

When that broke out in 1939 the ICA took a different attitude from that it had shown to the First World War. This time it was not detached and was totally opposed to German, Italian and Japanese aggression. It therefore fully supported the Allies', namely Britain, France, USA and USSR.

The ICA's head office was in London. Although at war, the United Kingdom remained unoccupied. The British delegation was the largest to the ICA formed substitute Central and Executive Committees. These retained effective links with American and Canadian ICA members and directed their representation in early moves to found the United Nations (UN) and its programmes for post-war reconstruction. All were fully reported to and endorsed by the ICA's first post-war congress in Zurich, Switzerland in 1946.

I had decided to make 1950 the end of my research. By then Cold War issues had become clear and positions taken on them by the ICA. In that process there had been a notable debate at its Prague congress of 1948. Neither east nor west affiliates held their punches and different definitions of democracy and co-operation were fiercely debated. Nevertheless an obvious wish to remain together produced an uneasy truce.

It compounded the compromise taken in the 1920s when the alliance had debated whether Soviet co-operatives remained true co-operatives. My research suggested two possible reasons for the compromise. . Each was only ever hinted at and never publicly discussed. One in the early 1920s was the maintenance of trade, between Britain and the Soviets. The other was the fear that if expelled Soviet co-operatives could form a "red International Co-operative Alliance". They remained in the ICA. When the USSR became one of the main allies during the Second World War their position was strengthened.

Despite renewed tensions during the Cold War, commitment to world peace remained. ICA congresses and meetings of its central committee regularly passed peace resolutions. I remembered immense drafting difficulties in the early 1980s when I became involved in these. Even with American and Soviet affiliates they were drafted and passed. Co-operatives' commitment to peace illustrated a strong ideology.

Overall my research brought great satisfaction. Within parameters agreed with my supervisors I worked by myself without the diversion of internal politicking. I enjoyed unearthing insight into how countries, organisations and people responded to war and worked towards peace, and regeneration. A personal lesson has since remained and arose at a session with Alan. He queried the Rochdale Pioneers' acknowledgement of members' "self-interest". This came in their 1860 almanac and read that the pioneers would "by a common bond, namely that of self-interest....join together the means, the energies and the talents of all for the common benefit of each." I said that this linked mutual action to individual benefit and was basic to co-operative ideology. Where a co-operative no longer met a need, or where that need was met by competitors, then members' "self-interest" shifted or disappeared and loyalty weakened. I believe lack of attention to this contributed to the later degeneration of British consumer co-operation.

My research was considerably helped by the detailed reports of ICA congresses and the minutes of Central and Executive Committee meetings. They had a Hansard quality. Indeed proceedings were recorded by two retired Hansard parliamentary reporters whose verbatim accounts became the basis of extensive minutes and reports. Accountability was important in an international non-government organisation comprising movements from different nations and political systems. I found in the 1980s that delegates needed minutes to show that they had acted as mandated. Detailed minutes and reports later helped my research.

We hoped I could complete my thesis by late 1994 and thus be in time for the alliance's centenary a year later. It might also be possible to produce a book version. The schedule was maintained apart from assignments in Mongolia and Egypt. However difficulties arose towards the end when my second supervisor unexpectedly made fundamental criticisms. I was upset because I believed she should have made these far earlier. Alan became an effective peacemaker and put in extra hours to help me complete shortly before Christmas 1994. Nevertheless I feared the disagreements reduced hope of a clear award. One could be delayed if examiners requested amendments or additions.

My viva on 24 February 1995 at the Open University seemed to go well. I even enjoyed the questions and discussion. When asked to withdraw I expected a long wait. It actually proved quite short which increased fears that an award would be delayed. I was therefore amazed to spy a bottle of pink champagne on the table when I returned but diplomacy suggested I did not see it. It was in fact a straight award. No amendments or additions requested. Smiles and laughter all round while Alan poured the champagne. Once we left and were in the corridor I gave him a big, big kiss! As soon as we reached his office I telephoned Bernard to tell him that Dr. Rhodes was calling. Wonderful Bernard! He was never jealous and was as happy as I was.

At 60 I expected no career benefits. Happily there were some. One was being appointed Visiting Research Fellow in the Co-operatives Research Unit at the Open University. It was an honorary position I held for 17 years. It brought many stimulating and intellectual rewards including membership of the Research Committee of the International Co-operative Alliance.

An early meeting of that for me proved difficult. It came during the centenary congress of the International Co-operative Alliance in Manchester in 1995. Events leading to the incident began some months earlier when Sven Ake Boke, the committee's chair telephoned me at home. Dr. Saxena, previous ICA director had married a Swede and they were now living in Canada. He had asked Sven, also a Swede to approach me to ask for a copy of my thesis. Although complimented I shrank from the cost I would incur of photocopying and posting 400 pages to Canada. I did not yet have e-mail; that came some three years later. However, past regard for Dr. Saxena led me to agree. When he acknowledged I was a little discomfited in that he wrote as if I had spontaneously sent him the copy to seek his approval, and not in response to his request through Sven Ake Boke.

Worse was to come at the actual research conference in Manchester. Saxena participated and rose to criticise my thesis, its recently published book version and the paper I had just presented. He argued that as ICA director he suffered from the Alliance's cold war fudge of a universal membership. His comments were based on his experiences between 1963 and 1981 and argued that there should have been separate western and communist international co-operative alliances. He did not speak of events in the period of my thesis 1910 to 1950. I was so shocked that I did not accept the right to reply given by Sven Ake Bok, the Chair. I was so aggrieved that Saxena had given no warning of what he would say. I might hold a Ph.D but in many ways I was still an academic apprentice.

I was further upset when Saxena's criticism was headlined in the Congress newspaper next morning. Nursing this in a quiet corner I was joined by Prof. Ian MacPherson, Canada. He kindly tried to cheer me adding that this "was all par for the course". In other words, welcome to academia.

CO-OPERATIVE RESEARCH CONFERENCES

Besides overseas assignments during the 1990s I also went abroad to conferences. Three were particularly memorable. One was in Tokyo in 1992 when I was an observer at an ICA Congress. Seeing Tokyo was a big attraction but the main one at the congress was a debate on the continuing review of ICA Co-operative Principles. Originally led by Sven Ake Boke, Prof. Ian Macpherson, Canada had taken over and was making a major speech.

I also returned to Mongolia at the request of the Co-operative Branch of the International Labour Organisation (ILO) in 1996. The ILO held a conference to review co-operative development in the country. The UNIFEM project with the Mongolian Women's Federation on which I had been employed was included and I was asked to give a paper. It was great to return to Ulan Bator but I found many changes the most notable of which was the decline of the Mongolian Women's Federation. This meant that our project had had little success. Apart from that I was delighted to learn of the continued growth of workers' or producer co-operatives and to note the birth of a consumer co-operative movement.

Mongolia was still moving from a command to a market economy. I became aware of the transition in many ways but two remain vivid. The conference was held in the offices of the Ministry of Labour but I never used the same toilet twice. Broken and unrepaired plumbing led to big problems and we were directed to wherever a toilet worked. Each was used both by men and women giving "unisex" added meaning. I never used the same toilet twice!

Another memory was an excellent lunch in a Korean restaurant. I could not help but recall an Indian International Voluntary Overseas worker arriving one evening during my earlier time in Mongolia and asking for directions to the nearest Indian restaurant. We had to tell him there were only two restaurants in Ulan Bator, both in hotels, and neither Indian.

Quebec was the venue for another ICA congress in 1999 where again I was an observer. I attended with long-time friend, Muriel Russell. We shared a hotel room and as past secretaries to the ICA's Women's Committee participated in its meeting. The timetable also allowed me to join the meeting of the Research Committee.

Three memories remain strong. One was meeting old friends among whom I was particularly pleased to see Robert Beasley and his wife Betty. As director of the ICA, Robert had extended my contract for me to try to trace the missing parts of its library. In Quebec we exchanged memories and perceptions of events at that time.

A sad memory involved Jack Shaffer. He was suffering from a degenerative disease but had just completed a most valuable *Historical Dictionary of the Cooperative Movement.* It was in fact launched at the Quebec congress. Since then I have used it much and admired its quality. Jack and I first met at meetings in Geneva of the Committee of Promotion and Advancement of Co-operatives. Both the Co-operative Branch of the International Labour Organisation and the International Co-operative Alliance were heavily involved in this and Jack was its co-ordinator. It was good to still have time to thank Jack and to congratulate him on his excellent dictionary.

The other strong memory was the opening of the Quebec congress. A lover of western films, my spine tingled when distant Indian drums sounded and red Indians danced down the aisles towards the stage. Lights, costume, dance and music created a particularly evocative atmosphere.

CO-OPERATIVE ASSIGNMENTS IN EGYPT

As far as overseas assignments were concerned, after Mongolia Egypt was where I spent most time in during the 1990s. I spent four months there on three assignments for the Plunkett Foundation in 1993, 1994 and 1997. The European Union (EU) had appointed it to monitor and evaluate its Food Sector Development Programme which focused on Egypt's dairy sector. No national distributive system existed. Milk was sold by pedlars on street corners where customers used their own receptacles to collect. The project included the breeding of cattle, kinds of cattle suitable to Egypt, care by owners and vets, feedstuffs and the building of a profitable dairy system.

The Plunkett Foundation recruited three of us. Our leader was Basil Cracknell, an evaluation expert recently retired from the Overseas Development Administration. The dairy expert was John Jenkin whose family had owned and run a dairy business in Eastbourne before selling to one of the national dairy multiples. I was to focus on the role of women and co-operatives.

Basil, John and I became good friends. I learned much. As leader Basil handled difficult situations well. I recall one when we were publicly berated by a senior Egyptian official criticising our first report. I wanted to reply but held back because Basil sat quietly and said nothing. He avoided an open dispute but over the next few weeks he refuted each criticism and tempers were lowered. In any event there was a sneaking suspicion that the senior official had wanted to show his authority to junior colleagues.

I found changes in Egypt since my first visit in 1987. They were now more co-operatives independent of government. Naturally this was to be welcomed but I felt that the Food Sector Development Programme was distancing itself too far from figures previously involved in government/co-operative relations. These included Mrs. Sohier and a number of co-operative leaders and members I had previously met. I felt it would be useful to know how they viewed the shift but difficulties were put in my way.

Understandably the project had people they wished us to meet. That was reasonable but ran the risk we would hear only favourable and possibly prejudiced accounts. We also needed to speak to others and those I had met on my previous visit in 1987 were obvious examples. Among these was Mrs. Sohier whom I valued in her ability to approach women in co-operatives. Her father had been a village elder and she was good at meeting village women without antagonising their men who invariably kept nearby. After some project reservations I was able to meet Mrs. Sohier again.

Anxious to retain good relations we were particularly careful over religious observances. Nevertheless an awkward situation arose at breakfast one morning in Alexandria. We were accompanied by an Egyptian project official who was also an Imam. He spoke little during breakfast and I sensed he was listening to a loudly relayed radio programme. Not realising this Basil asked for it to be turned down as he found it intrusive. No one disagreed but our project official looked distinctly unhappy.

I have to say Muslim religious observances rather pleased me. Early awakening to the first muezzin call of the day somehow comforted. The midday one could disrupt work but we knew to wait its passing. Many more Egyptian women now wore head scarves or veils including Mrs. Sohier; she had not worn one in

1987. I was intrigued with their great diversity of colours and styles suggesting rampant femininity and competition.

Tradition and religion obviously played a big part in women's lives. For example when Mrs. Sohier invited us to lunch in her flat male relatives needed to be present. Since our original meeting in 1987 she had suffered two tragedies: the death of her husband and the possible divorce of her elder daughter although she appeared happily married. Sadly she had lost a baby she had been carrying and complications led to a hysterectomy. Mrs. Sohier fainted when she received the news because this meant that her daughter would be unable to have other children. Her husband could not therefore pass on his blood line with her. His family was likely to demand they divorce so that he could remarry but it was unlikely that Mrs. Sohier's daughter would be able to do so because she could not to have children.

In wider relations it was interesting to find that when meeting rural women perhaps in barns and stables, men hung on the door watching and listening. Their wives carried out dairy functions but there was a growing practice of some to also raise poultry from which they kept the proceeds. . Invariably these women were poor but an unexpected situation arose with one who was wealthy. We interviewed her because she had applied for a loan from the revolving loan fund set up under the project. There were suspicions though that she had not applied and that the application in her name had been made by her husband. He had also applied for himself which meant that he could be receiving two loans.

Their house was large and reflected affluence. A servant took me and my interpreter into an elegant salon and offered us freshly made lemonade in gold rimmed glasses. When the couple appeared I was impressed with their dignity and manners. I was taken to see their cows which were unusually well kept and sheltered from strong afternoon sun in clean byres. Back in the house I had difficulties questioning the wife. Her husband remained and my male interpreter refused to translate some questions. It was difficult but we needed to establish whether she had her own bank account, owned cows and managed her dairy revenues which would have been unusual for an Egyptian housewife, even a wealthy one. Eventually we decided that her husband had applied for two loans when he should have applied for only one for himself.

We met interesting exceptions to women's subservience though. One was in the finance department of a co-operative union where a woman was in charge. She sat at a large desk on one side of the room and opposite her sat four men at smaller desks. They appeared to do very little and she did most of the work. On another occasion we met a stout, loud voiced matronly woman heading an artificial insemination centre. Her English was good so we had no difficulty in understanding the insemination procedures she described in a very matter of fact way. But we found it incongruous.

Tradition shaped many things besides relations between men and women. I was disconcerted when we had lunch one day way out in the country near a small pyramid. We ate in the upper floor of a large barn. Cheese, bread, honey and water melon were placed before us. I was uncertain what to do when accompanying Egyptians rose and left the table with food still on their plates. Their places were then taken by others who finished what they had left. Eventually Basil, John and I realised we needed to follow suite and did so. On other occasions we had seen that food left from meals was wrapped and taken to the needy en route to our next engagement.

Sometimes this wish to share spread to employment. A wealthy and high class farmer planned to improve his cattle but he also aimed to employ more than the increased business would justify. In other words he wanted to benefit as many as possible. Fortunately our figures persuaded him otherwise.

There were other examples of a seeming failure to anticipate unintentional consequences. One rose from an earlier national plan that set high value on education and determined student numbers in various disciplines. It had then been decided to train 40,000 vets and students were directed in that direction whether they wanted to be vets or not. Over supply was eventually reached. We met some who had been employed but had little aptitude.

The worst example of unintended consequences I came across and suffered was on a recent desert settlement. It had been set up to house unemployed graduates who were encouraged to raise cattle and supply milk. Obviously there was no fresh grass but the budget included the cost of animal feed and roofed pens to house cattle. Not taken into account was a changed eco system. It was not an oasis and the absence of trees meant that there were no birds. Consequently it was a flies' paradise. There were millions and millions of them. Attracted by new meat they swarmed towards us as we left the car. Accompanying Egyptian officials laughed at my flailing hands and arms. Locals seemed to have acclimatised.

Throughout our three Egyptian assignments Basil and John were agreeable colleagues. Our hotel was comfortable but not luxurious. We became known to staff which prompted excellent service. We ate breakfast and evening meals together. Something like "The Last of the Summer Wine" developed in our ramblings and personal reminiscences. We chose to walk to the project's office about 15 minutes away. On days we undertook visits a car collected us, invariably early. I found the Egyptian working day difficult. Work began early and continued, apart from prayers, until around 2.30pm. Lunch was taken then and this would be the first food since a very early breakfast. I quickly became used to carrying a banana to eat sometime during a morning. Because of the heat there was no work after the late lunch. We might have expected perhaps a couple of hours in the evening but that did not happen. However, Basil, John and I got together to discuss a day's findings and future work.

Basil proved a wonderful friend during our last visit in 1997. It was in March and we were surprised how chilly it was. We needed to buy additional warmer clothes. John returned home for Easter because he was worried about his wife who had become unwell. Basil and I stayed and on Easter Saturday the project manager invited us to lunch. Afterwards he took us on a long walk in Cairo.

On our way back to the car I suddenly fell and broke my left wrist. Fortunately this was at one of the very rare sets of traffic lights in Cairo. Had it been anywhere else in the city I could easily have been run over, the traffic is so lethal. I feared I would be sent home but fortunately the hospital to which I was taken operated the next day.

Payment up front was required which Basil arranged along with setting in action insurance claims, telephoning the news to Bernard and the Plunkett Foundation. Happily I was not to be medically evacuated. I left the hospital with a plate in my wrist, heavily bandaged and in a sling. The next day though I could join a visit to the Nile Delta and later that week we flew to Aswan: security problems made it impossible to go by road.

Happily I was able to complete the assignment although a wrist in plaster caused difficulties that remained even when I returned home. I could not drive so Bernard did much local shopping. Neither could I type. This presented problems in completing a commission already received which had a deadline.

I reckon my four Egyptian assignments to be on par with others that were long term. Each required learning how to live in a different location and how to adapt to new cultures and faiths. Seeing how peoples gravitated to and maintained faith impressed and taught me greater tolerance. Their cultures enriched and added some wonderful memories.

At home research and writing were the main activities and an assignment in the mid to late '90s renewed earlier political interests.

WRITING 'AN ARSENAL FOR LABOUR'

I had joined the Co-operatives Research Unit as a Visiting Research Fellow and the Political Committee of the Royal Arsenal Co-operative Society (RACS) had asked the unit if they could propose a historian to record the society's political actions. Two of us were short listed and interviewed. This was in the room in the Fabian Society where I had worked some 40 years earlier: it had been considerably refurbished. The other candidate was a lady who was a local historian and therefore well qualified in other ways.

Bernard and I long remembered the occasion for other events. The interview was on a Friday evening and we had decided to spend the weekend in London. We were shocked next morning to learn of the assassination of Isaac Rabin Israel's Prime Minister the previous day. Over years we had followed events in Israel and in co-operative circles had made a number of Israelis friends. My key ring was a gift from one. But as far as the interview was concerned I had been successful. A decision had been made with me as author to commemorate Royal Arsenal's political activities from 1896 to 1996. A budget for research and publication with Holyoake Books of the Co-operative Union was agreed.

The Royal Arsenal Society had merged with the Co-operative Wholesale Society in 1985 and became part of the CWS's South East Region. A decade later it was decided that its distinct political tradition needed to be recorded. Unlike all other retail societies it had directly affiliated to the Labour Party. Others through the Co-operative Union and its Co-operative Party negotiated electoral agreements with the Labour Party.

An immediate question was the availability of archives. Fortunately Ron Roffey, retired society secretary had saved a large part of them. When he saw files being discarded he tried to save whatever he could. He had assembled records, books and numerous artefacts such as old delivery bikes and stored them in an upper area of the society's central department store in Powis Street, Woolwich. Across the road was the society's earlier central store built in 1906. Above its massive front door was a statue of Alexander McLeod, a prominent leader in the establishment of RACS. Topping him was the slogan "Each for All and all for each". We decided to have a photograph of this building on the front cover of the proposed book. The old central stores reminded me of a gentleman from English Heritage I had met at one of the Consumer Conferences organised by the Education Department of the Co-operative Union some 20 years earlier. He specialised in historic co-operative architecture and the RACS early central store was probably already in his portfolio.

I was very happy to catch up with Ron Roffey. Our paths had crossed over the years, he having been a second year student at the Co-operative College at Stanford Hall when I was in my first year. He had been a popular student and his agreeable personality helped him rise within Royal Arsenal to become its secretary. I was now immensely grateful for the records Ron had saved.

They helped in many ways. I had not previously studied a single society and needed to become clear on RACS's wide-ranging services and democratic structures. The latter proved fascinating and included a number of member constituencies. One was catholic and another comprised branches of the Co-operative Women's Guild. Prominent in the latter was Mrs. Corringham who had been Bernard's landlady when he was Research Officer of the Co-operative Party in the mid 1950s. She lived in Kennington Road just south of the Thames. RACS records showed she had been nominated several times for election to the RACS board by the women's guild but always without success.

RACS operated in a highly politicised and working class area of south London. Like other retail societies it needed to keep watch on the activities of local councils and parliament that could affect its operations. This was defensive action but the society's environment also pointed it towards more direct political action.

Its direct affiliation to the Labour Party stemmed also from developments in the London Labour Party. Herbert Morrison (1888-1965), a Labour leader and minister contributed much to these during the inter-war years. His influence in RACS was indirect and channelled through friends rather than through direct participation. Nevertheless he frequently spoke at its public meetings, attended many of its events. He lived at three addresses in its area, the first being leased from the society. The RACS Funeral Department conducted his funeral in 1965.

Minutes of the society's Political Committee showed that Morrison urged the society to directly affiliate to the Labour Party. It took a position that held for some 70 years that there should be only one party of the left in Britain. It therefore believed the Co-operative Party to be unnecessary. Such a position drew it more towards the state socialism adopted by the post-war Labour Party rather than to the more collective form of social ownership advocated by the Co-operative Party. That strenuously argued against the proposed nationalisation of insurance including Co-operative insurance and other mutual insurance societies.

Researching and recording this tradition made a most interesting and happy assignment. I enjoyed working closely with Ron Roffey whose efforts to preserve RACS's archives I greatly admired. They brought home to me once again the need for concerted action to preserve co-operative archives.

Preparing the manuscript was complicated by my breaking my left wrist in Cairo. Happily a long time co-operative friend, Marion Rilstone, came to the rescue. She had been Bernard's secretary in the Co-operative Party in the mid 1950s and now prepared my manuscript.

Am Arsenal for Labour was launched in 1998 with Baroness Thornton hosting a reception in the Attlee Chamber in Westminster. As Glenys Thornton she had been the first woman to be appointed RACS Political Secretary in 1981 when I was with the national Co-operative Development Agency. We had then established links working with pre-co-operatives in RACS's area. The launch was a happy experience enabling me to thank all those who had assisted my research, particularly Bernard. He stood by me as I spoke. I was happy he could make this occasion: he had felt unable because of his stoma to travel to Brussels for the launch of my ICA book at the European parliament.

TRAN SIBERIAN RAILWAY JOURNEY

Neither did Bernard feel able to join a group of us who decided to celebrate the new millennium with a Trans Siberian rail trip between Moscow and Beijing. When in Mongolia I had been fascinated by accounts of colleagues who had travelled to Ulan Bator by train from Moscow. Urnaa Uranchimeg had recounted the six day journey to university in Moscow while the wife of farmer Nick Guyler, the Voluntary Overseas worker specialising in agriculture, travelled in the opposite direction when visiting him.

Nine of us planned to make the trip with stopovers in Irkutsk and Ulan Bator. Our flights would be to Moscow from Heathrow and back to Heathrow from Beijing: the rest would be by train. Sadly Basil Cracknell with whom I had worked in Egypt had to withdraw at the last minute after being diagnosed with cancer and needing surgery. The rest of us had co-operative interests and we arranged to visit co-operative organisations en route.

At Heathrow we thought we might lose someone else. Pam Walsh with whom I would be sharing throughout arrived wearing a Safari jacket. It had many pockets which she filled to avoid carrying a handbag. The trouble was she could not find her air ticket or remember in which pocket she had put it. A ridiculous situation arose with seven of us unzipping her: I could almost see her being upended to see what would fall out. Pam was near to tears. Happily, being in a party and with the rest of us having our tickets, a duplicate was issued. We all flew to Moscow. When we returned home Pam found her air tickets on her kitchen table! Later on the Trans Siberian train I chuckled several times at how near she had come to being upended.

The travel firm *Steppes East* did a wonderful job making the booking and arrangements during our 18 day trip. We were met at stations and guides showed us around places we visited. The train journey began Sunday afternoon in Moscow and in the morning Pam and I returned to Red Square. We wanted to visit Lenin's tomb and worship in a Russian Orthodox Church. We were surprised to find two churches on Red Square. Stalin had had one knocked down to facilitate military processions but it had been rebuilt. The other to which we actually went sided onto Red Square. We were bowled over by its beauty, superb choir and music. Worshippers stood during a long service while others came and went. It was difficult to follow because part of the service was conducted behind the altar and could not be seen. The church differed from those in Western Europe, being square and with a perimeter corridor running all the way round which one crossed to enter.

From a co-operative point of view the highlight of our time in Moscow was a visit to Centrsoyus, Russia's central union for consumer co-operatives. It meant much to me to renew contact with past members of the Women's Committee of the International Co-operative Alliance when I had been its secretary some fifteen years earlier. Centrosoyus had kindly arranged for us to visit retail societies during stops on our train journey. We had kept in mind the co-operative tradition of exchanging gifts and we carried a supply. At different times each of us made presentations. Happily and in another co-operative tradition we were all well used to public speaking.

The six day train journey began on Sunday afternoon with our Moscow guide handing us bottles of Russian 'champagne' as we boarded the train. We enjoyed four adjoining compartments with two of us in each. At the end of the carriage was a samovar kept filled by a strong looking woman attendant. We could make tea whenever we wished. At the other end was a toilet and wash room. Remembering the lack of bath and sink plugs in Mongolia I had come prepared with a spare one. We used it immediately because the wash basin indeed lacked one. It was soon lost though. Returning from her ablutions one morning Pam realised she had left it and although she had immediately returned, it had already disappeared.

Today there are luxurious trans-Siberian rail journeys but in 1999 our journey was hardly that. The adjacent dining car could not always serve meals. Warned, we had taken some personal rations with which we enjoyed our Russian "champagne". Nevertheless we developed good relations with the cook and waiter who always welcomed us whether they had anything to serve or not. They were friendly whereas our carriage attendant never smiled or sought closer relations. I once tried to take her photograph but she turned her back. I remember her well enough though, particularly her peroxide hair.

Train stops were exciting particularly as we moved into Asia from Europe. I had always argued that European Union was like a peninsula off the west of Russia which spanned the top of Europe, the Middle and Far East. Actually seeing this was exciting. At each stop food sellers lined the platform to sell home cooked items that I would not risk. Local populations looked poor and security was tight. At one stop Pam and I decided to look for a post box to post cards we had written home. Not finding one on or near the platform we went upstairs to cross a bridge into a larger part of the station. Another peroxide blond strapping woman appeared, barring our way. With the strongest of good international relations we smiled broadly and waved our cards. Fortunately we had stamped them. She took them from us and we returned to our platform and the train wondering if they would ever make it home. They did and we sent mental thanks.

Ekaterinburg was a historic stop as it was the place where the last Tsar and his family were imprisoned and later murdered. Irkutsk was also memorable because we left the train for several days including an overnight in a hotel beside Lake Baikal, the world's deepest lake. It was late June and the weather was superb. We enjoyed a good sail. In the morning Pam and I climbed a very high hill topped with numerous prayer flags. The walk up was memorable, with the lower areas being wooded and having numerous unfamiliar flowers. One appeared to be an oversized buttercup but was almost orange rather than yellow. Others from our party had made it to the top and when we joined them we respected the prayer flags and looked down and enjoyed a new view of Lake Baikal.

Back in Irkutsk we visited a regional consumer co-operative. I recall the lady interpreter glorying in the greater consumer freedom she now enjoyed. She complained that in the past she could only buy the same slipper in either pink or blue. Now she could have slippers in different styles and colours. Earlier in Moscow the deteriorating political situation under Yeltsin coloured many things. We had been surprised at the openness of condemnation. Despite political unrest greater consumer choice was welcomed.

We also visited a fur trading co-operative. Taken to one of its sale rooms we saw a great variety of furs, many unfamiliar. They brought home the region's diversity of furred life. We were allowed to try some on and many photographs were taken.

Problems were to arise on the next stage of our journey to Ulan Bator, just 24 hours away. Our guide in Irkutsk had been kind and efficient showing us the beauty created by rich Tsarist exiles sent there over centuries. When she asked if I would write her a letter of thanks I readily agreed. I later realised she had been trying to protect herself from complaints about the problems shortly to arise.

The train from Moscow had been a Russian train while our next one would be a Mongolian one. We soon realised that our compartments were not in first class as booked all the way through. The Mongolian woman train attendant woman hung back in apparent deference to two Mongolian men who were hurrying us onto the train. I tried to explain that we were first class and our Irkutsk guide explained that although there were no first class compartments we would be only two to a compartment. I got on to check and unfortunately the others followed and the carriage door was closed behind them. Our Irkutsk guide promptly disappeared and there could be no more help from her.

Each compartment was packed with trade goods. We insisted they be cleared but the fourth was not. We soon realised we had to be careful. Mongolian traders had piled the train with merchandise purchased in Russia and were keen to prevent disruption. In a nearby compartment an apprehensive Dutch couple told how they had been attacked. He showed us a weal on his neck. Goods in their compartment left them little space. Our party decided to try to settle into three compartments. It was not comfortable and in anger one of the men went to what should have been his compartment and physically emptied its goods into the corridor. The row between him and several Mongolian traders was memorable for its theatrics without language.

Further chaos arose when we arrived in Ulan Bator. Because we were four hours late the platform into which we should have drawn could not be used: a later scheduled train was now in it. We were therefore shunted onto a track with no platform and we disembarked onto a waste ground between rail lines.

Climbing down from the train the colleague who had emptied his compartment of trade goods had his wallet stolen from his back pocket. It contained cards and money and we wondered whether it was retribution or opportunistic theft. It brought home that we were at risk and not all were wearing money belts although I had strongly urged that everyone should.

Once off the train there were further problems we were in a precarious position. My dear friend Muriel, then 82 stood with her shoulder bag looped round her shoulder and hanging down her side. I urged her to hide it under her coat. Remembering old western films with wagons circling to defend against Red Indians, we drew into a group, backs facing outwards. Handbags and items that could be snatched were held in the middle.

We realised our courier would have difficulty reaching us through the crowds. Passengers were queuing to move to the rear of our train and round the back of another to reach a platform. We were aghast to see some crawl through the wheels of a train to take a short cut to the platform.

Eventually our courier and coach driver did get through to us. Warm and relieved introductions were exchanged but new problems arose. One was how to get our luggage to the coach outside the station. The courier feared that once cases were loaded, they might be stolen from the coach. The driver could not stay with the coach because he was needed to carry luggage. Eventually it was agreed that he and Alan Rhodes would take what they could and Alan would then stay with the coach. He was the tallest and broadest in our party but he later recounted how the jostling crowd had even knocked him to his knees. The rest of us tried to organise the remaining luggage so as to leave it as light as possible for those least able to manage. We then forced our way behind the stationary train, onto the platform, out of the station and to the coach where Alan was relieved to see us.

Except for our friend whose wallet had been stolen and his need to make quick contact with his UK bank to cancel his cards, our troubles were over. I was confident we would be safe and well looked after at the Ulan Bator hotel to which we were being taken. En route I was fascinated to see the town centre was being modernised. There were new banks in tall buildings with much glass and an increased number of shops. Ulan Bator was becoming more commercial.

The hotel had also been brought up to date. On our beds Pam and I found complimentary baseball caps. We were all comfortable and much to our collective relief the stolen cards had been cancelled. Communications had obviously improved from my first time in Ulan Bator when Nick Guyler was thwarted in a telephone call to the Ministry of Agriculture in London.

En route Bernard and I had kept in touch by fax which was then in vogue and we had had several telephone calls. One he made to the Ulan Bator hotel amused because it went through not to Mrs. Rhodes but Mr. Rhodes, Alan. Until then there had been no confusion arising from having two people in a small party with that name, although not married! In any event Bernard and Alan were pleased to speak. Their paths had crossed many times in co-operative work after Alan had been Bernard's assistant when he was the Co-operative Union's Sectional Secretary in its Leeds office in the late 1950s. I had met Alan then shortly after he and Margaret had been joined by their baby daughter. I had a fond memory of his opening our present of a knitted matinee coat and the incongruity of man with broad shoulders and large hands politely admiring such a small item.

Alan was a railway enthusiast, hence his enthusiasm for the trans-Siberian trip. He was looking forward to the train changing gauges at the Mongolian/Chinese border. Like Bernard, Alan's wife, Margaret had not kept well and had decided not to join us. She was obviously concerned for Alan because she had packed him a supply of plastic knives and forks to keep in his lapel pocket should he have difficulty using chop sticks. In fact we would only be given them in China but could still ask for cutlery.

By the time Alan retired he had risen to become secretary to Co-operative Retail Services (CRS). A great pleasure of days of continuous rail travel was to chat with friends and I recall an afternoon Alan spent with Pam and me recalling experiences with CRS and how its board responded to increasing difficulties.

We had a wonderful time in Ulan Bator. I met old friends with whom I had worked closely in the UNIFEM project seven years earlier. It was good to see that several had put on weight. Food supplies had obviously improved. I hoped other things had as well. I recalled how most Mongolian women had then lacked sanitary supplies. Urnaa had told me that when interpreting for Mongolian officials abroad, she would take a collapsible case in which to bring back a year's supply of sanitary towels.

It was sad to see that the Mongolian Women's Federation had further declined. Now a voluntary organisation rather than a state subsidiary its revenue was much reduced. It had moved from the offices I had visited three years earlier and was now in an even poorer house with only one secretary.

Our stay in Ulan Bator included a number of outings. One was on a picnic hosted by the young consumer co-operative union. It became memorable not least for the beautiful in wide open countryside to which we were taken. We could see for miles in any direction. Suddenly from the west a lone but saddled horse bolted at great speed towards to the east. It seemed to have unseated its rider and literally taken to the hills. It was a magnificent sight. Half a minute later we saw a rider chasing it, obviously hoping to rein it in. We never knew the outcome as both quickly disappeared into the vast distance.

Picnics are a Mongolian tradition, even in freezing weather when vodka and other spirits keep people warm. I heard that the British embassy followed suit and a tale came down about one of the first British women to work in Mongolia as a university lecturer. She was also believed to have worked for British intelligence and passed information during embassy picnics. She and the ambassador would meander onto a dry and frozen river bed to talk where they could not be overheard by man or listening device.

Our picnic was superb with a wide range of food and drink, spread out on cloths on the grass and us sitting on brightly coloured woollen blankets. In the shade of a tree though, a sheep was tethered. We were proudly told that he would be our lunch. Delicately, one of our men explained that Britons did not like to see animals killed. Our Mongolian hosts smiled, possibly believing we were giving thanks.

I had already learned what would happen and so was somewhat prepared. Along with others though, I looked away. The sheep, lamb or goat would be taken onto a man's lap, belly up. A long knife cut would be made down its front to enable a hand to enter and massage the heart until it stopped, usually within a few minutes.

Later our group had a fierce debate as to whether this was kinder than our slaughter methods at home. We finally agreed that it was. Until minutes before death the sheep had rested in the shade of a tree, perhaps missing its friends but nonetheless appearing content.

After it was killed we were taken on a sight-seeing trip for around about an hour. I have to admit though that after the recent slaughter I was too preoccupied to remember much of what we saw. When we returned our hosts had already cooked the sheep in a metal milk churn with embers beneath and above the carcass that had been cut into small pieces that would be easy to eat. Knives and forks were offered. Despite the drama I had to admit it was very tasty.

The next day we left Ulan Bator with some concern as to whether there would be further difficulties on the train. We need not have worried. It was a Chinese train and when we reached the platform we found well-tailored uniformed train guards waiting to usher us to our compartments. These were clean, comfortable and elegant. We were back in first class and not competing for space with trade goods.

At the frontier we had a long wait due not only to the usual procedures but also to engineering. The body of the train was lifted so that its wheels and under-carriage could be taken away and new sets were fitted to enable the train to travel on a changed gauge. Alan our railway enthusiast stayed wide awake despite it being the early hours of the morning. The rest of us yawned, chatted and occasionally put our heads out of the window to see what was happening.

Later and well into China and desert, we caught occasional sight of remnants of the Great Wall. The rail track then climbed into hills up which the train laboured. There was great excitement as it actually passed through the Great Wall and descended to a plain that led to Beijing. We marvelled at the engineering.

Arrival in Beijing was safer than at Ulan Bator but still a little confusing. We were not met and wondered how long we should wait for the courier before making our own way to the hotel. Eventually our courier arrived and introduced himself. Our luggage was then loaded into a massive high sided trolley wheeled by a disproportionately small Chinese lady wearing a pointed hat, presumably some kind of uniform. I marvelled she could handle such weight. Later I was sorry for her because on leaving the station a porter pushed her out of the way and took the trolley only a short distance before putting his hand out for tips. The tiny lady who had done the work got nothing!

The hotel was excellent; modern, clean and elegant. We all used its basement swimming pool. A number of trips had been arranged, including one to the Great Wall and to a union of workers and productive co-operatives. Here we were on the far side of the world but strangely we felt at home. Not only were we speaking co-operation but the organisation's offices seemed familiar. Several of us commented how they reminded us of those of the British Co-operative Union in Manchester. Both had similarly heavy oak doors.

After a few days we flew home. Boarding the bus to the airport taught me an interesting lesson. Unwittingly I had left hotel staff too small a tip. They took exception and climbed into the bus to hand it back to me. It was a genuine mistake. I had not realised there were small and larger version of the same denomination with smaller ones having half value and I had given these. It taught me that the Chinese would not be backward in coming forward if they had not received due reward and that this could have future implications for trade. It also reminded me of an incident during my 1996 visit to Ulan Bator. On the return journey through Beijing the desk clerk at the hotel where I was staying overnight asked to see my passport. This was automatic and not worrying but I was shaken when he said he could not admit me because my visa had been cancelled; and indeed it was. Most fortunately the ILO office was open and I asked to speak to them. They confirmed to the desk clerk and to me that I was there legitimately and that if I had any further problems I should speak to the ILO Regional Officer who had permanent accommodation in the hotel. I was then allowed to stay but was worried if I would have difficulty at the airport. I did not. The cancelled visa had been only in respect of entering China from Mongolia. I then suspected that the hotel desk clerk had assumed I was a mature lady travelling by herself from whom he could manipulate a personal under cover payment. Fortunately I was covered by the ILO. However, remembering that incident, as well as being overcharged by a taxi driver on my first visit to Beijing in November 1991, an unacceptable tip being returned showed that the Chinese had a sharp eye for reward and that could have wider implications such as trade.

The drive to the airport reflected other changes. The B type road I had first travelled on only eight years earlier was now a massive commercialised highway that was adorned with considerable advertising. It reflected the directions in which

China was moving. Changes to the airport confirmed. It had been massively modernised and vastly extended to become a major international hub.

Our flight home was uneventful. Bernard met me in at Heathrow along with relatives of others. We were happy to return having enjoyed a momentous journey through Europe, Asia and the Far East. It helped us celebrate the close of the century and approach to a new millennium.

Apart from his health problems Bernard and I had found the 1990s a memorable decade.

Chapter Eleven

LONG FAREWELLS

The year 2,000 heralded a number of farewells, making one long one that was both personal and organisational. Bernard still participated in various meetings and also kindly read and commented on my writings that were mainly papers for co-operative research conferences and a longer work, *Empire and Co-operation.* That had come about quite unexpectedly.

WRITING EMPIRE AND CO-OPERATION

India's first co-operative legislation was passed in 1904. A century later its Society of Co-operative Studies began a work on a history of Indian co-operation and sought help from the UK Society for Co-operative Studies (SCS) to identify and transmit relevant Westminster sources and to possibly give financial help. The former was agreed but because the British Empire had encouraged co-operatives in around a quarter of the world's population it was feared a dangerous precedent could be set if financial help was given. That was therefore refused but help with Westminster papers could be given particularly if SCS undertook its own history of co-operation in the whole of the British Empire.

The idea was born and my offer to work on it was accepted. It was also agreed that the Co-operative Research Unit of the Open University would support and that Prof. Roger Spear would read and comment on drafts. Our work took around ten years. We had under estimated how much work there would be and other events also intervened.

An early difficulty was trying to understand how two such diametrically opposed forces such as imperialism and co-operation ever came together. Whereas imperialism sought foreign domination, exploited local populations and resources and imposed forms of government, co-operation was voluntary, democratic and self-managing. Imperialism was considered by some to be the most noxious form of capitalism while co-operation was strongly anti capitalist in its collective ownership and mutuality.

Research justified my horror of empire but it also forced me to recognise the diversity of the British Empire. I had to admit that it was not wholly bad. It was less centralised than some other empires having come about in varying circumstances over some centuries. Consequently territorial administrations could differ although operating under broad Westminster parameters. Adding to the diversity was two civil services, one Indian and the other Colonial. Each was responsible to Westminster but with separate objectives, systems of recruitment and culture.

Co-operative ideas could creep into such diversity. They encouraged different forms in different settings: thrift and credit societies in India, Ireland and the British West Indies, farmers in Ireland and Rhodesia and retail societies in the potential dominions of Canada, Australia, New Zealand and South Africa. All this was helped by the fact that the British consumer co-operative movement was proving credible. It was innovatory in advancing an economic system of self-help and mutuality in which wage earners with no factors of production other than their labour entered new economic activity. Its evolutionary nature helped it become acceptable to British middle and upper classes then frightened by European revolutions. Co-operatives also became acceptable because they taught their members business and organisational skills which helped build civil society.

So in various ways the empire could assimilate co-operatives and in return its size and spread helped them spread far more widely than might otherwise have been the case. It did this through its massive movements of populations such as Britons settling elsewhere in the empire and others serving in its imperial armed forces and Colonial and Indian Civil Services. These widened knowledge and experience of co-operatives from what they had learned back home.

Other population movements included indentured Indians recruited to fill the void left by the outlawing of slavery. These landed up in East Africa, the British West Indies and south-east Asia. An irony of history is that the Windrush generation achieved a full circle in bringing back to Britain knowledge of thrift and credit co-operatives that their forefather had learned in India under its first co-operative legislation in 1904.

Co-operatives also developed in the empire through paternalistic influence. Important figures were the fourth Earl Grey (1851-1917) Sir Horace Plunkett (1854-1932) Lord Anthony MacDonnell (1844-1925) and Lord Wenlock (1849-1912). Grey was Administrator of Rhodesia and later Governor General in Canada and behind the scenes in both was highly influential in their co-operative development. Lords MacDonnell and Wenlock were much engaged in India's early co-operative development while Plunkett pioneered agricultural and thrift and credit co-operatives in Ireland.

Each accepted empire, Plunkett perhaps less so. He came from an Anglo/Irish aristocratic family but held no title himself. Extensive and dedicated public work did however bring him a knighthood. He proved a notable co-operative builder. Besides leading moves to establish co-operative support organisations in Ireland he recognised that knowledge was essential to co-operative development and founded a co-operative library which later became the Plunkett Foundation. This gathered extensive information on colonial co-operatives which analysed and distilled in publications and from which it advised the Westminster government and colonial administrations on possible new co-operative legislation. In addition the foundation brought co-operative leaders together. A notable event was a major conference it organised in 1925 during the Empire Exhibition at Wembley. It also organised seminars for colonial co-operative registrars on home leave from the Colonial or Indian Civil Services and all in all became a valuable resource.

Sadly Sir Horace Plunkett died in 1936 but his work helped explain how empire and co-operation had come together. Other evidence pointed in a surprising direction, namely the Westminster government. The French have called Britain the *perfidious Albion* and this seemed justified in the late 1930s when the threat of war prompted the British government to improve relations with its colonies because their manpower and other resources would be needed if conflict did break out. It therefore increased emphasis on their economic development in which of course there was a place for co-operatives. This emphasis strengthened under the post-war Labour Government. Territories preparing for independence could help prepare civil society through the business and organisational skills that co-operatives practised.

This development led to colonial administrations increasing recruitment from local populations. The colonial office then sent around 30 of these serving in Departments of Agriculture or Co-operative Development to study each year at the UK Co-operative College. Their courses should really have been with the Plunkett foundation but it lacked the residential accommodation that the Co-operative College could provide. Nevertheless the Plunkett Foundation made significant contributions as did the Colonial Office. During Christmas and Easter holidays overseas students visited a number of British consumer and agricultural co-operatives.

In the 1950s and '60s a number of British co-operators went to work in British territories moving towards independence. The Colonial Office recruited them as co-operative registrars or assistant registrars. Some were my friends from Co-operative College student days and kindly agreed to my recording interviews on these experiences. I had not planned to interview Trevor Bottomley but was urged to do so. Our relations were not good since our bust up at the International Co-operative Alliance some 20 years earlier. Eventually I agreed and Trevor and I met for lunch in London. Relations thawed when I became amused at his assuming the position of boss and I his secretary taking dictation. Happily our mutual co-operative interests and enthusiasms further warmed relations. Trevor became a great help. His support was ongoing in giving information and commenting on draft chapters. I came to enjoy and value his friendship over the years that followed.

Empire and C-operation was eventually finished and published by John Donald of Edinburgh in 2012. Reviews were favourable. Its research and writing had given pleasure and had shifted some prejudices and I had learned how some diametrically opposed ideas could come together for mutual benefit. It had taken over ten years to prepare but other events had also intervened including preparing and presenting papers at various co-operative research conferences. Many of these were organised by the research committee of the International Co-operative Alliance. Some were held alongside ICA congresses. I stayed on for these, attending as an observer.

FURTHER INTERNATIONAL CO-OPERATIVE RESEARCH CONFERENCES

I represented the Co-operative Research Unit of the Open University at these conferences. During the 17 years that I was a Visiting Research Fellow I attended these conferences in Cork, Oslo, Seoul, Bologna, Colombo, Quebec, Saskatchewan, Oxford, Limassol, Victoria on Vancouver Island, Lyon, Oxford, Prague, Pune, Stockholm and Marburg. Topics included co-operatives and peace, consumer co-operation, paternalism in the early British consumer co-operative movement, international co-operative trade and fair trade, the importance of co-operative archives, Indian co-operative history and co-operatives and British imperialism.

I made many friends at these conferences and we often met for dinner in nearby restaurants to catch up with each other's work.

The conferences also usually included study visits. The conference in Seoul was memorable because it was held in the largest conference centre I had ever seen. It had four identical entrances on four main streets and was an immense square with several large auditoria and smaller meeting and administrative rooms. I mused on its architecture as I sat signing copies of my earlier book *The International Co-operative Alliance during War and Peace 1910-1950* which the ICA was re-launching.

By contrast the smallest conference room I experienced was in the library of Marburg University in Germany. In 2004 Prof. Hans-H Munkner called a conference to commemorate the centenary of India's first co-operative legislation. Only nine of us participated which justified the limited space and made it more informal and quite cosy.

Prof. Munkner's had become an eminent authority on co-operative legislation in developing countries. He had also built a strong co-operative studies department that had produced a number of notable contemporary co-operative leaders.

The central presentation was made by Dr. Madhav Madane, chair of the Indian Society of Co-operative Studies. His paper and others added sources for E*mpire and Co-operation.* Professor Ian MacPherson, head of the co-operative studies department at Victoria University, Vancouver Island gave valuable information on the role of the fourth Earl Grey in Canadian co-operative development while the paper presented by Dr. Ake Eden from Gothenburg University, Sweden challenged mine entitled *British Liberalism and Indian Co-operation* on many points. His Ph.D thesis had been on the British East Africa Company and he was vehemently hostile to the British Empire. He largely dismissed the influences I attributed to Lords Wenlock and MacDonell in helping establish some Indian co-operatives before the 1904 legislation but partly accepted my assertion that a number of senior Indian Civil Servants had become enthusiastic co-operators and helped encouraged co-operatives in India and elsewhere in the empire.

The conference was helped by enjoyable coffee breaks. Hans and his daughter were enthusiastic cooks and prepared some wonderful cakes. Adjacent to our meeting room was a large wooden balcony and we could walk out onto it with coffee and cakes and overlook trees and hear many birds sing. Nature healed lively debate.

Several months after the Marburg conference another was held in Pune, India and was organised by the Indian Society of Co-operative Studies. I was delighted to be invited and to meet many Indian co-operative researchers. Their papers comprised the major part of the conference, particularly those arising from their history of Indian co-operation which neared completion. Other papers fed in from the Marburg Conference and were given by Prof. Ian MacPherson, Prof. Han-H. Munkner, Dr. Ake Eden and myself.

This was my first and only time in India apart from flight changes at Mumbai. I arrived shortly before midnight and would have preferred to spend the rest of the night at an airport hotel. Instead I was persuaded to allow a car to meet and transfer me straight to Pune. This may have been because traffic would be lighter and less scary. Despite learning to manage Egyptian traffic, the Indian version scared me witless. Vehicles drove at speed between each other, without keeping to lanes and ignoring most signs. Wing mirrors were folded back to avoid being knocked off by passing traffic and so gave no protection. Perhaps this chaos worked because all drivers developed a heightened sense of risk; eventually I decided that if Indian drivers knew what they were doing, then I could only trust and hope.

We arrived in Pune around 5am and I was taken to the agricultural college where the conference would be held and where guests would be accommodated. I went straight to bed but could not sleep. The drive had shaken me on top of which the college was waking and much was going on around me. Eventually I got up and had a late breakfast.

239

I arrived two days before the conference so as to be able to visit a number of co-operatives. These and drives to them made big impressions. I was struck by the juxtaposition of wealth and poverty. Directors of a women's co-operative bank wore much jewellery but I gathered that most of the bank's members were poor and were encouraged to save. Madhav Madane drove me to some co-operatives in his Rolls Royce. I wondered how on earth he could ever risk it in such horrendous traffic. Moreover it was ostentatious. That made me uncomfortable particularly when we were passed by a family of five crammed onto a moped.

The juxtaposition of wealth and poverty shocked in other ways as when we left a restaurant and found children on the street corner scavenging waste paper. Another occasion occurred when we had tea and cakes in a quite luxurious patisserie. Our window table on the first floor enabled us to see the street below where I saw a woman pull up her sari and clamber into a roadside skip. She was also scavenging. On another journey Madhav criticised a newly built estate of luxury houses because the shacks their servants would build nearby would spoil and devalue the area. I realised that better off Indians took surrounding poverty for granted despite seeing a role for co-operatives.

I valued the visit. It taught me much and proved complementary to the earlier conference at Marburg. By the mid 2,000s though, events at home were impacting on conferences and other work.

PERSONAL FAREWELLS

I believe it was in late middle age that I began to look around my friends and wonder who might be the first to die, and how. A friend thought me morbid when I observed that we unknowingly passed the anniversary of our death each year without realising it! As it turned out some departures were more difficult to accept than others. They made me realise that friends were important as Bernard and I had no close family.

A great loss was the unexpected and premature death of Pam Walsh. Our friendship had grown from my student days at the Co-operative College in the mid 1950s when Pam had been on the secretarial staff later becoming secretary to the college principal. After retirement she continued to live in her flat at the college. She was still physically active in her late 70s, gardening and cycling most places although she did mention possible hearing loss. I must say that I took little notice but later wondered if that contributed to her terrible accident. Riding her bike she turned right to enter Stanford Park and was hit by a car coming behind. She was badly injured and airlifted to hospital in Nottingham where a leg was amputated; she died three days later. A friend who then saw her said she looked at peace, despite her terrible injuries. Pam gave to many charities and it was perhaps appropriate that one was air ambulance.

She had strong religious faith and regularly worshipped at the parish church of Stanford on Soar for decades which helped to explain that it was packed for her funeral. When I arrived it was standing room only. Sympathy was also a possible reason because at that time it was believed that her accident had been caused by careless driving. Later her inquest showed that she had caused it by turning right without properly checking. I then suspected that her deteriorating hearing could have been a factor.

Pam's faith and gentle nature helped heal. I recalled many happy times together including sharing a compartment on our Trans Siberian trip during which there was an amusing incident. At lunch one day Pam told how she had walked into a street in Oxford and had been injured by a passing cyclist. She was hospitalised and left several days later in a car sent by Leicester Co-operative Society to take her back to Stanford Hall. Pam always tried to make conversation so she asked the driver which department he worked in and he replied the Funeral Department. She was being taken home in a funeral car. We had a great laugh but I later wondered if the Oxford accident presaged how she would die.

Other funerals were also memorable. That of Dr. Robert Marshall in 2005 brought together many past Co-operative College students while another in 2919 revived other co-operative memories. It was of Marion Rilstone, long-time friend and began with the hymn "These Things Shall Be" by John Addington Symonds (1840-1893). This traditionally opened co-operative congresses and although later dropped it was good to reminded of it and to know that it still meant something to Marion. The fervour with which it was sung at congresses reminded you of "Onward Christian Soldiers" with a rousing tune and words reminding you that co-operation was about ideology, morality, freedom and fraternity. I was touched that Marion recalled this.

Of course my biggest loss was Bernard in July 2005. It is difficult to write about even now because he had been the central person in my life for 45 years. We had been lucky, even blessed. Many marriages work out less well for many different and often unintended reasons. We had had strains and disappointments but had survived and become inter-dependent. There was no one else to whom I could speak in quite the same way. A loss of personality was also involved. You built up a joint personality over years together but when that finishes the survivor has to develop a new one.

Bereavement led me to wonder if Bernard had feelings about our age difference but had never said. I remembered years earlier being sorry for a middle-aged friend whose husband was 10 years her senior. A similar difference had never seemed to be an issue for us. Bereavement and retrospection though, led me to wonder how he felt as he declined but I still remained active. He never said and perhaps balances between partners shift with time. In early years I readily accepted his judgements while in later ones my being able to do things that he no longer could was a comfort to him.

Bernard's decline began five years earlier. It was slow and we adjusted in different ways. We no longer took holidays abroad but enjoyed breaks in London with the theatre, good meals and shopping in Oxford Street. Frequent places of worship became St. James in Spanish Place and the Church of the Immaculate Conception in Farm Street.

A terrible irony was that no diagnosis was given for Bernard's decline. Added to this was his life-long prejudice against the medical profession. I cannot remember any other similar prejudice he held and being highly rational he often laughed at its ambiguity. Recurring pain was not explained and suggestions began to be made that he was perhaps imagining when early stages of Alzheimer also appeared.

Imagine my horror when an autopsy was required and showed that he had died of Pneumonia, an ulcer and cancer of the bowel. The last two had never been diagnosed. His pain had been genuine and it must have been terrible. I had strong motive to call for an enquiry but my nerves were shot to pieces. I also doubted if it would be possible to apportion blame between so many doctors who had examined Bernard and requested tests and scans, yet the ulcer and cancer remained undetected. When told it was a matter of hours before he died I asked from what he was dying and the doctors even then could not say. Hence there had to be an autopsy.

Afterwards I heard a lunchtime mass in the church in Birkenhead where we was married and in the evening another in a church in Manchester where we had worshipped when courting and later living there. I had hoped to go to confession but was crying too much to do so. Then and for months later I cried to depths I had never previously known.

Gradually adjustment came. Work helped. I continued to prepare and present conference papers and to research *Empire and Co-operation*. A year to the day that Bernard had been rushed into hospital I participated in a conference on co-operatives and peace at the Centre for Co-operative Studies at the University of Victoria, Vancouver Island. Several of us had taken the train from Toronto to Vancouver. As much as anything though, I recall the misery of the anniversary.

CO-OP FAREWELL

The longest, and in many ways the saddest farewell has been the loss of British consumer co-operation. It has vastly changed and now bears scant resemblance to what Bernard and I first knew. Of course change is to be expected with those in wider society and economy but sadly those in British consumer co-operation have been of decline. They have emerged over decades and while Bernard and I were sometimes unhappy about them, we could see reasons for them. We therefore acquiesced but in any event opportunities to advance alternatives declined alongside those of democracy and member influence.

I believe the decline in democracy to have been fundamental. It has been argued it is a consequence of creating larger societies to meet the competition of competitors in larger markets. This is reasonable but I recall that when I joined the London Co-operative Society (LCS) it had over a million members yet remained democratic through its federal structures and procedures. I came to know many fellow members through events and made quite a few friends.

Gatherings varied in size with many in co-operative halls and other properties. Bernard and I first met in a hall over a row of LCS shops. I also recall arriving at our local Co-op Hall for what I thought would be a Co-op. Party meeting. I was wrong because it was a half yearly meeting of members and was completely full. Three officials sat at tables by the entrance checking share pass books and because I did not have mine I could not remain. Admittedly in those days in the early 1950s such meetings did not compete with TV and leisure activities that would later increase. They nevertheless reflected member interest and loyalty as well as the accountability of elected committees and of managers.

Alongside democracy there was also a decline in fraternity. By that I mean solidarity, friendliness and shared beliefs. In our earlier years the movement was very friendly. It has become less so. Earlier you made personal friends and came to know others through meetings or conferences or items in the Co-operative News. I met few leaders but I knew what positions they were taking on issues aired in the Co-op News, Agenda, Management and Marketing and later the Journal of Co-operative Studies. Each aided informed opinion and therefore democracy. Readers also came to know figures they might not know personally and some undoubtedly drew followings.

Their co-operative credentials and those of personal co-operative friends aided cohesion. I first met Muriel Russell at a Co-operative Education Convention. We smiled at each other and nodded heads across a room before actually speaking. She was well known. Although married she was enrolled at the Co-operative College in its first year at Stanford Hall. Women then and particularly married women were less readily advanced yet she won her place. She later became prominent in the Co-operative Women's Guild as well as an elected member of the Management Committee of the famous Enfield Highway Co-operative Society. At the time we first met she was the first Women's Officer of the International Co-operative Alliance (ICA). Of course I was far less renowned but Muriel knew me as a fellow past student of Co-operative College, as an occasional contributor to the Co-operative News and as the Co-operative Union's Sectional Education Officer in Scotland.

From the mid 1960s onwards co-operatives increasingly appointed outsiders, attracted by their supposed retailing expertise. It seemed to reflect a growing lack of self-confidence although this was hardly voiced. A tradition was breaking and a number of consequences followed. Outsiders needed to learn co-op traditions but some proved unsympathetic. Divisions arose and were sadly apparent in letters of sympathy I received after Bernard died. Some from past work colleagues wrote of feeling 'alienated' and had either opted for early retirement or were hoping for it.

An equally damaging effect of outsiders came in opening trade to non-members. It fractured members' relations and benefits, damaging their sense of identity and loyalty. Their sense of belonging declined as they, along with non-members judged co-op stores in the same way as they judged competitors' stores. These external influences could readily be seen.

However I believe more profound though less criticised ones came from the 1950s Independent Co-operative Commission. My doubts developed slowly over many years. Yet at the beginning Bernard and I were ready to accept its recommendations. We had high regard for Hugh Gaitskell who chaired the commission and Tony Crosland who was its secretary.

My doubts evolved from two influences. Years later I read a Co-op. College paper written by Bert Youngjohns on *Co-operation and the State.* I was shocked by the vehemence with which he concluded that the movement had been attracted to political action in the late 19th century because it was losing its self-confidence. I disagreed; the movement was then growing rapidly but had already recognised that it could not do all things. It should contribute to education, employment and health but overall responsibility for these should the state's thus justifying political action.

What has remained with me though is Youngjohns' identification of a growing lack of co-operative self-confidence. Hardly recognised and seldom acknowledged I believe this recurred in the 1950s and led to calls for advice from an Independent Commission. It then grew stronger as societies in responding to the commission's proposals and merged but felt the need for new expertise in the bigger markets in which they were competing. This accelerated the recruitment of managers and officials from other businesses and opened trade to non-members.

I believe that the earlier movement had a hidden advantage, namely subliminal propinquity. By that I mean the number of co-operative properties they saw around then, not only shops but also halls and facilities for entertainment and social activities. The place names in their co-operative's title also reinforced subliminal propinquity with names like London, Enfield, Chelmsford, Colchester, Loughborough, Nottingham, Manchester and Salford, Liverpool, Birkenhead, Leeds, Bradford,, Harrogate, Ayr, Falkirk and Stirling. Football teams kept their place names but retail societies lost theirs. I cringe when I see how present societies spanning many counties and even a national border. Focus and identification has been lost.

This has also happened in other ways. The focus on retailing has meant that co-operatives wider social activities such as choirs, brass bands, music festivals and co-operative amateur theatricals have declined. Co-operative education was refashioned to become Co-operative Member Relations. This may have seemed minor but it reflected a shift from the movement's earlier belief that it needed to propagate its principles and values. In earlier days the Co-operative Union had run a Propaganda Department but the term became somewhat discredited with the use of propaganda in Nazi and communist regimes and was dropped. Yet the co-operative movement had a distinct message comprising as it did a form of collective social ownership that differed from other forms of state and private enterprise.

An unfortunate consequence is that some present day co-operative enthusiasts advocate vague ideas that could be expressed more firmly if they knew more of earlier co-operative propaganda. The concentration on shop keeping seems to make this unnecessary and has faded co-operative identity further.

Within this has been a further decline, namely that of knowledge of earlier co-operative innovations. A notable one for me was federation under which primary retail societies collectively formed secondary societies such as the wholesales as well as smaller more local ones. These provided specialist services such as bakeries or laundries that a single society would find too expensive to undertake. Co-operative federations had existed since the mid 1800s and were owned and democratically controlled by their primary member societies. Out of them grew the co-operative principles of co-operation between co-operatives.

Yet federation in theory and practice fell into disuse as new dynamics emerged with the Co-operative Group and regional societies spreading geographically across counties and a border.

Another dynamic was the creation of co-operative chains. Shoefayre was an early one. While appropriate to the changing co-operative framework and brand advertising it is debatable how successful they have been compared with the previous system. In that member loyalty had been strong and reduced the cost of advertising. Members became familiar with the names of co-operatively produced goods of assured quality. From Rochdale onwards retail societies observed the principle of not selling poor or adulterated goods. Members also enjoyed some price advantage through wholesale and society dividends.

A fundamental change occurred with amalgamations and the creation of ever larger societies. Earlier primary societies had been universal providers because they met members' needs from cradle to grave. A decline in this universality prompted a further decline in member loyalty and the economic advantages that brought. Members and non-members increasingly saw their societies as just another retailer and loyalty was replaced by competition, "where has the lowest price?"

British consumer co-operation has changed fundamentally. Bernard and I lived and worked through those changes. We acquiesced with their inevitability from acceptance and implementing of the recommendations of the 1950s Independent Commission. Preparing this joint autobiography though has prompted deep reflection.

I have sadly noted that many leading contemporary co-operative leaders do not value the movement's history. In any event many histories of it have been written. I would now like to see a new type that records what the movement achieved in its first century, to note how it increased a new kind of wealth and among poorer classes not previously engaged in economic activity. It would be illuminating to produce a thematic guide to its annual congresses to see which issues arose and with what frequency.

Sources for such studies could be the Annual Report of the Co-operative Union that was presented to congresses and the reports of those congresses. Accountability and democracy led to those reports being highly detailed in statistics and accounts of activities. Such studies could take the form of dissertations or Ph.D theses but above all I hope they would be undertaken with academic rigour.

They would complement earlier histories and also show the modern movement how and why its earlier version achieved long-standing success. It is up to them what lessons they draw. I anticipate two, namely the merits of economy and localisation. Both are appropriate in an ecologically challenged world. There will of course be others which illustrate the importance and significance of co-operation.

FINAL PERSONAL THOUGHTS

There are strange twists in Bernard's life and mine. A fundamental one was that he really was the academic. In his final months when we spent much time on medical appointments doctors and other clinicians often commented on his lively mind and wide vocabulary. One even shared his enthusiasm for Roman history. Sadly he never completed his Masters on entertainment in that. The Co-op proved a greater attraction. By contrast I started in the Co-op but landed up in co-operative education and later Co-operative history.

Our co-operative enthusiasms bred compatibility. This helped us adjust to each other's quite different work schemes but always with interest and pride. We made many wonderful co-operative friends and I hope I have brought some to life in this joint autobiography.

Bernard was better at quips than I am but I hope he will endorse my saying that we joined the Co-op and saw the world.

Printed in Great Britain
by Amazon

66954784R00154